CLASSICS IN PSYCHOLOGY

CLASSICS IN PSYCHOLOGY

A NOTE ABOUT THE AUTHOR

EDWIN B. HOLT was born in Winchester, Massachusetts, in 1873. He was an undergraduate at Amherst College, but transferred to Harvard, receiving his A. B. in 1896. Thereafter he studied with William James and Hugo Münsterberg, receiving a doctorate in psychology in 1901. Holt taught at Harvard until 1918, and later served for ten years as a Visiting Professor of Psychology at Princeton where he was widely acclaimed for his brilliant lectures. Holt died in Rockland, Maine in 1946.

Though he conducted a number of research projects, Holt is best known for his theoretical contributions to psychology. One of the first American scholars to assimilate Freud, he reinterpreted psychoanalysis in objective and physiological terms. Similarly, he sought to explain conscious phenomena, such as memory and cognition, in terms of their behavioral manifestations. Holt was in sympathy with the new behaviorism and led the fight to rid psychology of its metaphysical and idealistic aspects. Nonetheless he avoided atomistic reflexology and anticipated the more sophisticated forms of behaviorism which emerged in the 1930s and 40s.

THE CONCEPT
OF CONSCIOUSNESS

BY

EDWIN B. HOLT

ARNO PRESS

A New York Times Company

New York ★ 1973

Reprint Edition 1973 by Arno Press Inc.

Reprinted from a copy in
The University of Illinois Library

Classics in Psychology
ISBN for complete set: 0-405-05130-1
See last pages of this volume for titles.

Manufactured in the United States of America

———————◆———————

Library of Congress Cataloging in Publication Data

Holt, Edwin Bissell, 1873-1946.
   The concept of consciousness.

   (Classics in psychology)
   Reprint of the 1914 ed. published by Macmillan,
New York.
    1. Consciousness.   Series.
[DNLM:]
BF311.H62 1973   73-2969
ISBN 0-405-

THE
CONCEPT OF CONSCIOUSNESS

THE CONCEPT
OF CONSCIOUSNESS

BY

EDWIN B. HOLT

NEW YORK
THE MACMILLAN COMPANY
GEORGE ALLEN & COMPANY, Ltd.
1914

HUGO MÜNSTERBERG PROFESSORI
HUNC LIBRUM
AUCTOR
D.D.

Νῦν δὲ περὶ ψυχῆς τὰ λεχθέντα συγκεφαλαιώσαν-
τες, εἴπωμεν πάλιν ὅτι ἡ ψυχὴ τὰ ὄντα πώς ἐστιν. πάντα
γὰρ ἢ αἰσθητὰ τὰ ὄντα ἢ νοητά, ἔστι δ᾽ ἡ ἐπιστήμη μὲν
τὰ ἐπιστητά πως, ἡ δ᾽ αἴσθησις τὰ αἰσθητά. πῶς δὲ τοῦτο,
δεῖ ζητεῖν.

De Anima, 431, b. 20-24.

PREFACE

In view of the diversity of philosophical essays a writer may well at once say something of his purpose, and of what the human interest of his effort is to be. Pragmatically speaking, one seems to distinguish two kinds of philosophers. There are on the one hand those who, looking on the world about them, the folded earth and the brave canopy of heaven, desire to account for all this and to see behind the maddening variety that unity which something prompts them to believe is there. So sane and wholesome seems this desire, so proper as a philosophic aim, that one could wish all lovers of knowledge passionately possessed of it. But on the other hand one beholds the high pontiffs of philosophy, builders of massive systems, constructing their edifices not as a frugally devised and modest housing for the data of experience, to hold them compact and demonstrate their kinship, but rather as ' a kind of marble temple shining on a hill,' pompous monuments dedicated ostensibly to Academe and Dialectica—but with the pontiff's name engraved not small upon the portal.

So ornate and splendid are these systems of philosophy and so replete with this and that, that a mortal once beguiled by them becomes henceforth a stranger to the

initial problem—which was to trace, mayhap to reproduce, the plan and framework of our concrete world,
to show the unity that lies behind such prodigal variety.
These great systems come to be an end in themselves,
pieces of virtuosity often so express and cunning as to
dumbfound every visitor, yet to the mind of the pious
and sober wayfarer, for whom philosophy is an avenue
and not a goal, they are ostentatious and frivolous—
useless save as show-places for the philosophic tourist.
And the student who is captivated by such an archi-
tectural triumph, who lingers hat off and commentary
in hand around, say, the mausoleum of Hegel, has
forgotten his errand in life. For philosophy, I conceive,
is not a free play of the creative imagination, however
nicely logical, loosed from all mundane reference; it
is, as Professor James has said, not a ' clear addition '
erected on high over the plain of our mortal experience,
not " a classic sanctuary in which the rationalist fancy
may take refuge from the intolerably confused and
Gothic character which mere facts present." Philosophy
is grounded in these facts, it is everywhere knit close to
the mundane fabric, and as soon as these ties are loosened
philosophy as little fulfils its function of service to
human beings as would a successful airship to the
leafy denizens of the forest. For the love of knowledge
commits us to a quest after coherence, demonstrable
structure, unity—and this not aside from what we
are wont to call the facts, not a detached mass, howsoever compact, floating loose and free, but a unity

within the facts, the unity of the facts. And these facts are the concrete whole of experience, and conspicuously though by no means pre-eminently that domain that is called the physical world. That demonstrable coherent structure toward which philosophy should lead is not the structure of a philosophic system, but the structure inherent in all *being*, running through everything that is.

Clearly the present volume will not aim to be a system. But it does profess not to forget the initial quest of philosophy, and toward this goal it seeks to indicate some little way of advance. Its scope is limited, for it proposes only to give a consistent account, a definition, of one very common yet perplexing feature of the universe—consciousness. Of course, this has been defined many times before, and much discussed, yet so often without consistency and so strikingly without agreement that the last word, very obviously, has by no means been said.

But if to define anything is, doubtless, to point out by word or gesture that which is its essence bared of all its accidents, how can a human being comprehend and define consciousness, when his own entire experience is just a case of it? Can a part include a definition of the whole, or a person step outside his consciousness in order to survey it? Yet we all do persist in discussing the subject, and even this would be not merely unwarranted but sheerly impossible if by principle consciousness could never be defined. And so, although

the experience of anyone is indeed conterminous with
his own consciousness, yet it must be that somehow
within this experience there is some necessary distinction
between subject and object. Somehow that which is
called the knowledge relation may lie within one consciousness ; one experience may witness the knowing
process. This comes about most significantly, I think,
when one individual observes a fellow-man together
with some section of their common environment, and
then further observes a division of this environment
into two parts, one of which is, while the other is not,
he somehow knows, accessible to the experience of his
fellow. Thus the prompter from his station at the side
of the stage sees a portion of the painted scene that
is presented to persons whom he sees in the audience ;
but he also sees much else behind the scenes that he
knows these others cannot perceive : so too the present
reader, doubtless, will note from time to time, along
with that which I as writer have intended to say, sundry
stylistic shortcomings, which the reader will know that
I am unconscious of, else must I have remedied them.
Howsoever one may interpret such a situation philosophically, one certainly meets it very frequently in daily
life. We often know something of both the contents
and the limitations of another's mind. And this is at
least to say that somehow one consciousness may
overlap another. The knowing process is similarly
known when one's present consciousness recalls an
incident of one's own past, and now supplements that

memory with items which one had not known then. Without such glimpses of other minds, or of one's own mind in the past, this knowledge of knowledge, in short, the attempt to define consciousness would indeed be vain in principle. But we do have these glimpses, and to describe this matter more fully is the aim of the following chapters.

In referring to other writers I have consistently not prefixed their titles. This is good usage, to be sure, in the case of authors who are not living: but I have omitted titles in all cases, because literature, after all, is gathered from quarters so remote that it is impossible to know the age and state of health of every contributor. Such untitled mention is a trifle strained, I confess, in the case of three or four more immediate colleagues, gentlemen with whom it is my happy privilege to rub elbows nearly every day. Yet on the whole I find consistency no such intolerable bugbear; and, besides, esteem begets in general a certain licence.

Every reader who knows the works of Professor James, Professor Royce, and Professor Münsterberg will be aware how much I owe to them for my general drift of thought. The definition of consciousness proposed in the following pages is in no small part inspired by the Radical Empiricism of Professor James; and is, I believe, throughout consonant with that view. To Professor Royce, and to studies undertaken with his guidance, I owe my notions of the conceptual nature of the universe—a verity which to me argues not for idealism, but for a realism of perhaps, even, a thoroughly naïve sort. And to Professor Münsterberg, it will appear, I owe my ideas as to the purpose of psychology and the way, more particularly, in which that science may hope to fathom the relations between the body and the soul. To him also, as is lightly hinted in the dedication, I owe indeed the project of this volume. To my mathematical friend, Professor E. V. Huntington, furthermore, I am deeply indebted for penetrating and salutary criticism, and to my friend Dr. H. M. Sheffer for what I must account a very happy invention, the application to some entities, with which we shall have much to do in the following pages, of the term ' neutral.'

EDWIN B. HOLT.

HARVARD UNIVERSITY.

[The manuscript of this book, as it is here printed, was completed in the autumn of 1908.]

CONTENTS

xvi   *Contents*

CHAPTER X

CHAPTER XI

CHAPTER XII

CHAPTER XIII

CHAPTER XIV

CHAPTER XV

THE CONCEPT
OF CONSCIOUSNESS

CHAPTER I

THE RENAISSANCE OF LOGIC

WITHIN the last two decades the scholarly world has witnessed a revival of interest in logic. The subject of formal logic, which for many years had progressed very little if indeed at all, has been taken up once more, and this time by investigators whose first interest is mathematics rather than philosophy. And a region has been discovered which lies between our older logic and mathematics, adjacent to both and so closely related that the two are now seen to be a single science. In so far as the two older disciplines are to be kept distinct from each other and from the intermediate realm, this last is called the Algebra of Logic or Symbolic Logic. Now the recent investigations in this field have brought out a number of new truths and laid a new emphasis on certain others, which seem to me to bear importantly on philosophy as a whole, and especially on epistemology. And it is on those theories of knowledge which are involved by the idealistic philosophies ; in short, it is on idealism that these investigations cast their most searching light.

This light is by no means a favourable one, for it

B

reveals idealism, as it seems to me, resting insecurely on a fallacy or two. And it may or may not be a mere coincidence that one observes on several sides of the philosophic world a tendency to dispute that claim which idealism, of one form or another, has laid to being the beginning at least of a final solution of the world-problem. With the objections which by and large have been raised against idealism we have here no immediate concern, for it is the purpose of this book first to survey briefly the findings of modern logic, and then to examine, with as little bias as may be, their bearing on epistemology. Yet it is fair to say at the outset that if anyone has foreseen the outcome of such an inquiry, that person was Avenarius.[1] For whatever may be the other merits or the defects of that author's Empirio-Critical theory, and I believe that the defects are several, he was the first in modern times to ' exclude the introjection.' And this exclusion we shall see is one of the lessons of modern logic.

In order to understand the consequences for philosophy of modern investigations in logic, we must take a brief and tentative survey of what symbolic logic is and

---

[1] The most extended English exposition of Avenarius' theory is so far that of W. T. Bush : " Avenarius and the Standpoint of Pure Experience," Archives of Philosophy, Psychology, and Scientific Methods, No. 2, New York, 1905. For other expositions, aside from the original volumes of Avenarius, the reader is referred to that author's briefer statement, " Der Gegenstand der Psychologie," Vierteljahrschrift für wiss. Philosophie, 1894–5, Bde. XVIII–XIX ; to F. Carstanjen : " Richard Avenarius' biomechanische Grundlegung " u.s.w., München, 1894 ; to H. Delacroix : " Esquisse de l'empiriocriticisme," Revue de Métaphysique et de Morale, 1897, t. V, p. 764, and 1898, t. VI, p. 61 ; and especially to J. Petzoldt : " Einführung in die Philosophie der reinen Erfahrung," Leipzig, 1900.

of what it has learned. The first new truth depends on the discovery that logic and mathematics are one ; and that logic is not the science of ' correct thinking,' merely, but that it is a science of what *is*. Algebra, geometry, and the other mathematical systems have never seemed describable, quite, as systems of correct thinking : their validity has been too objective for this, and too independent of whether this man or that, or whether whole generations of men, *thought* in such a way or not. And whether a more than individual being ' thought' in that way has seemed to most mathematicians a meaningless inquiry. Mathematics has always dealt with something that clearly is more than the mathematician's mere thought, with something, that is, which either is so or is not, and is inexorably the one or the other. In questions of logic, moreover, thought, in order to be ' correct,' had to proceed in certain ways, had to conform to laws, and so there was at least a presumption that logic too was a science of something ' correct,' of something at least not identifiable with thought ; since thought might be correct or incorrect. And now logic and mathematics are seen to be only different branches of one science, and this united science would call itself a science of *being*[1] rather than a science of correct thinking. Thus one of its exponents, Bertrand Russell, has said that " truth and falsehood apply not to beliefs, but to their objects ; and that the object of a thought, even when this object does not exist, has a Being which is in no way dependent upon its being an object of thought."[2] What thought is and

---

[1] We neglect for the moment what philosophers may say to this.

[2] " Meinong's Theory of Complexes and Assumptions," Mind, 1904, N.S. vol. 29, p. 204.

how it is related to its objects are strictly other issues, and the new logic believes that it deals with no such entities as thoughts, ideas, or minds, but with entities that merely *are*.

We now turn to the science itself, its methods and its results. The following account, derived mostly from recent papers on mathematical or symbolic logic, does not presume to be an adequate summary of that so actively growing science. If summary at all, it is one merely of such fundamental truths as are now firmly established, and as seem to have a serious bearing on philosophical theory and procedure.

In their article on symbolic logic Huntington and Ladd-Franklin, after mentioning the researches made in the latter half of the nineteenth century, say that, " The first result of these inquiries was the recognition, more clearly than ever before, that every mathematical theory is based on a small number of fundamental hypotheses, or postulates, from which all other propositions of the theory can be deduced."[1] Moreover, it is generally accepted, as by Russell, that " Since all definitions of terms are effected by means of other terms, every system of definitions which is not circular must start from a certain apparatus of undefined terms." And it is desirable " to make the number of undefined ideas as small as possible."[2] The plane geometry of Euclid is a familiar example of such a mathematical theory. Available editions of Euclid are in the light of modern knowledge uncritical to the last degree, and

---

[1] Edward V. Huntington and Christine Ladd-Franklin : " Symbolic Logic," The Encyclopedia Americana, New York, 1905, vol. ix.

[2] B. Russell : " The Theory of Implication," Amer. Journ. of Math., 1906, vol. 28, p. 160.

the apparatus of undefined ideas is usually disguised under ' definitions ' and ' axioms.' Thus the ' axiom,' of somewhat doubtful authenticity, that " a straight line is the shortest distance between two points " is strictly speaking neither a self-evident proposition nor yet a definition. The straight line in Euclid is one of the undefined ideas, and this so-called axiom serves merely to point out to the reader, and to name, a familiar instance of one of the entities on which the geometry is based, an undefined idea that it takes ready-made. The truth needs to be emphasized that whatever reference is made in a mathematical system to these undefined entities is solely by way of pointing out (or exhibiting) and naming that which is intended. If terms are defined by means of other terms in the system, the pointing out and designation of terms is not properly definition, and in the following pages it will often be referred to as ' exhibition '; a term that has some ulterior advantages.[1] The ' postulates ' in Euclid, although marshalled inaccurately, are correctly propounded as fundamental hypotheses.

Now in regard to the building up of any deductive theory Huntington says : " The first step in such a discussion is to decide on the *fundamental concepts* or *undefined symbols*, concerning which the statements of the algebra are to be made. One such concept, common to every mathematical theory, is the notion of a class (K) of elements (a,—b,—c,)."[2] . . . " Having chosen

---

[1] Oddly enough, in view of the quotation just made from Russell, that author nevertheless includes this process under definition (" Principles of Mathematics," p. 27). It is hard to see how he can consistently do this.

[2] E. V. Huntington : " Sets of Independent Postulates for the Algebra of Logic," Trans. of the Amer. Math. Soc., 1904, vol. 5, p. 288.

the fundamental concepts, the next step is to decide on
the *fundamental propositions* or *postulates*, which are to
stand as the basis of the algebra. . . . Any set of
consistent postulates would give rise to a corresponding
algebra—namely the totality of propositions which
follow from these postulates by logical deduction."[1]
Thus the fundamental entities are of *two kinds*, the
elements or terms (' undefined symbols ') which if not
exhibited have at least to be named ; and the propositions or postulates (or hypotheses) from which the
entire algebra follows by logical *deduction*. This distinction is of the highest importance, because the terms
or elements play, if one may speak figuratively, a
passive part in the system ; while the propositions, one
is bound in spite of the metaphor to feel, are the *active*
factors. This opposition of active and passive is perhaps
not generally recognized and may at first seem highly
fanciful. Nevertheless the strictest logicians have not
been able to avoid language that implies just this
opposition. The postulates it is that yield, by deduction, the subsequent portions of the system. We shall
meet with this distinction again, and anyone who has
not now and then been aware of logical *agency* should
well consider what it is, for instance, when he is drawing
an ellipse by the analytic formula (proposition) that
makes the two ends meet. This same fact of agency
can be detected in any deductive system.

Some ambiguity may arise on two points. One is the
place of what are called relations, the other is that of
existential postulates. Spatial, temporal, and many
other relations, such as those of whole to part, likeness
and unlikeness, are familiar to everyone ; and in sym-

[1] *Ibid.*, p. 290.

bolic logic, if one were to accept the views of Kempe,[1] terms and relations or ' form ' would be the sole substance of logic. Yet clearly in a deductive system which is expressed in words rather than algebraic symbols, relations (such as A within B) must become propositions (A is within B). And although many words convey relations in non-propositional form, complete accuracy of form would probably require each relation to be expressed in a separate proposition. Thus— stones down from the wall—means at the least—stones were on the wall, and, stones fell. In our present provisional scheme, then, which confessedly sacrifices much detail to the purposes in hand, relations may be classed as propositions. Relations, however, like any propositions can themselves figure in a system as merely passive entities or terms ; their relational or propositional content being irrelevant to the system.

As to existential postulates, if they merely enumerate certain terms and state that these exist, they serve simply as an alternative way of stating that the system starts with these terms as the fundamental, given elements. But such propositions, that *enumerate* all those terms whose existence they predicate, and we

---

[1] For important discussions on relation, see A. B. Kempe : " A Memoir on the Theory of Mathematical Form," Phil. Trans. of the Royal Society, 1886, vol. 177, p. 1 ; " On the Relation between the Logical Theory of Classes and the Geometrical Theory of Points," Proc. of the London Math. Soc., 1890, vol. 21, p. 147 ; Charles S. Peirce : " The Logic of Relatives," Monist, 1897, vol. 7, p. 161 ; Josiah Royce : " The Relation of the Principles of Logic to the Foundations of Geometry," Trans. of the Amer. Math. Soc., 1905, vol. 6, p. 353 ; and see specially, it being the most easily read, A. B. Kempe : " The Subject-Matter of Exact Thought," Nature, 1890, vol. 43, p. 156.

shall later meet another kind of existential postulate, are so sterile of deductive consequences that one may question if it is not more justifiable to keep these postulates apart from the rest, or else, as is often done, to do away with the propositional form and merely enumerate the elements in question under the head of Given. It is, of course, pure redundancy formally to enumerate the given terms and then later to postulate their logical existence.

Now while postulates or propositions seem to be the active portion of a deductive system, they are nevertheless powerless without the passive terms. It may be doubted whether any proposition or relation can even subsist without involving the existence of some terms ; but apart from this, the more terms the proposition has to bite on, as it were, the more can be deduced. Now the number and the kinds of terms to be found in a deductive system, specially in the less exactly formulated systems, are often far more than was at all indicated in the initial enumeration of the undefined Given. Thus in mathematical physics the laws of force yield deductions only when various masses are given in the system between which the forces operate, and these masses are often hypothecated *ad libitum ;* the laws of wave-transmission afford deductions only when points are present between which propagation of waves takes place ; or again, in geometry, from the definition of two lines that are everywhere equally distant from each other, interesting truths can be deduced about angles *if* a line is given cutting these parallel lines. Thus at the beginning of each new theorem in Euclid there is an enumeration of the Given, and there are here brought in many complicated figures whose existence in the system was not previously suspected by the reader, and which were apparently not implied by the elements and propositions originally postulated as the basis of the geometry. Such figures are the trapezoids, decagons, etc., whose existence seems hardly deducible from the fundamental apparatus assumed at the beginning of Euclid's treatise.[1]

Does now such discovery in a system, of terms that are not exhibited at the outset with the undefined Given, necessarily mar the deductive purity of the system ? Or can these new terms be yielded by deduction, just as new propositions are deduced ? Firstly, it is undoubtedly common enough to find systems in which new terms are arbitrarily imported whenever the framer happens to want them, regardlessly of whether they strictly ' exist ' in the system or not. Such terms certainly do mar its logical purity, although the blemish can usually be removed by an appropriate enlargement of the fundamental Given. But secondly, new elements can be deduced. Given, the class (K) of elements (a, b, c, — — —), and the proposition that, Every element unites (in a relation called, say, ' + ') with every other to form a new element;—then clearly as many new elements or terms are deductively generated in the system as there are different pairs of simple terms.

And this is definition in its stricter sense. The compound elements (a + b, a + c, b + c, — — —) have somewhat different properties from the simple elements (a, b, c, — — —), and the class of elements (a + b, a + c, — — —) has to be defined and named (as, say, ' dyads '). The definition would then read : Dyads are

---

[1] Recent revisions of Euclid have remedied this defect.

pairs of simple terms connected by the relation (+).
Where there are different kinds of dyads there will be
correspondingly several definitions. In this way " all
definitions of terms are effected by means of other
terms," and " every system of definitions which is not
circular must start from a certain apparatus of undefined
ideas."[1] This definition of ' definition ' preserves the
traditional meaning of the word ; as when triangle is
defined in terms of plane and lines, starch in terms of
carbon, hydrogen and oxygen, or government in terms
of laws and prerogatives.

Terms so compounded are obviously more *complex*
than the simple, fundamental terms which enter into
their composition. And familiar and unimportant as
it may seem to be, this difference between simple and
complex entities is a most significant fact. The relation
of simple to complex is an asymmetrical relation ; and
the definition of complex elements in terms of simple
is an *irreversible* process. The mere existence of a plane
and lines does not require the existence of a triangle,
but the existence of a triangle does require that of a
plane and lines. Carbon, hydrogen, and oxygen, can
be without being starch, while starch cannot *be* without
being these three elements. Logically speaking the

---

[1] Although, as mentioned in a previous note, Russell elsewhere
says (" Principles of Mathematics," vol. i, p. 27) that " many
notions are defined by symbolic logic which are not capable of
philosophical definition [in terms, presumably, of other ' notions '],
since they are simple and unanalyzable," it seems better to call this
not definition, but exhibition. For if such ' notions ' or terms are
not exhibited, they can scarcely be said to have been in any wise
grasped or fixed. The mathematical point is such an instance : it
is not defined, but the so-called definitions serve merely to *point out*
(to the onlooker, confessedly,) as best they can the entity postulated.

difference is, that from a + b the existence of a and b can be deduced directly, while from a and b the existence of a + b can be deduced only by means of an additional proposition. This fact, true as it is of both the material and the mathematical realms, argues a *structure* to the existing universe, and one that is ultimate, whereby entities are ordered in a series of graded complexities ; a true hierarchy of being that may well suggest Plato's ' realm of ideas.' The reason for which this feature now interests us is that in discussing consciousness we shall have to ask whether it is a simple or a complex entity. If complex, it can be defined ; if simple, it may be exhibited, but cannot be defined.

Thirdly, the existence in a system not only of complex, but also of new simple terms can be deduced from a certain kind of proposition, namely, the kind that postulates a recurrence. A simple illustration is—' A repeats itself.' Now the second A, being an A, must also repeat itself ; and so on without end. The variety of such recurrent propositions is seemingly as endless as the series of terms that each generates. Such processes can also generate propositions that are new, as well as terms.

Among recurrent processes is one of special importance, the principle of so-called mathematical *in*duction. Of this principle Poincaré has said that it is " at the same time necessary to the mathematician and irreducible to logic."[1] By ' irreducible to logic ' he undoubtedly means that mathematical induction is not a case of deduction. It has been asserted so persistently that deduction yields no more than what is ' wrapped up '

---

[1] H. Poincaré : " les Mathématiques et la logique," Revue de Métaphysique et de Morale, 1905, 13-ième année, p. 817.

in the premises, that the idea has become widespread that nothing novel can be deduced, in short that deduction is an essentially sterile principle. And to this idea may be attributed the above-quoted judgment of Poincaré. Yet deduction is scarcely to be defined as *any sterile* logical process. The essence of deduction lies in the logical *necessity* with which consequences, whether seemingly novel or not, follow from premises. Therefore any cases that are found in which the necessary consequences seem novel, cannot for that reason be denied to be deductive. Now the proposition for mathematical induction reads, in general, If X is true of the nth term, it is true of the $n+1$th term (where X is any particular relation or proposition) : and no one denies that from such a premise logically necessary conclusions can be drawn. And it seems equally impossible to deny that in this case *in*duction is a misnomer for deduction. Indeed, of induction as a whole, Russell says : " What is called induction appears to me to be either disguised deduction or a mere method of making plausible guesses."[1] In fact, all the recurrent types of deductive process, including ' mathematical induction,' show how fertile and laden with novelty deduction can be ; and afford also perhaps the most striking instance of that logical *agency* that was spoken of above. Deduction doubtlessly yields no more than is ' wrapped up ' in the premises, yet the most surprising things often come wrapped up : nor are the wrappings usually supposed to detract from their novelty. The fruitfulness of recurrent, or as Royce has called them, of ' self-representative ' processes, has been so cogently set forth

---

[1] B. Russell : *op. cit.*, p. 11.

in that author's Supplementary Essay,[1] that we need
hardly dwell further on the point. But one of Royce's
illustrations is so striking that it may well be quoted.
The system of whole numbers, he says, is generated
by a repetitive process, and yet " they do not prove to
be a monotonous series of contents, involving mere
repetition of the same ideas. On the contrary, to know
them at all well, is to find in them properties involving
the most varied and novel features, as you pass from
number to number, or bring into synthesis various
selected groups of numbers. Consider, for instance, the
prime numbers. Distributed through the number-series
in ways that are indeed capable of partial definition
through general formulas, they still conform to no single
known principle that enables us to determine, *a priori*,
and in merely universal terms, exactly what and where
each prime shall be. They have been discovered by an
essentially empirical process which has now been
extended, by the tabulators of the prime numbers,
far into the millions. Yet the process much resembles any other empirical process. Its results are
reported by the tabulators as the astronomers cata-
logue the stars."[2]

That peculiar agency, once again, which seems
inherent in recurrent and other deductive processes is a
feature that is especially worth noting. The given terms
and propositions *generate* what we know as the system
of valid deductions or ' consequences.' It seems to be
this relatively independent activity of the system itself
that the mathematician or logician follows, as he would

[1] J. Royce : " The World and the Individual," New York, 1900,
vol. i.; cf. especially pp. 490–538.
[2] J. Royce : *ibid.*, p. 576.

trace the course of a river, when he ' deduces ' by ' logical necessity ' hitherto hidden features of the system that he is studying. For at bottom ' logical necessity ' is the term of the conforming thinker, for that which logically *is*. Everything which is not logically necessary, in a system, is found in the end not to have being in that system ; for the latter contains only so much as the given terms and propositions do generate, and to this alone does the thinker find it ' necessary ' to conform his thought. Necessity seems not to be a fundamental category, but a derived one, though exact and proper in its place. And similarly, too, deduction is the thinker's name for his own act of conforming his thought to the relatively independent activity of the propositions that generate his system. Deduction would in the end depend on this activity for its meaning. But with this understood, I shall continue to use the term, for after all we are here attempting to conform our thought. The present point is the activity itself. Of this there are few more striking illustrations, aside from the recurrent processes above cited, than the generating formulæ of analytic geometry. Given a surface and the formula of any curve, however complicated, and the entire curve forthwith *is :* and the geometer follows after with his deductive thought to learn what this is.[1] Thus if " a point moves in a plane keeping everywhere at an equal distance from another

---

[1] This angency has been very interestingly instanced by Sheldon, who finds that the ' idea of more ' necessarily engenders a further train of ' ideas.' Wilmon H. Sheldon : " A Case of Psychical Causation ? " Psychol. Review, 1901, vol. 8, p. 578. We shall find reason later, however, for disagreeing with Sheldon's interpretation of the case as one of psychical, instead of propositional efficiency.

point (the centre"), a circle forthwith *is*, and is in a sense that would not be without this formula. Another instance, in a very different field, is the case of the characters ' given ' in a drama or novel. It was Émile Zola, I believe, in one of his *préfaces*, who first insisted that the dramatist is not his own master, that he merely watches to see what his personages with their given temperaments and in the given situations *must* do, himself having no further part in the matter than to set on paper the ensuing events. The novelist and dramatist, like the mathematician, are onlookers at the logical spectacle. But the instances of propositional activity are innumerable : they can be found in any even fairly coherent universe of discourse, in any realm of thought.

The upshot of this consideration of the potency and the fruitfulness of deductive processes is that we must quite dissent from seeing any dilemma in the following statement of Poincaré : " The mere possibility of mathematical science seems an irresolvable contradiction. If that science is deductive only in appearance, where does it get that perfect validity that no one thinks of setting in doubt ? If, on the contrary, all the propositions that it enumerates can be derived from one another by the rules of formal logic, how is it that mathematics is not reduced to an immense tautology ? "[1] Its terms and propositions *are* derived from the given terms and propositions, but this implies no tautology. Why should it ?

A last feature to be noted of propositions, whether repetitive or not, that yield deductions is that

---

[1] H. Poincaré : " sur la Nature du raisonnement mathématique," Revue de Métaphysique et de Morale, 1894, 2-ième année, p. 371.

they show how actually the Many can be One. A
series of elements is in itself many, but is unified
in the one proposition that generates it. This solution of an ancient and vexatious problem is the
contribution of Royce, and the reader is referred to
that author's notable Supplementary Essay above
mentioned.

Briefly to sum up, then, this sketch of what mathematical logic is ; we have found that its subject-matter
is systems of being or, as they are often called, universes
of discourse. Any system of being, if it is a coherent or
true system, arises from a certain Given consisting of
terms and propositions, which generate of their own
motion all further terms and propositions that are in
the system. The Given together with these latter are
the system. The act by which the thinking mind explores those parts of the system that ensue from the
Given is called deduction by logical necessity, or simply
deduction. It is ordinarily asserted that inconsistent
propositions cannot be, that is *are* not, together in one
system. Furthermore, the fundamental terms are
undefined ; but they have being in the system, and if
they are also to have being in the exploring mind of the
individual who apprehends the system, they have
somehow to be exhibited to that mind. But this
exhibition is a psycnological and not a logical consideration. Other terms may be defined ' in terms of ' the
fundamental terms, and in that case the former are
essentially more complex entities. The relation of
simple to complex is asymmetrical, and it would not be
possible truly to define simple terms by means of others
that are more complex.

In this account more emphasis has been laid on

activity of propositions than would have been laid at the present time by a specialist in mathematical logic, more perhaps than such person would find at all just. Thus Kempe has stated definitely that exact thinking is purely a matter of the ' form ' of thought, and in the point manifolds which Kempe has so ably discussed all appearance of activity has been as far as possible suppressed. This author seems to have gone further than anyone else, recently, in conceiving of logical systems as absolutely static ; although most other logicians seem to neglect activity or change (even as concepts) with remarkable steadfastness. And thus it has been charged against logic that it conceives of any system as ' a dead and finished product instead of a living and moving process ' ; whereas, in fact, " the whole *is* not, if ' is ' implies that its nature is a finished product prior or posterior to the process, or in any sense apart from it. . . . Its ' parts ' are through and through in the process and constituted by it."[1] In so far as this criticism means that logic has unwarrantably neglected the concept of activity, it seems to me just, for on that topic logic is strangely reticent : and hence, as it seems to me, is hardly prepared to discuss motion as the physicist meets it, or even as the mathematician has to use the term. One cannot imagine, for instance, how logic would attempt to discuss critically the movement (all too easily assumed as self-evident and free of logical difficulties) of a point along a locus ; and logic would be even more helpless in face, say, of the ' ephemeral,' a concept nevertheless with an indefeasible meaning. Yet in order to make up for this deficiency, logic needs

---

[1] H. H. Joachim : " The Nature of Truth," Oxford, 1906, p. 76.

C

only to recognize, as it seems to me, and to study further the intrinsic activity of propositions. Unlike motion in space, this activity does not of course involve time ; but time involves it, being a special case thereof. Logical activity is neither spatial nor temporal.

CHAPTER II

OBJECTIONS TO THE PROGRAMME OF LOGIC

WE cannot, I regret to say, advisedly pass at once from this brief outline of logic to those epistemological considerations which are the immediate object of our interest and the actual topic of our discussion. For in the first place we must consider some objections of a fundamental nature which philosophy has urged against the programme of logic above outlined; and in the second place we must consider some of the conclusions to be derived from this programme, for these are in several cases at variance with tenets which are more or less popular, and more or less frequently and unconsciously used by us in philosophical argument. And several of these less popular theorems of logic are indispensable lemmas to our own further discussion. Thus the programme of logic must be defended and then expanded, before we can enter with secure steps the field of epistemology. And I crave the reader's indulgence in behalf of these further preliminary considerations, should they for the moment appear to be wanting in relevancy and interest. The lemmas are indispensable and our later need of them guarantees at least our later interest. Let us proceed, then, in the next three chapters, first to the fundamental objections which philosophy has urged against the general programme of logic, and secondly to some conclusions derivable from this programme which have a bearing on philosophy and epistemology.

The most sweeping objection, and one that is urged, I believe, in some form or other by every species of idealism, is that *being* is not the fundamental category. Therefore, of course, any philosophy is shallow and trivial which takes mere *being* for its foundation stone. In the philosophy of Descartes, since at first he was assured of the being of nothing but himself, and of himself solely because he could ' think,' *esse* is secondary to *cogitare ;* and later on *esse* is found to be secondary to *cogitari :* in the philosophy of Berkeley *esse* is secondary to *percipi :* in that of Kant *being* is secondary to *being real :* in Fichte *being* is secondary to *being willed :* and in Hegel it is secondary to *being thought by the Absolute.* Thus the mere logician, fancying as he does that *being* is the most fundamental of all categories, is as ignorant of the serious problems of philosophy as the sanguine digger for gold who expects to unearth the precious metal everywhere. The stupid fellow delves in *being* for his treasure, whereas the mother store is in *being real* or *being perceived* or *being willed* or *being thought ;*—according to one's bias. This question of venue is clearly one of prime importance.

Now it is certain that the fundamental category must include all entities and all processes whatsoever ; its name must have a universal denotation. But that which denotes everything cannot especially denote any-thing, that is, can connote nothing. That which all things are is not a feature or property by which some things are distinguished from any others. And furthermore, the universal predicate cannot be complex, for then it would have parts which would be entities and of which the universal predicate could not be predicated. Wherefore, aside from the fact that *being real, being perceived, willed,* and *thought* do mean something special and hence are not universal predicates, they are again not universal predicates because they are not simple. Is it not evident that *being real* or *being thought* or *being* anything whatsoever is both a more complex and a more special thing than merely *being?* *Being,* which connotes nothing, denotes everything and by virtue of this is the one universal category.

As to *being real* (like *being true*) we know that there is the opposed category of *being unreal* (and *untrue*); so that some additional determination over and above *being* is needed to make an entity real or unreal (true or untrue). *Being real* connotes more than *being;* the former is more complex than the latter. But to *being* there is no such negative category : *being not* are words without meaning, printer's ink and nothing more. The proposition, for instance, that ' A is not ' is either elliptical (and means ' A is not here,' ' is not in this system,' *et cætera*) or otherwise it is self-destructive and false (like the sceptical proposition—" It is true that there is no truth "). For the printed symbol A stands for some entity which we may call A's meaning, and if there *is* a meaning for A, then A's meaning *is,* and the proposition that ' A (i.e. A's meaning) is not,' is self-contradictory and hence false. If, on the other hand, for the printed A there is no meaning, the proposition is meaningless ; it is printed symbols and nothing more. *Being not* are always meaningless symbols. There is then no category negative to *being,* but there is a negative to *being real,* and it is *being unreal.* Both the real and the unreal *are,* and hence *being real* connotes something more special and denotes less, than *being*. *Being* is simpler than *being real* ; it includes *being real* and more besides : but *being real* does not include all *being*. Hence *being* is the more fundamental category.

As to *being thought* or *being willed*, both are processes, and are clearly more special than *being*. And moreover if ' thought ' and ' will,' as intended by idealism, mean anything at all comparable to what these words ordinarily and properly connote, they are active processes which are much more complex, even, than the activity of simple logical propositions. Thinking and willing are special cases of activity ; and the special case, while it denotes less, connotes more than the general, and is therefore more complex and less fundamental than the latter.

It is said, to be sure, that the human mind ' knows ' nothing except that which it thinks ; so that for its knowledge at least there is no negative category of *not being thought*, opposed to *being thought*. There is, however, even for human knowledge, just such an opposed category, and it is encountered in the ' unthinking,' the ' thoughtless,' the ' unconscious,' and the ' inanimate.' And then in order to make room for these in idealism, recourse is had to ' some other than the merely human thinker and willer,' to some sort of Absolute. Now if anything more is meant or connoted by the ' Absolute's thought ' or ' will ' than logic means by entity and proposition, that is to say, by *being*, then by just so much do these former categories fail of being fundamental. If no more is connoted by them, then idealism has chosen its terms most ill-advisedly. The latter case would be a less serious predicament, but there can be no doubt that it is in the former case that idealism actually finds itself. The one character common to all forms of idealism, as the name itself suggests, is the fundamental position ascribed to one or other of the functions of mind—to thinking, perceiving, knowing, valuing or willing; and, to glance at the genetic aspect of the matter, the peculiar charm of idealism, its huge vogue with the philosophical masses, has resulted from its subtly animistic flavour.[1] It has profited, genetically speaking, by an intimate, egocentric appeal over and above whatever argumentative cogency it may possess. The critical aspect of the case, however, is that the fabric of idealism is reared on a set of pseudo-fundamentals. The simple entities of logic are more fundamental than the pseudo-simples of idealism, and logic offers a more thoroughgoing analysis of the world of experience than does idealism. The important question remains, whether logic is able to discover a principle of unity in this world.

We have found that *being*, as we have it in logic, is not so superficial and insignificant a category as is sometimes alleged, but is fundamental, and we must next ask whether logic offers, in order to unite its simple elements, an adequate principle of unity: and by ' adequate ' I do not mean adequate, perchance to some human craving for a unified universe, but adequate to account for as much unity as the universe actually exhibits. The pious desire for a unified universe is no guarantee that the universe is really a unit. There seems, however, empirically to be a degree of unity, and

---

[1] Richard Avenarius was the first, I believe, to point out that idealism is a sort of anthropomorphism, which, although refined and rarefied, is not incomparable with that of theology : " Der menschliche Weltbegriff," 2te Auflage, Leipzig, 1905.

we may ask whether logic has a principle to account for that. Now there is a considerable weight of opinion that logic has not such a principle : it is urged that the relations of logic are ' external ' to the terms, and that they do no welding. Thus it is argued that " a simple entity cannot *as such*, and considered *as such*, be related to anything. If we identify, distinguish, or in any way relate A and B—two simple entities—we have *eo ipso* retracted their simplicity ; and their simplicity never existed, if their nature justified our proceedings."[1] The assumption on which symbolic logic proceeds, that although in a system the terms are united by relations, yet each term has being in itself and ' independently ' of the other terms—this assumption by insisting on such an *externality* of the relation shows itself to be nothing in the world but a ' problem to be solved.'[2]

[1] H. H. Joachim : "The Nature of Truth," Oxford, 1906, p. 11. It is not the invariable rule that an Hegelian disciplines himself to brevity and clearness of expression ; but this volume of Joachim possesses every merit of style, not to mention the distinction of its thought, and I shall venture to refer to it extensively.

[2] And Joachim very happily illustrates the futility of simple parts that are supposed to have being independently of their system, by reference to so-called absolute moments of time and absolute points of space. "What an absolute moment or an absolute point may be, how it is distinguished from other absolute moments or points, how it is recognized, or how anything can be said about it which will serve to fix its absolute individuality : of all this I am ignorant, and I have not yet found any one to enlighten me " (*ibid.*, p. 45). How such a point can be identified is perhaps irrelevant to whether it can *be*. We believe that some things are, as for instance various heavenly bodies, without our being able to distinguish them. But the issue seems to me here to have been confused between absolute points and absolute individuality of *position*. If we grant for the moment that all points absolutely and severally *are*, it still remains clear that any one of these is not a position. By ' here ' in space or ' now ' in time, we certainly mean a *relation*

It seems to be implied here that logic assumes that any and all entities, and propositions, already have and always have had being, and are stored away somewhere waiting for the algebraist to come and place them like blocks in this or that systematic order. Thus he hopes to get a true system, whereas he really gets nothing but a collection of juxtaposed but otherwise strictly un-related entities. The relations are external, as were the relations between the Herbartian ' ideas.' But the epithet ' external ' is rather confusing, for it implies reference to a possible ' internal ' relation, and since the simple entities that logic presumably ' externally ' relates have neither outside nor inside, the term is at best a misleading figure of speech. We are, however, all familiar enough with the way in which this word is interpreted, from Bradley's " Appearance and Reality." By external relation between two terms, the monadistic theory, Bradley means simply and solely a third *term* that does not relate, but separates the other two. But then, he says, if the given two are nevertheless by hypothesis related, there must be further two relations to relate each with the intermediate relation-term. Then these two new relations again do not relate but separate, and so more are required (by the hypothesis), and so on *ad infinitum odiosum*. Thus for Bradley a hideous scorbutus

between this point or moment and other points or moments ; and in the end, doubtless, position in time or space would not be " abso-lute" except with reference to *all* the points thereof. But this would not prevent each several point from having *being* and a fixed individuality (though not of position), and indeed I cannot see how we could ever mean ' here ' and ' now,' relative to the remaining points, unless this point of space and this moment of time did have its individual *being*. This consideration brings us back to the ' problem of external relations.'

breaks out everywhere to disfigure the appearance of reality.[1] By what right Bradley posits a relation and then instantly declares it to be a term, and having posited that it unites at once declares that it separates, we may leave for the super-ingenious to discover. But what else can the relation be, except it be a term ? it might be inquired : and the answer is that just possibly it is a relation. It may be that the ultimate components of a universe, whether they are ideal or other, are of at least two distinct types—terms and relations. Much if not all of our experience speaks for this, and logic has proceeded (correctly, as I think) for the time being to assume it.

Now as to the objection that if terms have being, severally, they simply cannot be related, it is to be admitted that if ' severally ' meant ' absolutely independently ' the hypothesis itself would deny the possibility of a relation. But on the other hand the proposition that ' a simple entity (x) *is*,' assuredly says nothing at all as to whether it *is* independently or otherwise. " But a simple entity," it is objected, " cannot *as such*, and considered *as such*, be related to anything." Now to me it is not as such self-evident that the propositions that A is after B, A is over B, A is within B (here B is not simple) and A is next to B, in all of which A may be simple, involve any internal contradiction ; and the only arguments that I know for supporting this objection are essentially like that of Bradley just cited. But by the same showing A could no more be related to anything else, if it were complex. Apparently, then, there is no

[1] For an interesting discussion of the monadistic and monistic theories of relation the reader is referred to Russell's " Principles of Mathematics," p. 221 *et seq.*

such thing as relation anyhow. It is perhaps the fatal objection of Hegelianism that in endeavouring to explain, it frequently explains *away ;* and this outwits the purpose of the argument.[1]

We are not, however, with regard to the being of terms and relations, to suppose ourselves so disastrously at variance with the Hegelian doctrine, for if we were to concede everything except the one ineffable whole of the Absolute (though to be sure we shall never be able to compass this with our merely finite minds) we shall presently learn, concerning any set of judgements, that the " context, as a concrete unity of significance, invests the several enunciations—*so long as they are not severed from it*—with determinate meaning : . . . the fuller significance, which is affirmed in the system of judgements as a whole, is affirmed in its many different ' moments ' or ' emphases ' as the determinate relatively-partial meanings of the several judgements."[2] And here are our old friends again. We cannot for the nonce know whether ' moments ' are the terms, and ' emphases ' the propositions, but we do not need to, for both are back again as ' partial meanings.' It is denied to logic that propositions and terms have being, but to the initiates the mystery is promptly unveiled that as to the Absolute system as a whole, " as a *concrete* unity of significance, its identity is, so to say, ' many-faceted,' and it can obtain adequate expression only through the different affirmations emphasized in the various con-

---

[1] For a discussion of external and internal relations the reader is referred to Bertrand Russell : " On the Nature of Truth," Proc. of the Aristotelian Society, 1907, N.S. vol. 7, pp. 28–49. Cf. also H. M. Sheffer : " A Programme of Philosophy Based on Modern Logic," Doctorial Thesis at Harvard University, 1908, pp. 23–28.

[2] H. H. Joachim : *op. cit.*, p. 103.

stituent judgements of the system " (*ibid.*, pp. 103–4).
And indeed : " Any constituent judgement of the
system *in vital coherence with the other constituents* affirms
a determinate meaning, because it is the emphatic and
concentrated affirmation of a distinct [! !], though in-
separable, feature of the fuller significance " (p. 103).
The words which the author has italicized add nothing,
because ' the other constituents ' are no less than *all*
that is contained in the Absolute, and so infinitely much
our finite minds cannot apprehend ; so that whether
our partial meanings do cohere vitally with the Absolute
or not, is for ever beyond our ken.   In all exactness
Hegelianism here makes a vulgar concession to the
general, for if a constituent judgement, i.e. proposition
or term, has meaning *only* because it coheres inseparably
and vitally with the one organic whole, the Absolute,
it will have no meaning at all *for us*, because in our finite
minds it coheres inseparably with nothing so immense.
Strictly, for this reason, Hegelianism should assert that
it finds no meanings whatsoever in any and all propositions or judgements ;   and to this many non-
Hegelians would possibly assent. In short, we have been
told that while relational coherence is a problem to be
solved and one that presents insuperable difficulties,
' vital ' coherence is the most obvious thing in the world,
needing not to be questioned.   Just how far the partition of the Absolute may go and yet leave the parts
each with a ' partial meaning,' Hegelianism seems not
to say : but logic, which in the meantime has been
cutting no such intellectual antics, does say ; it may
go as far as simple terms, and simple relations or
propositions.
   If there were validity in these objections to logical

relations, we should be forced to inquire what unity it is that the Absolute is supposed to confer on those 'moments' or 'emphases' of our universe which to mortal mind seem so 'distinct' and discrete. Discrete elements are not made a unit by the assertion that they 'cohere vitally' in the Absolute whole. If no principle of coherence can be exhibited this Absolute remains for ever a mere aggregate of truly unrelated elements. Now the objection that logical relations do not relate, or unify, is not valid, because every logical system of terms in relation is generated by a proposition or set of propositions, and herein lies their unity. The terms in relation are the explicit variety that is implicit in the unity of the proposition. And here it is interesting to note that the one actual demonstration of the unity which may be attributed to the Absolute, that of Royce in his Supplementary Essay, shows this to be the unity of a *Kette*, a recurrent *logical* process. Any series of logical elements, howsoever many they are, is unified in the *one proposition that generates it*. And a logical system is not a mere aggregate of terms plus an 'external' scheme of relations, but is in a very exact sense the production of one or of some few purposes, and has a true teleological unity.[1] The many grow out of the one. And while the system, any system, as a whole has *being*, the several elements or 'moments' (if one prefers) have also determinate character and *being*. Indeed, the dispute so industriously fostered by Hegelians as to the independent being of terms and propositions, is precious and pointless to the last degree. Logicians speak of terms and propositions and say simply that these *are*:

---

[1] Concerning purposes and propositions, and "final purposes," more will be said in a later chapter.

and by this nothing more is meant than is meant by Hegelians when they say that ' distinct ' moments and emphases *are*. If the entities are ' distinct,' and the opponents seem to grant this, it is all that logic needs. Moreover, deductive systems are strictly or even 'vitally' coherent, and undoubtedly their *being* depends on the Given group of propositions. Modern logic does not assert the storehouse theory of being that has been imputed to it. And thus we can heartily agree with Joachim when he says of every ' significant whole ' that : " Its organization *is* the process of its self-fulfilment, and the concrete manifestation of its individuality. But this process is no mere surface-play between static parts within the whole : nor *is* the individuality of the whole, except in the movement which is its manifestation. The [significant and united] whole *is* not, if ' is ' implies that its nature is a finished product prior or posterior to the process, or in any sense apart from it."[1] Such indeed is the significant principle of unity which logic offers : an explicit variety of terms is implicit in one proposition ; an explicit and highly diversified system is implicit in a set of very few propositions. And so far from this principle being inadequate or inferior to some other, it is, so far as I can ascertain, the sole principle of unity amid variety that has ever been discovered.

Such is the logical principle of unity, but it is a different, and, indeed, an empirical question how far our universe is actually a coherent and unified whole : a question which we shall later consider.

We have considered two philosophical objections to the programme of logic ; the first, that *being* is not the

---

[1] Joachim : *op. cit.*, p. 76.

fundamental category, and the second, that logical relations do not relate, i.e. that logic has no principle of unity. I have tried to show that both objections are unfounded. Let us turn to a third objection.

Logic believes that systems can correspond by a one-to-one relation, one with another : they may be, even, ' isomorphous.' And furthermore, it is believed that logical systems may be profitably studied because they have some definite ' application.' Any theory or law in physics from which deductions may be drawn, is in so far a deductive system, and it is said to ' apply ' to the motions of concrete objects which the physicist is studying. So too, Euclidean space is said to apply to, and to explain, the space in which we live. There is clearly a notion of correspondence here between two systems, one a concrete and ' actual ' one (whatever that may mean) and the other, not a system of ' thought,' for we have seen that logic rightly denies this, but a logical or conceptual one. The ' actual ' system is presumably more complex, contains irrelevancies or at least qualities which can be abstracted from it to leave as a skeleton—the purely neutral system. The two are then identical so far as structure goes ; while one, the ' actual,' merely has additional matter laid on to its fundamental structure. This difference is like that between two pictures which are identical, save that one is coloured and the other is in black and white.

But this notion of a one-to-one correspondence between the elements of two such systems is not so free of difficulties as it may at first seem. In a discussion of ' truth as correspondence ' Joachim brings up some arguments against the notion of one-to-one correspondence which, although I am not asserting that corre-

spondence is truth, concern us here on behalf of the
possibility of correspondence itself. First of all, in so
far as logical systems are applied or correspond to ' real '
or ' actual ' systems, it is urged that the notion of a
' real' system, to which the logical system corresponds,
is fraught with vagueness and cannot be made precise.
I readily grant that there are difficulties enough here,
and especially if the logical system is supposed to be a
' thought' system in the current dualistic sense. But
I have already contended that this dualistic sense is
incorrect; that the subject-matter of logic is not
mental and that deductive systems have a being which
thought conforms to, but which is not essentially
thought-being. Undoubtedly the mind apprehends the
deductive, as likewise the ' real ' system : but this is a
different issue and is to be discussed further on. On the
one hand, then, there is a purely logical or neutral
system.

How, now, does this system differ from the ' real '
system to which it is ' applied ' ? What is this latter, and
in what sense is it more real than the former ? If by
' real ' is meant some reference to that physical *Ding an
sich* or matter which Berkeley opposed and successfully
demolished, but which I believe is still the notion practically held by all but the most advanced of natural
scientists, we must admit, or rather assert, that neither
system is more ' real ' than the other. But as Joachim
says, " In general we take the simpler or more abstract
expression as the representation of the fuller, or more
concrete, expression of the idea " (*op. cit.*, p. 17) ; this
latter being the real system. And this is all, I think,
that the word ' real ' ordinarily means in this connection.
This is, however, by no means enough. A distinct

theory of reality is, or ought to be, implied. And whatsoever this 'real' system is found to be, it will undoubtedly be a part of that larger system which includes
all that *is ;* a system that includes both the 'real' and
the 'unreal.' But real and unreal are distinctions
that are logically later than our present plane of argument and I have not (either now or later on) any theory
of reality to offer. The word is bound to mean something,
doubtless, and whatever this meaning is, the 'real'
system, like the deductive logical system, will be a part
of the realm comprising all that *is :* so that if correspondence is possible at all, there should be no difficulty
with correspondence between logical and 'real' systems.
Provisionally it should seem that of any two systems
which, although in some way distinguishable, yet express the same purpose or have the same deductive
structure, that would ordinarily be called 'real' (by
contrast) which is the more concrete, elaborate, and
complete.

But Joachim urges two objections against correspondence itself. The first of these seems to me to be
purely psychological. As to the truth of a correspondence between two systems, that is as to its exactness
or completeness, he says : " But if we are driven thus
to emphasize the embodiment of purpose, the teleological structure, in both factors, it seems clear that
' truth ' of a narrative or portrait—or even of a reflection
—becomes increasingly dependent on the nature of the
' recognition ' by the apprehending mind. We can no
longer suppose that the mind plays the part of the
absolutely disinterested spectator, and *in no sense*
' makes ' the facts. On the contrary, the mind sees what
it makes by its interpretation : and the ' truth ' of the

D

corresponding factor varies in degree with the nature of the recognition which the mind brings to bear. What the painter sees in the face, *that* he expresses in his portrait ; and the portrait will be more or less ' true ' or ' faithful ' according to the painter's insight, and, again, according to the mind of the spectator who sees and compares both the original and the picture " (*op. cit.*, pp. 15–16). Might one not in precisely the same way urge, that because in viewing a church one spectator notes the scheme of counter-balanced strains in the vaulting, another the merits of the colour schemes in the stained windows, and a third the historical importance of the inscriptions on the tombs,—that these apprehending minds ' make ' by their interpretation the church ? The fact seems to be too obvious to be worth articulation, that the entire object is so complex that each mind can apprehend only a part, but a part that is there.[1] If a complicated system embodies many purposes (and at present we seem to experience relatively few systems that are generated by a single purpose or proposition, and that are therefore strictly unitary) it follows that a simple system can correspond to but some special part of a more inclusive and elaborate whole. And we have already considered the objection that no such special parts have being. Nor does the apprehending mind ' make ' the part that it apprehends ; it *selects* such part. How it does so is, of course, the psychological but not epistemological problem of attention.

It seems to me that this objection loses sight of a truth that Hegelianism ought most of all to keep

---

[1] If so special a matter as illusions and hallucinations is meant, it cannot be discussed here, but will be in a later chapter on " Error."

steadily in view, namely, that since the simple entities of a system have meaning only by inseparably cohering in a purposeful whole, then wherever any cohering parts *are* there *is also present* the purpose in which they cohere. So that the apprehension of this purpose by the mind of the spectator is anything but that mind's fabrication of an 'interpretation.' It must apprehend the purpose far more readily than the mere 'emphases' or 'moments' that fulfil and embody the purpose. Surely this objection cannot be urged by an Hegelian.

Even in his objection Joachim admits that the spectator sees and *compares* both the original and the picture, and comparison is possible, obviously, only where there *is* correspondence. In regard to the general contention (which may be met in the most diverse writers) that the mind makes or constructs this and that, as e.g. the laws of nature, it should be remarked that the terms 'make' and 'construct' are worthy of careful scrutiny. It may well be questioned whether they ever mean more than that this or that (which 'is constructed') merely *is :* although the terms profess to imply some how and whence of its being.

The second and more serious objection to the notion of correspondence is, briefly, that if two systems are sufficiently alike in structure to be said to correspond, they cannot correspond because they will be nothing short of identical. This is really the problem of similarity in difference, or of particulars and universals, and it will require a chapter for itself.

Before we proceed to that subject, however, it seems proper here to justify my rather casual assertion that purposes and propositions are one. Psychological doctrines of purpose, confused as they are with theories of emotion, are of course not here in question ; nor yet is the older doctrine of ' final causes,' although these latter are doubtless in the end merely purposes. But it must be shown that any purpose which guarantees the unity of a coherent whole is essentially the same as a proposition, or if one prefers, the latter is the same as the former. It will be granted at once that so far as language goes the two are necessarily expressed in the same way ; for although " A purposes to do x " is not quite like " A does x," yet wherever a system is in question in which the purpose is fulfilled, and which coheres and *is* merely by virtue of the purpose, all that can possibly be said is that " A does x." Both purposes and propositions are strictly reducible to the formula that A is a certain function of x. Thus a circle is the fulfilment of a purpose which is expressed as " the point A moves in a plane at a constant distance from a point B " : and this is identical with the briefer genetic formula $x^2 + y^2 = r^2$. Both are propositions. But aside from language the identity of purposes and propositions is shown by the fact that the two generate the systems that ' fulfil ' them in precisely the same way, and in both cases alike one can ascertain only by logical deduction what the resulting system is. The system follows from the purpose by logical necessity exactly as it follows from the proposition. This identity makes it possible to reconcile ' final ' with ' efficient ' causes. And, lastly, since the term ' purpose ' has a vague though unnecessary suggestion of a personality back of it, and since we have so far found no reason for admitting such a notion in connection with logical entities, I shall continue to use the name proposition.

CHAPTER III

CORRESPONDENCE: THE PARTICULAR AND THE UNIVERSAL

IT is to be remembered that our thesis is not that correspondence between two wholes is truth, nor that it is knowledge, but that such correspondence is possible. The establishment of correspondences is strictly not a portion of logic, but the ' application ' of logic to anything whatsoever seems to depend entirely on the possibility of there being such correspondences. And logic avers this possibility. In regard to the relation of correspondence to truth, as when a theory is said to be ' true ' if it corresponds to some ' real ' manifold, it seems to me that nothing is here meant beyond the statement that the *correspondence* is true, i.e. that it *is* in greater or less measure. If that which is wanted, as truth, is an abstract system that corresponds in its structure to some more concrete ' real ' system, then ' truth ' is found if such corresponding abstract system is found. And truth means, as here appears, consistency; means, namely, that in the correspondence there is no feature of one system that contradicts any feature of the other. But for this, in this case, correspondence itself must be possible.

Now it is urged by Joachim that correspondence " is simply a name for identity of purpose expressed through

materially different constituents as an identical structure, plan, or cycle of functions " (*op. cit.*, p. 10). " Now
if there is *no* difference in the two factors, there clearly
is no ' correspondence '—there is identity. But if there
is a difference, e.g. what we loosely call a ' material '
difference, how can there also be identity of structure ?
For ' structure ' is a name for scheme of inner relations,
and relations which really relate different elements
cannot be identical, i.e. cannot be identical if the differences of the elements are differences of them *qua* related.
Or we may put the matter less abstractly. On the one
side we have a whole of experience at the level of feeling ;
and, on the other side, a whole of experience at the level
of reflective thought. To say that there is (or may be)
identity of structure is to maintain that these experiences
are different matters subsumed under an identical form.
And whatever may be said of such a conception in
general, at least it does not do justice to the unity of an
experience-whole. Whatever may be the case with other
' wholes,' at least a felt-whole, or again a thought-whole,
are not elements *together with* a scheme of relations. *Such*
wholes at least cannot be analysed into materials subsumed under an external form—i.e. a form which can be
what it is, unaffected by the differences of the material
which it unifies " (*ibid.*, pp. 25–6). Now we need not
dwell on ' felt-wholes ' and ' thought-wholes,' for,
firstly, we are now discussing correspondence of logical
systems, and secondly, such wholes of feeling and thought
seem, at least to me, to be the very ones that reveal
most unambiguously identical structures in different
materials. The same melody on different instruments
and in different keys, the same picture painted in
different colour schemes, the same dramatic or emotional

climax ' worked up ' in different ' situations,' the same
mathematical demonstration imparted algebraically
and geometrically, and even the same theory expounded
in different languages, are as clear cases as one could
well wish of felt-wholes and thought-wholes that are
identical in structure but different in ' material.'

The more serious objection is that " relations which
really relate different elements, cannot be identical, i.e.
cannot be identical if the differences of the elements are
differences of them *qua* related." I confess that I never
know what ' qua ' means, but if it here means that the
relations cannot be identical (either in two systems or
within one system) if the elements differ *by virtue of* their
being related, so much is to be admitted. By being in
relation entities have added to them a *position* which is
in fact different from each entity. But neither the
elements on the one side nor the relations on the other
need be severally different from one another. It is the
merit of that view which we have adopted of the many
and the one, that it shows how in fact the principle of
self-representation generates a series of identical terms
each one of which bears the same relation to the one next
preceding, but each one of which is in a different position
and hence distinct from the others. But because the
whole has being I cannot see why it should be denied
and not rather stoutly affirmed, that the simple parts,
whether terms or relations, also have being—and this as
' distinct ' as one pleases. It is true enough that no *one*
of the simple terms or relations has position, but position
is not being. Nor is it claimed that the several *positions*
are identical. The several terms and relations, however,
are by the very hypothesis of self-representation,
identical. In short, then, the elements do differ in

position by virtue of being related, while any two elements or relations, though not their positions, are identical.

Cases of different 'materials' in identical forms are so familiar both in everyday experience and in the field of logic, that it is hard at first to convince oneself that any ambiguity is involved. No contradiction is apparent in the statement that as two mountains are *together*, so are two mustard seeds together. As a design can be executed in wood, so it can be in bronze. As a+b is, so is c+d : or that just as A repeats itself, so B repeats itself.

This objection really and finally resolves itself into the problem of the particular and the universal. The difficulty as to the same structure subsisting in different materials, or conversely of the same material shaped into different structures, is nothing other than the difficulty of a 'universal idea' (whether structure or material) subsisting in different particular embodiments or manifestations. Now in the traditional treatment of this subject it seems to me that two problems have been fused :—one, that of particularity or concreteness proper as opposed to universality or abstractness ; the other, which we have just touched on, that of identity in difference, or of repetition. How, namely, can any entity, whether term or relation, simple entity or complex, be repeated ?

The self-representative system that combines the many in the one, involves in its being the concept of repetition ; of logical repetition, that is, which is of course neither spatial nor temporal in essence. Whether this repetition constitutes a ' problem ' or not, I do not know. It is conceivable that just as improved forms of the microscope are revealing complicated structures in bodies that have been supposed simple, so further variety may be found in the logical entities that we now suppose to be simple. But at any rate repetition, if it is to be explained, is not to be explained *away*. And the empirical truth will scarcely be denied, that in wholes, the partial meanings or distinct moments frequently recur. And having traced the objection urged against correspondence, to the problem of repetition, we may leave it. For our point is that the objection alleged against the *being* of two systems of identical ' form ' but different ' materials ' does not actually rest on the ' externality ' of such relational structures to the term-materials. It really rests on the concept of repetition. And this problem, if such it is, is contained in its boldest form in the assertion, which is not rejected by idealism, that ' A is A.' The coherence of many in one is satisfactorily explained, it seems to me, and not explained away, in Royce's treatment of that topic ;[1]—a treatment that shows how relations are not ' external ' to their terms, and that at the same time lays special emphasis on ' self-representation,' a concept that rests on the concept of repetition. And this latter, although it doubtless offers an enticing field of research, presents itself as an empirical fact beyond all gainsaying, and one that may be recognized without inconsistency. Entities when ' repeated ' are invariably repeated with a difference, usually with a conspicuous difference of context, and always with at least a difference of position ; in the last analysis, of course, *logical* position.

Since we have chanced on the problem of the parti-

[1] J. Royce : " The World and the Individual," New York, 1903, vol. i., the Supplementary Essay.

cular and the universal, proper, and since this will concern us further on, it seems allowable to consider it here. A classical treatment of it is to be found in Hume, who declared that a genuine universal exists neither ' *reali-ter* ' nor ' *mentaliter.*' For think of any triangle, whatsoever, he argued, and you will find it not to be the triangle universal. Rather you will find it to be a right-angled, an isosceles, or a scalene triangle ; and in spite of yourself, it has some vague, or even a definite size, and perchance even some hint of colour. You will find it always to be a particular triangle. This particular idea can become general only by being annexed to a general term. In reasoning the mind has to run over the different particular individuals designated, in order not to make a statement inconsistent with one or more of them. This quick review of all the individuals becomes finally habitual, and the general term serves as a cue to set off the reaction. The ' general term ' which thus acts as a cue is of course itself a particular— a special sound, a printed word, or an impulse of thought.[1]

This doctrine, as Joachim says of current theories of the judgement, is " a hybrid, in which psychical elements . . . are unwarrantably blended with the purely logical fact " ; and it is, in my opinion, not even a just psychological description of the matter. The mind does not habitually run over all or even several of the individuals designated. The account of Mill does not materially differ from this, and I presume that modern pragmatists would say much the same—that an entity

---

[1] This " general term " is, of course, equivalent to the " *nomina,*" " *voces,*" and " *human designations* " of Boethius, Roscellinus, and other nominalists.

is particular or universal according to the use or function
that it subserves. Now any such account of the particular and the universal reveals a stage of thought in
which psychology has been imperfectly differentiated
from logic ; and we have here to ask what the purely
logical distinction is between universals and particulars.
If we ask what is the empirical feature that distinguishes
these two, we shall doubtless agree that a universal is
capable of numberless repetitions (the distinction undoubtedly presupposes repetition), whereas a particular
is unique, it is the ' this and no other.'[1] The difficulty
then that presents itself to logic is not in universals, for
all logical entities seem to be universals, but in particulars. Can logic define a particular, unique entity ?
If we turn for a moment to the purely empirical aspect
of things we note that any distinguishable entity,
whether simple or a complex whole, is so far capable of
an infinity of repetitions, and for the most part we do
experience it repeatedly. So it is with any animal,
plant or chemical element, a geometrical figure, any
equation, or a mathematical ' point.' Any whole is
so far a universal. But now *within* any whole we find
that no part can be identically repeated. The molecule
of water, so far as its being goes, can be and is repeated
indefinitely ; but the molecule of water that is part of a
coherent explicit system, as it is in the chemist's test-
tube, is just itself and no other, identical with itself,
and different, at least in position, from all the others,—a
particular molecule. So the ' point ' that merely *is,*
swarms in infinite multitude : but any point in a
system is distinguished by its position from all the

[1] Cf. Josiah Royce : " The Absolute and the Individual," an
essay in " The Conception of God," New York, 1898.

others, and *it*—the point so related—can never be
repeated. Thus within any system each least part is a
particular; and on the other hand the system as a
whole can be repeated, and is hence a universal. If it is
asked, Is any entity, then, absolutely particular? the
answer would be that every least item in a system is
absolutely particular if that system as a whole is so
comprehensive that there is nowhere a repetition of it.
One of the most comprehensive systems that we know
is undoubtedly the corporeal universe in space and
time, and herein the significance of the *dictum* of
Schopenhauer, that space and time are the great in-
dividuators. Thus it seems that particularity or
individuality, like position, is a relative term. Just as
relative (partial) position is defined by adjacent portions
of a system, and absolute position only by the system
entire; so the relatively particular is defined by a
portion, and the absolutely particular only by the whole.
Complex entities are defined in terms of their simple
elements, and a system containing such entities is by
that fact more inclusive than a system composed solely of
simple elements, and for that reason its entities are less
abstract and more particular. Thus the canine is a
particular genus within the order of mammals, collie
is a particular species within the genus of canines,
and Aberdeen collie is a particular variety within
the species. And so, *con*notatively, Aberdeen collie is
both a more complex and more particular entity than
canine.

Hence logic and discursive thought can never seize
hold of true particulars. Even Aberdeen collie is a
general term that has various embodiments in different
living animals. The man of thought prefers the timeless

universals, and leaves the fleeting particulars to the man of action ; who on the whole has his predilection as well. Even our so-called judgements of fact and of perception, as Joachim explains, do not succeed in seizing the particular fact that they profess to fix for us. In the fabric of knowledge our " judgements of perception persist and cling to life. But the distinctive features of those judgements, their individualities, are lost, and the life, to which by a metaphor you may say ' they cling,' is *their* life which they formerly enjoyed. The sciences of botany, of the physiology of the senses, of the physical conditions of colour, etc.—these may be said to absorb and to preserve the ' truth ' of such judgements, as ' this tree is green.' But the sciences neither contain any judgements of perception *as such*, nor preserve their ' truth ' in an un-altered form."[1]

It will be objected against this view of the universal and the particular that it exalts to the high place of universals precisely those fragmentary partial meanings, artificially abstracted from the concrete living reality —those abstractions that so far from having universal significance have the barest minimum of it. This is partly true, but in ' fragmentary, partial meanings ' lurks an ambiguity. The main business of science is the analysing of concrete processes, and the abstracting therefrom of bare formulæ that by their logical activity produce a *corresponding* process bared of its concrete (and in the respect chosen) irrelevant trappings. If these formulæ are the ' fragmentary, partial meanings,' it has to be pointed out that they are the complete and the sole *connected meaning* of the concrete ' living ' whole.

[1] H. H. Joachim : *op. cit.*, pp. 112–13.

All such meaning[1] lies in order, deductive arrangement, and this is comprehended in propositions or laws. If *this* is the part abstracted, such part is no partial meaning, but is the whole meaning. And there is no pertinency in the epithet ' artificial,' for the propositions abstracted, I have tried to show, were truly within the concrete whole. A skeleton is not ' artificial ' because it is removed from the muscles and other tissues. On the other hand, whether in a logical system or the concrete physical universe, a detached segment of terms or ' moments,' if it is too fragmentary to reveal what its deductive order is, has of course very little connected meaning, but is in so far (relatively) without significance. Its universality, however, is not lessened thereby. And it is to be granted that according to the view here defended, the categories of universality and of significance are by no means identical. The more universal need not be the more significant. The contention that universals must have ' universal significance ' is true only because ' significance ' means here something quite different, namely *denotation*—an utterly different thing from the *connected meaning* of our present discussion. And, to resume, the least segment, however fragmentary, has *being :* and it is fundamental to the attitude of logic that both the significant and the insignificant have being ; in fact, that being is the one quite universal predicate.

On this *being* of ' detached ' and ' artificially ab-

---

[1] Of course we are here dealing with connected meaning, significance—in the last analysis, deductive fecundity—and not with meaning in the other sense, i.e. as that entity to which a printed symbol refers, for which in the interests of human communication it stands.

stracted ' parts, we must specially insist. By this it is
not said that they have significance, much less that they
have truth, nor yet that they are ' independent ' beings
in that sense which idealism so delights to impute to
logic, and then to attack. To deny that the ' emphases,'
' moments ' or terms have being, is to explain away
everything that *is* meaningless, problematic, or mysterious. Whereas it is just the mysterious, the proble-
matical, that philosophy sets out to explain, and therefore admits at the outset to have being. This being is
so far neither dependent nor ' independent,' but if the
issue is forced, logic would say indeed that this being is
independent, that is, that the being of one part is not
dependent on the being of another part. And logic is
quite right in this, for while the being of any part does
depend on the generating formula or proposition, and
can be deduced therefrom, it does not depend on any
other part : so that all entities among themselves are
indeed strictly independent of one another. But these
propositions, have they independent being ? To this
question logic seems to say,—Look and see. It is an
empirical matter. If you can find one proposition from
which all other logical propositions, all mathematical
manifolds, and all the laws of nature can be deduced,
you will have demonstrated the dependence of their
being. At present we know that such propositions have
being : but whether that is independent or dependent
we do not know. Meanwhile it is to be noted that none
are more eager than logicians to reduce the number of
seemingly independent propositions from which any
given manifold can be deduced, to discover that some
supposedly independent postulate of a well-known
system, such as Euclidean space, can be deduced from

one of the other postulates. Logic is eager for such
unity, and accounts the elimination of any 'independent'
proposition from a system, or the demonstration that
one system is deducible from another supposedly independent system, an important event. But, on the other
hand, *how far* this can go, how far the universe has unity,
is a question that awaits empirical investigation. And
such 'fundamental' propositions as philosophy has
sometimes offered, the *cogito ergo sum*, or the 'ego posits
itself within itself,' for example, are, besides being too
anthropomorphic, too premature and over-reaching to
be deserving of very serious consideration. Logic, itself,
moreover, makes no hypothesis that the universe *is* a
complete unity : and one may well doubt that such is
the case. For there are propositions that contradict each
other, and as it seems irreconcilably, whereas a truly
single proposition seems never to yield a contradiction.
The problem of error is a serious obstacle in the way
of the hypothesis that the entire universe is one deductive system. We shall consider this problem again.
Meanwhile all terms, whether significant or not, and all
propositions, whether contradictory or not, have being ;
and the more dependent these can be shown to be, the
better. But the dependence must be shown.

To return now to the general consideration of correspondence between logical systems, an attempt has been
made to show that correspondence involves neither
contradiction nor ambiguity. The objection that
correspondence implies simple beings, and that simple
beings cannot be related to form a system, we have seen
to be really the objection urged by Bradley against the
many being also one. And this difficulty we have overcome by showing that the many grow out of one genetic

formula, and even that in a self-representative series there are endlessly many terms that are identical except as to their ordinal position. Besides, it was admitted by our objector that partial meanings *are* as ' distinct moments ' or ' emphases.' And this is all that the correspondence notion requires.

We have laid no stress on the so-called ' reality ' of one of the corresponding systems, for this means merely that the ' real ' system contains more than the other that is said to correspond. The objection that the mind makes its facts by its ' interpretation,' we have found to be a misapprehension. The mind does contain a part of the more comprehensive system, but such part *is ;* and the selection is a question of psychology strictly. The objection that an identical structure cannot subsist in two different materials, that if two systems really correspond they are identical, we have found to be a re-statement of the problem of particulars and universals : a problem which is in reality two. The first, that of the repetition of identicals, is solved in the doctrine here advocated of the many and the one. The second, that of concreteness as opposed to abstractness, is not essential to correspondence : but since it will concern us later, I have advanced a certain view. This is, that any entity of a system in its position in the system, is a particular, for it can never be repeated but is just itself and no other—in that system. Furthermore, different systems are of different complexities, and simple systems can be and are repeated in more comprehensive systems, and position in the more comprehensive system confers a higher degree of particularity than in the less comprehensive, the less concrete. And since the corporeal universe is a very comprehensive system,

E

position in that system confers a very high degree of particularity—although perhaps not the highest. Thus particularity is a relative term depending on position in a system and on the comprehensiveness of that system. Discursive thought, at least, even in judgements of perception, never seizes absolute particulars. And we shall later find reason for doubting that concrete corporeal activity does so either.

I have attempted thus to defend the notion of correspondence, not because correspondence is truth, for I see no connection between the two except that in so far as a correspondence is, it is a true correspondence ; nor yet because correspondence is knowledge, for whether this is the case or not, we have yet to inquire : but because, as I understand the matter, correspondence is one of the fundamental facts of our world. And it is as essential for logic that the repetition of systems (with some difference of position, at least, and often with more salient differences) be acknowledged, as that the repetition of a simple entity (with a difference of position) be admitted. This difference of position (in the former case), we shall doubtless see, is often in a system yet more comprehensive than the concrete world of time and space. The other differences are logically of two kinds : firstly, the terms of a system may differ from those of another, although the form is identical, that is, the same proposition or set of propositions generates both. And, secondly, a system may be generated by the same propositions as another, *and* by certain additional (non-contradicting) ones. The former system then includes the latter ; as solid includes plane geometry. This is for us the most important case. But wherever two systems correspond there is *identity* in just so far as there is correspondence. And it must be urged once more that the repetition of identicals (with indeed some systematic difference of position) involves no contradiction.

It is true that in this general programme, logic assumes the *being* of many, so-far distinct propositions. But it does not assert that such being is ' independent ' in the sense so often imputed by idealism. On the contrary, logic is as eager to discover the dependence of any or all of these propositions on one fundamental proposition—if this is possible—as chemistry is to reduce the number of elements. But logic rightly insists that such reduction must be a demonstration, and not an assumption. If all propositions can eventually be deduced from one fundamental proposition, it will have to be shown how a unified whole can contain contradictions. In short, error will have to be explained *away*. Since contradictions certainly *are*, there is at least a prejudice in favour of supposing that the universe of being is not a thoroughly unified whole. Entirely coherent it surely is not.

Thus we start, provisionally at least, with a pluralism of terms and propositions, all of which have ' distinct,' though not necessarily independent, being. And so far as any of the terms are related to one another it is because their being is not independent, although the terms are distinct, but is generated by the logical activity of a proposition. Many propositions are also generated by other more fundamental propositions. And the dependent relation of one entity upon another, whether terms or propositions, is for discursive thought the *deductive* relation. This provisional pluralism, however, has nothing to do with the dualism of mind and matter, or any other pluralism of substance. If the terms and propositions of logic must be substantialized, they are all strictly of one substance, for which perhaps the least dangerous name is neutral-stuff. The relation of neutral-stuff to matter and mind we shall have presently to consider at considerable length.

These two chapters on correspondence grew out of our attempt to survey the implications involved in the general programme of mathematical logic, set forth in the first chapter. We turn now to some further implications of this programme.

CHAPTER IV

FURTHER IMPLICATIONS OF THE PROGRAMME OF LOGIC

WE have seen that the material of logic is universes of discourse, and that any such universe consists of some number of fundamental, mutually consistent[1] propositions and a class of fundamental terms, together with all such further propositions and terms as *are*, if the fundamental entities are; that is, all that can be *deduced* from the fundamental propositions. In brief, we may say that a universe consists of a number of fundamental propositions with the terms that they contain, and all that can be deduced from them. The whole work of logic is now to find out what can thus be deduced, making as certain as may be at the same time that the fundamental propositions are in fact consistent, for this cannot in general be ascertained *a priori*. The universe of discourse is then a system of which the unity or coherence is guaranteed by the fact that the very *being* of the system is generated by the fundamental propositions. And it is admitted that the coherence is more secure if the entire system is generated by one, and this demonstrably one, proposition; wherefore every effort is made to reduce as far as possible the number of supposedly fundamental and so-far independent propositions.

[1] We shall have to inquire whether in fact logic is right in saying that these must be consistent.

53

In the last resort, then, coherence is dependence of being on propositions, and the absolutely coherent system is one that is generated by the (logical) activity of a single proposition ; as is the number system. Since now this activity becomes for discursive thought deduction, it follows that all coherent thought is deductive. While some such thesis has been asserted by several philosophers, the assertion has never been so unqualifiedly made nor so well sustained as by modern logic. This is partly because in the past the whole scope of deduction has been thought to be comprised in the forms of syllogism, which are in fact a small part of deduction, and a relatively unfruitful ; so that deduction has often been minimized, as by Mill, because it could prove no more than was ' contained ' in the premises. And in further part, deduction has in the past shared the honours in coherent thought, with ' induction ' : and this latter, Mill, for instance, accounted by far the more important part of ratiocination. Thus the statement that all coherent thought is deductive has come to many minds as a novelty, if not indeed as an absurd heresy. For description and explanation, to cite examples, are coherent exercises of thought, and yet that either of them is deductive would not be generally conceded. In fact, mathematics and formal logic are probably the only long-established disciplines that are generally acknowledged to be deductive. Now description and explanation are instances to the point, since any treatise, as this on consciousness, while presumably aiming to be coherent, sets out avowedly first to describe and then to explain its topic. Are these, therefore, deductive exercises ?

Now a description may be coherent or incoherent ; it

may be chaotic and unintelligible, or it may give the facts so consecutively that they seem already half explained. And any such merit, clearly, lies solely in orderliness. But what is order ? In describing the shells of a particular species of mollusc found in a given locality, the biologist who would describe coherently, classifies them and reports them, for a mere instance, in the order of their size—the smallest first, then the next larger, and so on up. Now in this orderly arrangement of the shells it is logically necessary that any shell shall be succeeded by the one just next larger, for otherwise the collection is not ordered. From the fact that it is ordered in this way, can be *deduced* the fact that the shell or shells if any, coming after any particular shell will be larger than it. In this lies the deductive nature of every orderly arrangement ; and it is a property that holds as much for the classifier as for the chance comer who surveys the classification accomplished. It guides the one in classifying, and instructs the other as to what he may look for. In either case the order is deduced from a genetic formula or law. To be sure the proposition on which the deduction is based is not formally stated, but it is there ; the orderly arrangement whereby many have become in a very real sense one, *is* it. To consider for an instant the psychology of the situation, a moment's reflection will show that in any business of life whatsoever the presence of order means the presence of some principle on which the order is ' based,' and the order is merely the obedient fulfilment of the principle. Moreover, the principle on which the order is based is always, at least to some extent, in consciousness ; although it may be well out in the fringe. And until such principle is to some extent grasped by the mind, the most orderly arrangement has for that mind all the look of chaos. The intelligent visitor to a museum asks first of all—On what principle are these objects arranged? He really means to ask—What deduction is in operation here ? And unless he can ascertain this he will spend his time quite as wisely in scrutinizing random pebbles on the beach. The whole quest for a ' natural ' system of classification, notably in botany, is the quest for that deductive principle which will make one whole out of many facts. All ' suggestion ' in literature, too, is such an arranging of thoughts as makes the reader deduce conclusions from a proposition not explicitly stated. Thus in their orderly arrangement, which is really their deductive arrangement, lies all the coherence and intelligibility of a collection of objects. So, too, the coherence and intelligibility of a description lies in the deductive arrangement of the topics treated.

It must be said in passing that from the orderly arrangement, according to size, of the mollusc shells one cannot deduce that after any particular shell there shall *be* another coming. Of course no collection of natural objects, whether classified or not, guarantees its own completeness. This fact does not prejudice, however, the deductive relation holding between such terms of the series as are present. The proposition does seem indeed, in this case, not to generate the shells, but it does generate their order. We shall later see, perhaps, that even purely abstract deductive systems may be in this sense incomplete.

The case of explanation is far more obviously a case of deductive relation. Most persons will agree that any phenomenon is explained as soon as one has discovered

the law that governs it, or better simply, its law. But
now once the law of a phenomenon is known and the
phenomenon is caught at any particular stage, the
phases next to come can be *deduced* logically from the
law. If a falling body has at this instant a particular
velocity, its velocity at any subsequent moment can
be deduced from the law of gravity. That the body shall
continue to fall, or in general that a phenomenon shall
persist without interruption, is again not guaranteed
by the law. But as long as the process does persist, so
long can its course be deduced from the given law.
Herein lies the sole and the inestimable value of natural
laws. Of course very much more can be said, and in a
later chapter will be, about description and explanation ;
but thus much, showing their essentially deductive
nature, will now suffice.

It was just said that modern logic has shown that
deduction is a very much more powerful and fruitful
instrument than its few forms crystallized in the syllogism ever let it seem. But we shall not here study
the details of this discovery, because this volume, in
spite of its apparent digressiveness, aims at nothing
but a deductive account of the concept of consciousness.
Logic, on the other hand, has shown that deduction is
the alpha and omega of ratiocination, by discarding
altogether and with good reason the notion of ' induction.' And this point it concerns us to consider.

Induction, I believe, was said to be the process by
which human thought aimed at ' necessary or universal
truths ' ; and it was supposed that deduction, then
known as syllogistic reasoning, could not arrive at
universal truth, because the conclusion of a syllogism
is never more *distributed* than its premises. Deduction,

then, could never yield universal truths unless it started
with them. These induction must elicit. It is to be
inferred from this that induction sought propositions
of which the subject was universally distributed. And
the classic illustration shows this to have been the case :
induction would like to prove that " all swans are
white." Now this conception involves no less than four
distinct fallacies :—that a proposition can predicate
particular corporeal existence ; that necessity is universality ; and that this is the same as distributedness ;
and that necessary truth is the true correspondence of
an ideal to a ' real.' Concerning the first point, we have
already seen that no proposition, not even a judgement
of perception, can seize hold of corporeal existence nor
predicate this of anything.¹ The proposition that " This
tree is green " means no more than that " A tree is
green." If the judgement is uttered in a particular
spot in space, by a corporeal mouth and accompanied
by a specific gesture, ' this' tree may be referred to :
yet the *judgement* has not so referred, but the physical
hand pointing in a particular direction. The action, not
the judgement, has seized the particular existence.
Even less could the proposition " All trees are green "
refer to corporeal existence ; for here no comprehensive
gesture is possible. In fact, all propositions endure in a
way that cuts them loose from the ever-changing physical objects : whereas if corporeal existence were implied
by a proposition to-day, such existence must remain
fixed for ever. This fact may well bring us to pause with
the question, whether an impossible thing-in-itselfness

¹ For a more extended discussion of this point I beg leave to
refer the reader to the volume of Joachim already so often cited,
pp. 101–13.

is not essentially involved in our popular notion of the
' physical ' world.

In the next place, induction confused necessity with
universality and this again with distribution of terms.
We have already seen that necessity for thought is
logical or deductive necessity, and that this is the
dependent *being* of entities on a generating proposition
or law. It might have been true that all swans were
white, yet this fact would have been of vanishing
importance, for it gives us no assurance that all swans
must be white. Then, furthermore, according to that
view of the universal and the particular set forth in a
previous chapter, and it seems to me according to any
tenable view, the ' truth ' that " All swans are white "
would not be a whit more universal than that " A swan
is white." Either proposition as an entity thus isolated
is a universal ; and of the two the latter is actually more
universal than the former, for the latter permits of
more numerous particular exemplifications. Thus by a
double confusion the distribution of terms was mistaken,
in the theory of induction, for logical necessity.

In the third place induction assumed that necessary
truth is the true correspondence between an ideal and
a ' real ' system. Undoubtedly such correspondence
between abstract systems and portions of the concrete
world is sought by the natural sciences, and more or
less successfully ; and I have tried to defend the notion
of such correspondence as legitimate, showing that so
far as there is correspondence there is identity, and that
the repetition of identicals is no inconsistency. And
even did it seem to be an inconsistency it is a plain
actuality ; and we have not so far seen that consistency
can be demanded of our world. But if truth is merely

true correspondence, of what use is truth ? When we have the concrete particulars, why seek to parallel these with merely, and always only partially, corresponding or identical abstract entities ? Surely, and solely, because *necessity* could be traced among the abstract entities, as seemed impossible among the concrete. Of particular swans we might have *seen* only white ones, but this guaranteed nothing of the swans that one had not so far seen : whereas an ideal definition of swan might be framed such that all swans must by definition be white. *If* then the ideal swan corresponds to the real swan, all real swans are white. But this ' if ' of induction begs the entire issue : and strangely enough this very ' if ' was the chasm that induction, borne on the wings of magic, was supposed to leap. How it did so was a mystery, as Mill himself confessed, with a candour that will eternally attest the rare temper of his mind. For " Why," asks Mill, " is a single instance, in some cases, sufficient for a complete induction [the bridging of the ' if '], while in others myriads of concurring instances, without a single exception known or presumed, go such a very little way toward establishing an universal proposition ? Whoever can answer this question knows more of the philosophy of logic than the wisest of the ancients, and has solved the problem of Induction."[1] But logic to-day answers that no such chasm is ever crossed. The universal is not the necessary ; and *any* proposition by itself is a mere universal, while necessity is found in deduction alone. True necessity among particulars is not grasped by discursive thought, because particulars are not grasped ; nevertheless laws (propositions) are discovered (experienced) in

[1] J. S. Mill : " Logic," Book III, chap. 3.

particular objects and these laws, in themselves universal, yield necessary deductions which are, of course, universal. And so far as the necessary behaviour of particular objects goes, the 'if' above-mentioned for ever remains, because while the particulars will certainly obey the law that has been found, they may be *also* at the same time governed by other laws not so far noted. Thus a certain law of gravity has been found in falling bodies, and it is not a ' construction,' for it describes how bodies do fall, it *is* the course of their fall : hence we are certain that *if* a body falls under the influence of gravity *alone* it will move thus and so. But science never attempts to say that a particular body will fall uninterruptedly under that one influence. Hence the ' if ' that induction was supposed to overcome, always remains for science and for thought. We have seen that action but not thought can grasp particulars, and so in laboratories one undertakes to witness a particular body acting under the influence of one or of a limited number of laws. And here one is peculiarly liable to be baffled, and here one reverts to doctrines of ' error ' and ' approximation.' It is not that science is inexact or that its deductions are not necessary, much less that our thought is of a different texture from ' reality ' ; but it is simply that the entities of an abstract system are never so numerous and hence never so completely particular as the (partially identical) entities of the world of time and space. I have indicated thus much of metaphysics rather in advance in order to show that ' induction ' is no coherent process of thought ; and we shall return to a consideration of the concrete world, and the ' real,' in a later chapter. We do not in thought cross that gap which induction was supposed to cross.

Universals are ever with us, and necessity is always deductive necessity. As to truth it will doubtless be something more interesting than truth of correspondence. All coherent thought is then deductive : and we may now proceed to some of the other implications of our general logical programme.

The place in logic of the category of *substance* is of importance to us in the present inquiry. It seems to be an ingrained habit of the human mind, at least since the time of Locke, to conceive that pretty much every entity of experience ' inheres ' in something else, and this other an inscrutable something called ' substance.' What this relation (or do some perchance call it a process ?) of ' inherence ' is, and how it differs, say, from adherence, I venture not closely to inquire, but I gather roughly that inherence in a substance figures as a guarantee of existence, a sort of ontological endorsement. But further this substance category has been alleged, often surreptitiously or even inadvertently, as the basis of difference between two entities between which a difference has seemed certain, but the exacter nature whereof uncertain. Thus it is said over and over that, " Mind and matter are *toto cœlo* different." " How so ? " " Why, they are so utterly different that they can't be compared [!] : they are two different substances." And very frequently indeed, it seems to me, so-called ' generic ' differences are predicated solely, though perhaps tacitly, on the basis of ' substance.' Now in logic the question of substance is of the most trifling interest, if it can be said to be of interest at all ; for clearly in any system the fundamental entities, or the members of the fundamental class (K), are all of one ' substance ' and differ only in respect of position, *et cœtera*, being generated by some repetitive process ; while all complex entities, being defined in terms of the simple, consist likewise in the same substance. Thus any system contains certainly but one substance, and this, by reason of being everywhere present, is nowhere of interest. Nothing can be said, or thought, about it. Thus the substance of the points of Euclidean space interests no one, and perchance both the affirmation and the denial of it are equally meaningless. This identity of ' substance,' however, does not prevent the entities of different complexity from having very different properties, differences, in fact, which it is an important part of logic to investigate. We have seen that in a logical system complex entities, if present, are defined ' in terms of ' the simple or fundamental entities, which in their turn are not defined. And the relation of simple to complex is irreversible and ultimate, so that while the complex must be defined in terms of the simple, the simple cannot be defined in terms of the complex. And so strikingly different are the properties of entities which differ only in complexity or in form, that these differences would, in other fields of inquiry, be called differences of substance. Thus, for instance, it might well be said that the finite and the infinite numbers are different ' *toto cælo,*' different in substance.

Such marked differences between entities without differences of ' substance ' are found among the chemical compounds that are composed of the same kinds of atoms combined in different proportions, or indeed of the same kinds and proportions combined in merely different arrangements, as, for instance, the various members of the benzol-ring group. And of course the progress of science shows countless cases in which an

apparent difference of substance has resolved itself
into a difference of form but an identity of substance.
At the moment, indeed, we seem about to learn that all
of the chemical compounds and elements are really
but different forms of one substance,—and that a unit
of electricity. In view of these considerations one may
well query whether, as empirical knowledge advances,
many more supposed differences of substance will not
be found to be differences purely of form or complexity ;
whether ultimately perhaps all so-called substantial
differences will not be thus resolved. In any purely
deductive logical system, at any rate, indeed in the entire
domain of mathematical logic, no differences of substance are for a moment in question. If on a foregoing
page the substance of logical entities was called neutral-
stuff, this was in order to forestall any possible suggestion that these are either ' material ' or ' mental ' in
their ' nature ' (substance). For the mind almost
inevitably conjures up the notion of substance as if it
were an aid to thought : and in order to make sure that
this, in the case of our logical entities, shall not be
imagined as either material or mental substance, they
will be called oftentimes—a purely didactic expedient—
neutral entities. We shall take up this neutrality of
logical concepts again, as well as the notions of physical
and of mental substance.

We may well consider at this point a subsidiary
question, but one that is important for our future
discussion ;—whether do propositions imply the being
of their terms ? Concrete physical existence is not here
in question, for most propositions cannot profess to be
about concrete particular objects ; nor is mental being
in question, because logic, our present domain, does not

find its objects to be mental. And besides, all are agreed that if a proposition is in a mind, its terms are also in that mind. Do propositions then involve the logical being of their terms ? It is recalled that Mill[1] commented on the ' double meaning ' of the verb *to be,* saying that it asserts being when it is itself a predicate, but does not assert the being of the subject when it is a copula. But Mill clearly had in mind physical existence. Thus " Socrates is just," he says, does not mean that Socrates exists : nor does " a centaur is a fiction of the poets " mean that a centaur exists, " since the proposition itself expressly asserts that the thing has no real existence." Here ' real existence ' can mean nothing for Mill but physical existence at some time or other. This is a strange query for a serious logician to entertain, when certainly ninety-nine propositions in a hundred do not even profess to refer to so-called physical existence, and if there was to be such a query at all, it should have been as to whether a proposition *ever* implies the physical existence of anything.

In the strictly logical sense, however, Fichte and, after him, Herbart have also held the opinion that propositions do not imply the being of their terms. Fichte said that, " The proposition A is A is by no means equivalent to A *is.* (*Being* when posited without a predicate is something quite different from being when posited with a predicate.) Let us suppose A to signify a space inclosed within two straight lines, then the proposition A is A would still be correct ; although the proposition A *is* would be false, since such a space is impossible."[2] Here

[1] J. S. Mill : " System of Logic," Book I, chap. 4.
[2] Fichte : " Grundlage der ges. Wissenschaftslehre," Translation by A. E. Kroeger, London, 1889, p. 65.

F

the context shows that ' real ' space is not in question, but logical being alone. " The *content* of the proposition is not regarded at all : merely its *form*." It may be questioned whether this ' content ' can be considered, since the words ' a space inclosed within two straight lines' are utterly repugnant to the mind and unthinkable, and the term A has no significance. Some distinction should be made between the merely untrue and the meaningless, since words, being symbols, can slip their moorings and become mere printer's ink. And it seems impossible that these words are anything more, the real ' content ' being the mere letter A, a proper enough entity. Granting, however, that there were a meaning here, and hence a content, we have to ask concerning propositions (not whether they can be ' regarded ' apart from their terms, although an unbiased person will perhaps see that they cannot be even thought in that way, but) whether apart from terms they can anywhere be found to *be*. And we have seen already that neither propositions nor relations are ever found without terms. If then a proposition is, its terms are ; and a proposition involves the logical being of its terms. This is so whether the proposition is itself true or false, for untrue propositions have being, since otherwise they could not meet true propositions in contradiction. Therefore even the terms of untrue propositions also have being.

A rather more difficult case is found in propositions of the form A is not. Of these Russell says ; " ' A is not ' must always be either false or meaningless. For if A were nothing, it could not be said not to be ; ' A is not ' implies that there is a term A whose being is denied, and hence that A is."[1] Thus even here the proposition

---

[1] B. Russell : " Principles of Mathematics," p. 449.

implies the being of its term. And this interpretation is quite in accord with the self-evident truth that there is nothing that is not. But I believe that ' A is not ' is usually used elliptically, meaning that A is not in this universe of discourse, and implying that ' A is ' in some more comprehensive universe. Undoubtedly logic still has problems to solve in regard to negation in general, yet it seems sufficiently clear that propositions (and relations) always imply the being of their terms. As Russell has said : " *Being* is that which belongs to every conceivable term, to every possible object of thought— in short, to everything that can possibly occur in any proposition, true or false, and to all such propositions themselves."[1]

We have said very little about consistency among the propositions of a system. The general view is held that all the propositions of a system must be consistent, that is, must nowhere lead to a contradiction. Yet it is admitted that there can *be*, and are, different systems which are not consistent with one another. Thus two contradictory propositions are said each to have being if they are in different systems. Furthermore, it is unfortunately true that a logician in basing a deductive system on a number of ' independent ' propositions can generally not tell immediately whether these are or are not mutually consistent. He may follow out long chains of deduction from his premises, finding no contradictions, when unexpectedly and far distant from the premises originally assumed, a contradiction *is*. From this he recoils and says that it ' cannot be.' His effort then is to find that one fundamental proposition (or if not one, yet the least number of propositions) that

[1] *Loc. cit.*

can be discarded to eliminate the contradiction with the least further detriment to the system. This unhappy proposition is summarily ejected and declared to have no being in that system. But here I confess that it seems to me the logician forsakes his commendable objectivity of attitude. The offending proposition has been allowed to have being through a considerable number of deductive steps and has itself helped to contribute, perhaps, many theorems that are consistent with all the others, so that the summary ejection when at length (not temporally but ordinally) a contradiction *is*, has all the look of a capricious distaste for contradiction on the part of the logician. This is all the more apparent when, as sometimes happens, either of two propositions is equally the offender and the ejection of either would eliminate the contradiction with neither more nor less further mutilation of the system. Then it is purely arbitrary which proposition shall be said to have worked the contradiction, and which shall be denied to have being : yet the logician inconsequently rejects one or the other.

If the logician admits that *he is interested* only in groups of consistent propositions, no one can object ; for we all have our foibles. But then it must be recognized that this recoil from contradiction is purely a case of personal preference. Whereas in fact it is taken as a valid insinuation that contradictory propositions cannot *be* together ; although the logician admits that they can have being ' apart,' in different systems. But if they cannot be together, how came they to *be* so readily up to that deductive step in which they contradicted ; and more emphatically, how could they possibly *meet* in contradiction ? For if purely logical entities are to behave like Hindu conjurers, seeming to have being at a place where they really have none, we may as well resign our quest of any knowledge. Be it remembered, that we are not here speaking of truth, nor even of reality, but solely of *being* : and, for my own part, I cannot see how the contradiction of two propositions even remotely prejudices the *being* of either. And what else can we mean when we say that two propositions contradict each other, than that both *are*, and are contradictory ? The game of chess, which is a pleasant blending of free volition and lawful submission, will illustrate the point. Admittedly the rules of chess define a very large number of possible ' games,' and the players obey the rules, yet with each play the player voluntarily excludes a number of possible games, until at ' mate ' one out of all the possible games has been played and the other millions voluntarily excluded. Now the rules of chess are purposely framed to produce deductively contradictions : indeed, one rule takes account of these, for when two men have by the law of their moves a legal right to one and the same square, the second-comer ' takes ' the first-comer and this one becomes henceforth non-existent. And the whole point of the game lies in the special contradiction called ' mate '—and never effected out of deference to majesty. But if the players were to treat chess as the logician treats other deductive systems, they would eliminate altogether either whites or blacks and play a consistent but certainly less absorbing game.

The predilection in logic for consistency loses much of its august character from the consideration that no one can tell from the propositions themselves whether they will meet in contradiction or not. " The only known method for proving the consistency of a set of postulates is to exhibit something with reference to which they are all satisfied together."[1]   The something exhibited is *not propositions* but some system of *terms*, and this fact again emphasizes our distinction between these two types of entity.   The system of terms ' satisfies ' the set of propositions if these are ' true of ' the system or are fulfilled or embodied therein ; in short, if the propositions (or these with others besides) generate the set of terms.   It appears from this that propositions are likely enough to be inconsistent with one another, but systems of terms can embody no inconsistency. For inconsistent propositions no system of terms can be found that satisfies them, or, as the logician says, no such system ' exists.'   It seems permissible in this connection to call sets of propositions and systems of terms respectively the *im*plicit and the *ex*plicit portions of the realm of *being*.   If we grant, now, that truth is *consistency* within a system, and I do not see what else truth can mean (for even in a true correspondence two systems are one and hence consistent), we must recognize that truth is difficult of discovery.   And we must admit the grave doubt as to whether the world that we experience is wholly true.   Truth, of course, must not be confused with *being*.   And I cannot conceive by what right a human philosophy has ever announced that the Eternal Order is spherical, or self-contained, is one, is perfect, or is true.

----

[1] Cf. H. C. Brown : " The Problem of Method in Mathematics and Philosophy," Essays Philosophical and Psychological in Honour of William James, New York, 1908, p. 436.   A theory has been offered by Hilbert (" l'Enseignement mathématique," 1904) for testing consistency *a priori*, as it were, but this has not so far been accepted as sound.

One distinction, to return to our programme, between deductive systems in pure mathematics or logic and such systems ' applied ' to so-called real objects is that the fundamental propositions in the latter case are supposed to be not postulates but ' true ' propositions, that is, laws or facts. At least such is the case for any fairly well-established and verified system. Their being ' true,' however, does not hinder them from yielding by deduction other propositions, and these similarly are called facts. Applied deductive systems, also, involve terms which are in large part peculiarly susceptible of being taken and exhibited, that is, are material objects. Significant in some regards as is the difference between postulate or hypothesis and fact, it is in regard to deductive fecundity absolutely missing. And this absence of distinction is of all truths, perhaps, at the present time the most significant. Thus deductive sequences, whether hypothetical or truly corresponding to ' reality,' start from terms and propositions.

It may not be amiss here to point out one or two practices in discourse which, from the principles of deductive procedure just reviewed, can be identified as vicious; and which are not unknown in philosophy. One of these practices relates to definition of the terms of discourse. We have seen that terms must either be given as fundamental and simple, and in such case exhibited, or else must be defined by means of the fundamental terms, in which case the defined terms are complex. The relation of simple to complex is asymmetrical, and the process by which complex elements are defined in terms of simple elements cannot be reversed. It is not a matter of choice. And if it happens that the fundamental terms are otherwise known to

have internal configurations, such internal complexity
is no part of a system in which they are taken as fundamental elements. They are simple in this system. Thus,
for instance, bodies figure in a mechanical system as
simple masses, although the same bodies have in chemistry an elaborate molecular structure.

It is therefore of great importance to find out what,
in any particular field of investigation, are the simple
and fundamental elements, and what the complex or
derived. The deductions, if deduction is reversible, may
proceed from the complex to the simple, or from the
simple to the complex; but not so the definitions,
which must strictly observe the asymmetrical relation
between simple and complex entities. If this principle
is violated the result may be that the name of an entity
asserted to be simple will be found to denote so much
that it connotes almost nothing : that is, no propositions
or relations can be asserted about it. What should
then be a deductive system has a term or terms, but too
few propositions, or even none : and discourse must
stop. Since, however, in human practice nothing can
quell the flow of words, propositions *are* asserted of the
all-denoting entity, and these are subsequently found
to be false. Thus the rural preacher used to commence
his sermon by declaring that, God is all in all. If this
is true no more can be said—about God. But more is
said, namely that, God is good. Then it straightway
appears that some of the all in all is not good but evil :
whereon the preacher flies to cover : " Ah, here we
behold the foul traces of that evil spirit and enemy of
God, the Devil." Therefore God is not all in all, but
part in all. So the sermon proceeded by a series of trials
and errors ; and many persons will have in mind times

and localities in which this was the favourite form of pulpit discourse.

But if this was once, and to some extent still is, the theological fallacy, it is to-day a common epistemological error. Thus a fairly recent text-book, in discussing the science and method of psychology, declares that, " Consciousness can neither be defined nor described. We can define or describe anything only by the employment of consciousness. It is presupposed, accordingly, in all definition ; and all attempts to define it must move in a circle. . . . Consciousness is necessary for the definition of what is in itself unconscious. Psychology, accordingly, can study only the various *forms* of consciousness, showing the *conditions* under which they arise "[1]—and it is safe to say that among psychologists this is the commonly accepted view. The deductive system starts with consciousness, a class (K) of elements (a, b, c, — —) all of which are consciousness particles. This is possible, and there can be groupings of these that it is proper to call ' forms of consciousness.' But it appears at once that some of the elements, or groups of some, are *un*consciousness ! God is all in all, but the Devil is a part ; consciousness is all in all, but unconsciousness is a part. The fact is that either consciousness is a complex entity, not fundamental but definable in terms of simpler entities that are not consciousness, in which case unconsciousness can also be a complex entity in the system ; or else consciousness is fundamental and simple, is opposed by no negative category of unconsciousness, and can in no wise become the subject of further discourse. Another and a remarkable case of this fallacy seems to be that of Bradley's Abso-

[1] John Dewey : " Psychology," New York, 1898, p. 2.

lute,[1] ' in which ' all diversities and infinite *regressus* are ' transmuted ' into one whole : unless indeed the author should say in extenuation that he has here abandoned, with a sense of gladness and relief, all attempt to be coherent. In short, it is fallacious to assume an entity as fundamentally given in a system and hence simple, and later on in the discourse to discover that it has an internal variety which is responsible for some features of the system.

A second vicious method in discourse is the use of terms or relations which are neither defined, if complex, nor properly pointed out or exhibited, if simple. The vagueness that results from this is familiar enough to need no further comment ; unless, indeed, the mention of Spinoza's " Ethics " as an example, where in spite of the affectation of ' geometrical ' method the definitions are pure enigmas until the reader has made a considerable study of Spinoza.

Another abuse, although a less serious one, is the assumption of a large number of undefined terms or propositions. This in itself is not a fallacy but a risk incurred ; the danger, that is, that some of the entities assumed to be distinct will later be found to be partly identical, and that propositions assumed to be consistent will be found to be contradictory. Either of these is a logical disaster, and is always difficult to avoid. Therefore before the deductive system is framed, analysis should have gone as far as possible toward discovering what are actually the fundamental terms or propositions. In case of failure the fallacy committed belongs to the type first mentioned above.

In these considerations of the programme of logic and

---

[1] F. H. Bradley : " Appearance and Reality."

its implications, we have constantly found ourselves straying into the realms of philosophy, and we have now to approach that field avowedly. It has so far been aimed to show that all coherent thought is deductive ; that deduction employs terms and propositions ; that the latter, although unable to subsist without the former, have a property that unmistakably resembles what is ordinarily called activity ; that the repetitive or ' self-representative ' propositions especially have this property ; that terms differ intrinsically in point of complexity ; and that the relation of simple to complex is asymmetrical. Simple terms cannot be defined by means of complex terms, but these latter can and must be defined as aggregates of simple terms in some relation. It has also been shown, partly explicitly and partly inferentially, by the illustrations given, that when a system of so-called 'real' objects is to be described and explained this can be done not otherwise than by framing a set of terms and propositions from which all relevant features of the ' real ' system can be logically deduced.

If the question of substance is urged, we have so far found but one substance which, if it must be named, may be called neutral-stuff. This implies nothing about mind or ideas, nor yet experience, and so far as logic or mathematics goes this question is a pure irrelevancy. Lastly, every term or proposition, whether true or false, must be conceded to have *being*.

We have now to consider our world of experience, containing material objects, ideas and minds, and concepts, and to inquire what may be the place in this world of the entities that are called conscious. The first question is naturally that of substance, for we have seen that in a deductive system there can in the last analysis be but one substance, and any terms that seem to be of a special substance are really aggregates of simpler terms in some relation, and consist really of the same fundamental substance. Thus, if our world of experience is a coherent system, that is a deductive system, as partially at least it appears to be, it must be such a unisubstantial system ; it too must in the last analysis consist of but one substance. And this it might, as we have seen, without being a wholly unified or a wholly true world.

CHAPTER V

OUR UNIVERSE AT LARGE

IF in the present state of scientific thought one tries to find a common basis from which to view our world at large, and one that nearly everybody will at least provisionally accept, one can probably not do better than to adopt the position first taken by Avenarius, and to say that our world is a world of pure experience. And this is to be understood in a purely empirical way. The term includes, as we all know, all objects, whether we call them physical or mental, all 'primary' and 'secondary qualities,' all ideas, feelings and emotions, however vague, all truths and all untruths, reals and unreals. It includes, in short, whatever one happens, whether for a long or brief interval of time, to meet with. This is the attitude, I presume, of a somewhat naïve realism, and philosophically it declares almost nothing; but, as philosophy finds, it states a problem. We may, however, start with this promiscuous aggregate, and inquire whether it has any even partial unity, and whether it shows anything like the texture of a deductive system.

Seemingly free as this beginning is of metaphysic, one is yet instantly tempted to inquire with what propriety this unlimited range of objects is said to be the objects of *experience*. Is to-be-experienced their very essence; is their substance experience-stuff? It is just so in the case of the 'undifferentiated' objects of 'will' in Neo-Fichtean types of philosophy,[1] which are all so far neither physical nor mental, that one inquires why the 'will' is essential to them. Clearly Avenarius approached the matter with a somewhat social bias, having himself and other ' subjects ' in mind, and in so doing he conceded, at least verbally, a point that he ought never to have granted. For surely a purely naïve realist does not say, " *I* am experiencing all these things "; but he says : " All these things are." And for my own part I am willing to believe in the most unequivocal way that they simply are. For one has instantly to admit that one's own experience is a highly complicated aggregate of objects whose ' nature ' is not so far known or even questioned : and hence, as we have seen, an experience is not a simple entity but a complex of entities that are at least simpler than itself, and for this reason it is definable in terms of them, but *not* they in terms of it. They cannot be defined in terms of experience ; and such a definition attempted is actually equivalent to the assertion that the components of experience consist of an experience-stuff,—and this is false. Experience consists of them, in combinations, and if they have a substance, experience too consists of that same substance. If we would truly ' exclude the introjection ' we must do so at the outset, and there dismiss our deeply rooted psychological prejudices. Certainly it has been the vice of all latter-day philosophy, by which I mean idealism, in one way or another to try to define the simpler entities of being in terms of their more complex aggregates, wills or minds or experiences.

[1] As in Münsterberg : "Grundzüge der Psychologie," Leipzig, 1900, p. 46 ff.

Their substance has been said to be mental or ideal, whereas in fact minds or ideas are their substance and neutral. We have already seen the vice of this attempted inversion of the simple to complex relation, and have seen that so far the substance of logical entities at least is one, and that of that substance nothing can be predicated. It is, indeed, of vanishing importance. Avenarius, too, partly saw the error of this hysteron-proteron of definition and much of his work is free from it ; though at times he was still too much the ingrained psychologist. And it was he who first pointed out the anthropomorphic if not indeed the ego-centric, or solipsistic, quality of all doctrines of soul-substance. The soul-substance, he said, is the last relic of animistic philosophy. This point is of the utmost importance, and I must repeat that unless one will define laws in terms of government, carbon in terms of trees, and mathematical points in terms of dodecahedrons, one must not attempt to define severally the component entities that we experience in terms of experience, or of consciousness, or of mind. In short, then, a vast variety of component objects simply *is*.

It has been urged in this connection, of course, that there is another side to the matter ; that truth, for instance, " is actual as true thinking, goodness lives in the volitions and actions of men, and beauty has its being in the love of its worshippers, and in the creative activity of the artist. Truth, goodness and beauty, in short, appear in the actual world and exist in finite experience. To experience them is, no doubt, to transcend the purely personal, the merely finite experience ; but finite experience is the vehicle of their being. They live as the experience of finite subjects ; and their life

(at least on one side of itself) is judgement, emotion, volition—the processes and activities of finite individuals."[1] " Doubtless it is irrelevant to the nature of truth whether *I* know it or *you*. Truth is independent of the process by which *I* come to know it, and is unaffected by the time at which I know it. But yet this independent truth itself . . . lives and moves and has its being in the judgements of finite minds " (pp. 21-22).
. . . " — its being is essentially ' in ' and ' for ' and ' as ' the temporal and finite thinking of the individual minds. It is universal ; but its universality is stamped with the unique differences of the many minds, in whose thinking it is manifest. It is independent and dominates our thought ; but it is *in* and *as* our thinking that its controlling independence is exercised " (p. 164).

I scarcely know whether such argument will more incline or disincline the reader to acceptance. Certainly the argument holds as well for any of the objects of experience as for truth, goodness and beauty. Now we must gracefully concede that we are all individuals, and that no individual experience contains more than that which it contains ; and that an individual can know truth or any other object only when it is within his knowledge ; or lastly, to be very liberal, that all individuals can know anything only in so far as their knowledge goes. And since all the objects that I know are in the aggregate called my experience, it follows truly that every one of the objects that I know is a part of my experience. But that I know each object only ' *as* ' my thought, is simply false. I do not know it ' *qua* ' this or that, or anything other than just that which it simply *is*—in my immediate knowledge. One might

[1] H. H. Joachim : *op. cit.*, p. 21.

as well say that a single stone exists only ' as ' the
edifice, or a point is only ' as ' the epicycloid ; for a
stone *qua* edifice and a point *qua* epicycloid are no more
nonsensical than red or green, truth or beauty ' *qua* '
my or your idea. And, moreover, if truth, beauty and
all other objects live and move and have their being
in finite minds, it must be remembered that by the very
same token molecules, motions, forces and mathematical truths live and move and demonstrate their
being far less in finite minds than in earth and cloud,
in the planetary orbits, in lightning and the water-
fall, and in all the accomplished feats of engineering.
Joachim strenuously objects to, and derides, a statement
of Russell's that some propositions are isolatedly true,
and says that for Russell truth is a sort of grey paint
to be smeared on propositions before they can be true.
Yet Joachim and all idealists have their pale cast of
thought, with which all things must be sicklied o'er
before they can even be.

It is true that a reflective act can always be gone
through, so that on seeing a sinking ship one can say :
It is my idea that the ship is sinking ; or a second time :
It is my idea that my idea is that the ship is sinking.
And this can be repeated yet again, as Bradley has
sufficiently pointed out. For some minds, indeed, this
way lies reality. But in ordinary consciousness, I speak
empirically, one forgets to think that one is thinking, and
the sinking ship ' *qua* ' *sinking ship* is alone in mind. And
if one considers the two acts of perception and of reflection, one will see that if they are truly two then the object
of the one is necessarily different from the object of the
other act. " It is my idea that the ship is sinking,"
has a meaning only if it implies a contrast between ' my

G

idea ' of a ship and some other fact (which I do or may know), and which when known will not be my mere ' idea,' but will be the sinking ship. In general even the act of reflection involves a judgement about an entity which is not merely mental.

The whole error once more lies in an attempt to reverse the true order of definition, and the true order of being ; to declare that the complex entity, experience or mind, is a something of which the simple entities are composed ; while this something, if further examined, is found to be a *substance* and nothing else. Whereas, in truth, the complex entity is an aggregate of the simple ones (a vitally cohering one, if you will), and its substance is only their substance. The ' objects ' of experience together compose experience, and they have being, not *qua* experience, nor *qua* objects of experience, but *qua* themselves. In fine, the logically prior truth is that entities in infinite plurality *are*.

Now since a very early time these entities have been more or less sharply distinguished into two groups, the material and the mental—a distinction which, whether so acknowledged or not, is actually one of substance. And this distinction, partly, I think, because the ' plain man ' stoutly averred it and still so avers, has been one of the pivotal points of philosophical controversy. We are probably indebted to Protagoras for this treasured dichotomy of the universe, and in his day the difficulties attending thereon were presumably not patent. And in the time of Democritus the relation between the two groups of objects was easily explained ; all objects consisted of atoms, while minds were composed of the finest and smoothest of these, and matter was atoms that were coarser and rough. But it was soon

seen to be impossible to conceive this universe as a
multitude of dust dots, while the reasons for distinguish-
ing mind and matter remained as valid as ever. And
still through all transitions in our conceiving of matter,
this duality has successfully asserted its claims, and is
now closely woven into our language and thought.

Yet so intimate is the relation, obviously, between
mind and matter, that they cannot be merely distinct
and separate substances. And it has been incumbent
on philosophy to define the manner of their relation,
since related they are, and the extent of their distinction. In fulfilling this obligation philosophy has in
turn denied the being of one, and then of the other,
substance. In asserting that all objects are matter,
materialism failed, for it denied the being of mind ;
and mind is undeniable. But the assertion of idealism
that all objects are mental has for a long time been
sounding loudly in our ears. I cannot see that either
contention would be objectionable if only it left room
for the other class of things, that is, if only it took due
account of those daily recurring motives that force us
to distinguish after all two somehow contrasted groups
of entities (perhaps not different *substances*), the
material and the ideal. Nor can either theory, in spite
of its resounding advocacy, be accused of any fundamental partiality ; for if materialism denied the being
of mind, so too it really denied matter by erecting it
into a universal predicate, which by denoting everything
connoted nothing whatsoever ; and just so idealism,
in denying the being of matter, has left us no place in
which to look for our old and indispensable friends, the
ideas. The difficulty is that among our objects some
truly are material in a way that others are not, and

some are truly mental as others are not. And no monism is desirable if it is to be had at the expense of ignoring a distinction that each day calls on us anew to remember. And both of these forms of monism would explain *away* a distinction that it had professed to explain. The distinction between mind and matter is not to be wiped out, but to be made precise. We seek to know how the two are distinguished and how related.

The controversy has, as I have said, implicitly centred about the notion of substance : the fundamental error being the now popular one that the distinction between mind and matter is a generic distinction, a distinction of substance, and their relation, therefore, such as not to admit of articulate definition ; and the later errors being in declaring one of these substances void and the other valid. The concept of substance was explicitly enough used by the materialists, and it has been implicitly, if not explicitly, employed by idealists ; for the statement that *all* my knowledge is my idea, which is true of my knowledge collectively, would not yield the conclusion that each item of my knowledge *severally* is my idea, unless by the former had been meant that all my knowledge is composed of a substance called ' idea.'

The difficulties involved by a denial of either mental or material groups of objects, not necessarily as separate substances but as distinguishable groups, are most strikingly seen in that special field which treats of the immediate and concrete approximation of the two, the field of experimental psychology. Whatever his philosophy may otherwise be, the physiological psychologist finds himself, in considering the case of the individual on whom he is experimenting, forced to acknowledge there an experience which is ideal in a way that material bodies are not, and, on the other hand, a physiological organism and its surroundings that are physical in a way that the aforesaid experience is not.[1] This situation, although it is not the only one which presents the problem of knowledge, is the one, and this can be said without hesitation, which presents the epistemological problem more interestingly and more perplexingly than any other. Just here and nowhere else lies the very crux of any theory which professes to give an articulate account of the knowing process. Yet I know not where in epistemology prior to Avenarius the concrete nervous mechanism of the body is so much as mentioned. Epistemology has known nothing of the nervous system, has left its really crucial problem to the psychologist, in order to devote itself to morbid analysis of the reflective act, and to study of the so-called subject-object relation, and of knowledge in general, but always among disembodied knowers—a case of 'Hamlet' with the Court of Denmark left out. And furthermore, idealism, that philosophy which has done its best to convince us that the epistemological is the sole problem of philosophy, has never taken any thought for the body. Kant found the knowing process everywhere,[2] and

[1] Cf. Ralph Barton Perry : "Conceptions and Misconceptions of Consciousness," Psych. Rev., 1904, XI, p. 287.

[2] I know, of course, that no proposition can be framed concerning Kant which will not be hotly denied by ninety-nine out of the one hundred schools of Kantian interpretation. And some, of course, very deftly turn Kant into an 'objective idealist' by deliberately substituting other concepts for Kant's subjective ones. But in the sense of the present volume, the author of the following words is a subjectivist : " . . . so wird vielmehr klar gezeigt, dass, wenn ich das denkende Subjekt wegnähme, die ganze Körperwelt wegfallen muss, als die nichts ist als die Erscheinung in der Sinnlichkeit unseres Subjekts und eine Art Vorstellungen derselben " (Kritik der reinen Vernunft., A. 383).

seems never for a moment aware of those considerations which oblige the experimental psychologist to find this knowledge process *some*where. Nor can it be said in extenuation that epistemology, by taking account of the bodily tenement of the knower, would become physiological psychology, for if such were the case epistemology would be already indistinguishable from analytic and descriptive psychology, which like epistemology do not consider the nervous system on which an individual experience somehow depends.

Now the psychologist has not been able to evade the sharp confrontation of mind and matter that he finds concretely presented in his experimental ' subject.' And so in dire necessity, for philosophy has offered nothing adequate to explain the situation, he has resorted to the remarkable makeshift of the psychophysical parallelism, with what success everyone knows who has followed recent discussions of that theory.[1]   A severe and hitherto unessayed test of idealism lies in this concrete problem of experimental psychology.

Our starting-point, then, is not a world in which *all* is knowledge, but in which *some* part is knowledge, nor yet a world in which all is experience, as in Avenarius ; our point of departure is a world of pure being. Now we have already found that merely to take consciousness as a theme of discourse implies that it will be possible to frame a deductive system (although not perhaps with

---

[1] As good expositions of the complete failure of this doctrine, I beg leave to refer the reader to two recent books which in a way resemble each other, specially in the one constructive chapter with which each closes : Ludwig Busse : " Geist und Körper, Seele und Leib," and Charles A. Strong : " Why the Mind has a Body." A briefer and excellent discussion is also to be found in Ward's " Naturalism and Agnosticism."

mathematical formality) consisting of terms and propositions as premises, and themselves not ' conscious,'
not made of conscious or ' ideal ' stuff, such that all the
essential features of consciousness will follow as logical
consequences. It implies even more, for consciousness
is but the psychologist's name for the individual mind :
an explanation of consciousness, therefore, must also
explain mind and therewith the process of cognition.
But mind can hardly be explained apart from its supposed antithesis, matter. The task is thus a comprehensive one of epistemology, and the question is—Can
a deductive account of these things be rationally
undertaken ?

We need not ask whether such an account could
perhaps be achieved by a mind transcending that of a
human individual. Here an individual mind is to frame
the system, and an individual mind is to scrutinize and
pass judgment on it. This implies that an individual
mind is in position to survey a region in which the
process of cognition is going on. For is it conceivable
that a mind can describe something that is not in that
mind ? Now since the process of cognition assuredly
involves both a knower and a known, a subject and an
object, it is implied that an individual mind, witnessing
acts of cognition in order to describe the process, can
include both the subject and the object, and can watch
the changes in both. That is, other minds or parts of
them and objects or parts of them, must be included
within such an individual mind. Certainly one cannot
describe the cognitive process who cannot witness it,
any more than one can describe an eclipse without
observing it.

Now can one mind contain parts of other minds ? and

then, can it contain objects ? That a mind contains objects of some sort or other is admitted ; but that it can contain either the whole or parts of another mind is generally denied. Works on psychology unfailingly state that every consciousness is completely shut off from every other. No mind and no part of one, then, can be in any other mind. Individual minds are mutually isolated. If this is true, the proposed task of explaining cognition cannot be accomplished.

It is true that one generally further reads, that one mind can ' know ' another by ' inference.' But such a statement seems to contradict the previous one, that minds are isolated : and in any case the latter proposition cannot be here admitted to have a meaning unless we wish to move in a circle—are willing, that is, to say that an individual mind may hope to describe the knowing process because it can *know* other minds.

Of course, the doctrine that consciousnesses are mutually exclusive, and do not overlap or have common contents, has its roots in subjective idealism. It is a consequence correctly drawn by the subjective idealist when he attempts to face the concrete problems of physiological psychology. For a person who holds the doctrine, in any of its various forms, that ' the world is MY idea ' (even if he supposes that he can somehow avoid solipsism), has to say when he approaches the physiological aspect of cognition, that ' my idea ' is somehow or other in my brain. Then every individual's ' idea ' is in that individual's brain ; all brains are distinct and isolated from one another ; therefore each ' idea,' that is each consciousness, is distinct from every other. We must consider then at some length, as determining the bare possibility of our whole undertaking, whether it is true that ' the world is my idea.'

This might be meant, as we have already seen, in either of two senses. If one is walking in the wood, and remarks that " All this is Epping Forest," one may mean that this entire manifold of some square miles is the Forest; or else, that every twig and leaf which one sees, in short, every least *fragment* of the whole is Epping Forest. The former meaning is a true one; the latter meaning is absolutely false. Everyone admits that while a circle is a manifold of points, a single point is not a circle; while a house is a manifold of bricks, boards and nails, any single brick is not a house. Yet, if any even particular and concrete object of knowledge is in consideration, it is habitually said that every least component of experience is 'idea,' that is, that every twig or leaf is Epping. This is a monstrous fallacy, for the fact is that it takes *all* the trees and other objects and just that arrangement of them to make the forest, and it takes *all* the components of my experience together and in just their given order to constitute my idea, consciousness or mind. A part is not the whole, nor does a part derive its substance from the whole. Since then (it is falsely argued) my mind is the sum total of all the objects that I can experience, why, then of course, each one of the entities that I experience is my mind too, is mental, my idea :—every leaf is Epping Forest. This fallacy when committed by plain persons is called fetichism.

Briefly, and more strictly stated, the two meanings in question are these : if consciousness or mind is a class (K) of elements (a, b, c, — —), it may be understood either, that consciousness is the substance of which each element is composed, so that each is consciousness just as every molecule is matter; or else, that consciousness is the class entire just as a regiment is *all* the soldiers collectively, and no less. The statement that ' the world is my idea ' taken collectively and altered to read ' my world is my idea ' is true; but taken distributively it is false. The latter is the sense in which ' idea ' becomes a distinct substance. Let us see in which sense subjective idealism has meant this proposition.

CHAPTER VI

THE SUBSTANCE OF IDEAS

SINCE we cannot take up the several systems of idealism, we must if possible find one that embodies the essentials. Now in Berkeley are to be found the kernels, certainly, of the arguments that effectively predispose modern English minds toward subjective idealism; and these arguments are likewise, I believe, at the root of later German idealism. A brief examination of Berkeley will also throw light on several collateral contentions that we shall have later to consider.

Berkeley opened his "Treatise Concerning the Principles of Human Knowledge" as follows: "It is evident to anyone who takes a survey of the *objects* of human knowledge, that they are ideas actually imprinted on the senses; or else such as are perceived by attending to the passions and operations of the mind; or lastly, ideas formed by help of memory and imagination—either compounding, dividing, or barely representing those originally perceived in the aforesaid ways." This is good psychology and, for that matter, is almost precisely what Locke had said. But if the passage is to be taken as a piece of epistemology the phrase 'imprinted on the senses' is not allowable; for it cannot be construed so as not to refer implicitly at least to the physical organs of sensation, that is, to matter. And epistemology begins in a realm where as yet matter is not. Berkeley believed that he corrected this lapse, committed perhaps for the sake of clear exposition, by going on to say : " The ideas imprinted on the Senses by the Author of nature are called *real things ;* . . . yet still they are *ideas,* and certainly no idea, whether faint or strong, can exist otherwise than in a mind perceiving it."[1] And in another place he said : " To me it is evident . . . that sensible things cannot exist otherwise than in a mind or spirit. Whence I conclude, not that they have no real existence, but that, seeing they depend not on my thought, and have an existence distinct from being perceived by me, *there must be some other mind wherein they exist."*[2] In fine, the physical world, including the sense organs them-selves, is God's idea imparted to us.

From this it is perfectly clear that Berkeley means that the world is idea in the unallowable sense—every least fragment of the world, the world distributively, is idea. And why, once more, is it unallowable ? Why is the proposition true collectively, but false distributively ? Why must consciousness or mind be like the regiment, which is destroyed if the men are distributed to their homes, rather than be a fundamental substance of which every least thing consists ? This is the reason. Let it be granted that the world distributively is composed of ideas, that each least feature is idea. Then ' idea ' becomes at once the fundamental, undefined concept of which simply nothing more can be said. By being everywhere present, as logicians who love paradox are apt to say, it is nowhere present : it is the zero-class. If the several terms (a, b, c, — —) of a class are all

---

[1] " Of the Principles of Human Knowledge," Section 33.
[2] " The Second Dialogue between Hylas and Philonous."

' idea,' they are something else as well, for otherwise
they could not be a *and* b *and* c, and it is by virtue of
this something-elseness that they can enter into propositions. Of ' idea ' nothing can be asserted. Now
there would be no harm in this, for it is supremely
indifferent how the class of fundamental entities is
named, were it not that in the world as we find it ' idea '
or ' mind ' happens still to mean something, and the
term cannot be spared for this glorious sinecure of
fundamentum ultimum. There is a parallelism here with
the dim age of cosmological philosophy, when the
universe was conceived as consisting now of earth, now
of air, and now of water. But these praiseworthy
generalizations had soon to be abandoned because it
was seen that special parts of the universe really did
consist of earth and air and water. Logically stated,
and as we have already seen, the difficulty was that
entities which were really specific and complex, like
earth or air, had been assumed to be general and simple,
whereas experience presently showed that they were
to be found somewhere, but not everywhere, and that
they were not simple but could be analysed into components that were not earth or air. Symbolic logic and
the school of empirio-criticism have begun the demonstration that mind is not a simple substance, and that
it can be analysed into something else.

Now after subjective idealism has royally disposed
of mind and idea, it finds in the world such odd couples
as blindness and atrophied retinæ, dreams and indiges-
tion, hallucinations and cerebral tumours. In other
words, it meets the crux of physiological psychology :
and for subjective idealism this is a fatal crux. Within
the realm where all was supposed to be idea are found

instances of something that is even more peculiarly idea, that is, in fact, just that, and all that, which was originally meant by the term ' idea.' But ' idea,' if it denotes everything, cannot continue to denote anything especial. Berkeley met with this difficulty at once. In spite of his belief that physical objects are God's idea, he everywhere continued to use the term ' sensation,' with its several variants, which necessarily involves an antithesis between something which is mental and something else which is not so strictly ideal. He may have used the term at first for the sake of exposition, but he had to retain it or do violence to several urgent empirical considerations ; and so deeply was the notion embedded in his philosophy that the whole has been styled, by Fraser, ' theological or universalized sensationalism.' A notable instance of the indispensability of this antithesis between idea and not-idea is found in the " Essay toward a New Theory of Vision." Berkeley wrote this essay in order to prove that the soul, which perceives space, is not itself extended (any more than it is red or green). He showed " that distance or outness is neither immediately of itself perceived by sight, nor yet apprehended or judged of by lines and angles, or anything that hath a necessary connection with it."[1] The Theory, which is incredibly acute in view of the state which sense-physiology was then in, is the forerunner, or possibly the source, of the local-sign theory of Steinbuch[2] (erroneously attributed to Lotze), which declares that the perception of space, whether by sight or touch or other sense, is mediated by

[1] " Of the Principles of Human Knowledge," Section 43

[2] Johann Georg Steinbuch : " Beytrag zur Physiologie der Sinne," Nürnberg, 1811.

sensations which are themselves not extensive, but only intensive. Berkeley explained visual space perception by means of what would now be called the sensations of eye-movement. But our present point is that he stated his argument only by assuming outer objects in space, and inner sensations. He rather cannily admitted that he had done this, but observed that it should not be for an instant supposed that " that vulgar error was necessary for establishing the notion therein laid down."[1] It would be interesting indeed to see the demonstration after ' that vulgar error ' had been eliminated. In short, Berkeley's squandering of the term ' idea,' to denote everything whatsoever, and his later need of something specifically ' idea,' led him into an unctuous case of eating his pudding and digesting it, and then still discovering it on his plate.

The true difficulty with founding a philosophy on the proposition that all *esse est percipi*, is that it violates the rule of logic that was explained in the first chapter, that complex entities must be, and can only be, defined in terms of more simple ones. It seems incredible that anyone should ever have believed that *being perceived* is a more simple thing than *being*. For it is clear that the former is a relation between at least two terms, while the latter involves but a single term. It may be true that X is perceived, but only on the condition that X is. The statement that all that a person knows is the contents of his mind commands assent because it asserts merely the tautology that a person's mind is his mind. From this it cannot be concluded that any *part* of his mind is his mind, nor that any part is mental : and if one will but consider the little logical entities,

[1] *Ibid.*, Section 44.

and among these alone can *Being* be discovered weaving
her web (the old lesson of formal logic), one will see at
once that it is remarkably impertinent and meaningless
to say that the number seven, or the alphabet, or the
Pythagorean proposition is ' mental.' In this connection
Russell has said : " Although it was generally agreed
that mathematics is in some sense true, philosophers
disputed as to what mathematical propositions really
meant : . . . Philosophy asks of Mathematics : What
does it mean ?   Mathematics in the past was unable
to answer, and Philosophy answered by introducing the
totally irrelevant notion of mind."[1]   " Everyone except
a philosopher can see the difference between a post and
my idea of a post, but few see the difference between the
number 2 and my idea of the number 2.   Yet the distinction is as necessary in one case as in the other.   The
argument that 2 is mental requires that 2 should be
essentially an existent " (p. 451).

Now Berkeley certainly meant the proposition ' the
world is my idea ' distributively, and he himself was
unable to sustain the doctrine consistently.   And in
examining why he was thus unable, we have found why
subjective idealism is essentially and for ever a false
doctrine.   Whatever the *fundamentum ultimum* is of
which all terms or entities in the universe are composed
(if indeed that has any meaning), nothing can be predicated of it and nothing can be deduced from it.   Or,
otherwise, whatsoever name is given to the Class of all
classes, that name will denote each and every thing in
the universe, will therefore denote no one thing more
than another, and will suffer no predicates to be joined
to it.   Now Berkeley, and subjective idealists in general,

[1] *Op. cit.*, p. 4.

have supposed that mind or idea is the substance out of which each least term that is, is composed; whereas, in fact, *some* entities discoverable in the universe really are mind and idea, and some predicates can be asserted of mind and idea that cannot be asserted of other things. What these predicates are is in part the subject-matter of descriptive and physiological psychology. Berkeley, who was no inconsiderable psychologist, could not avoid contradiction; while Kant has avoided some difficulties, because for him the concrete problems of that special science seem not to have existed. In short, subjective idealism is a false doctrine because mind is really something, and hence everything it cannot be.

This final objection applies to all forms of idealism, whether ' subjective ' or not, and we might dismiss the matter were it not for a variety of that doctrine which has a somewhat different emphasis. This is the philosophy of Fichte, in which not mind but ' will ' is that which all things are. Now will can really no more be the ultimate substance than idea, and for the same reason. Will is really in the world, is a concrete problem of psychology, and relations can be asserted of it that cannot be predicated of other things. Correspondingly we shall find a flaw in the deduction. Yet the theory is interesting because, while most idealism insists on the importance and mental nature of *terms* in the universe, Fichte insisted on the importance of a principle of activity.

We have noticed above that of the two kinds of entity, term and proposition, the former, although indispensable to the latter, seems to be the passive portion of any deductive system, while some suggestion of activity or agency inevitably attaches to the

H

propositions. Activity is a better name for this quality than ' will,' because it is a vastly more general term. Wills are active, but so are machines, plants, energies, and the curious little entity ' A repeats itself.' Activity already denotes more and connotes less than will. But it is indifferent what this feature of propositions is to be called. Let anyone consider what happens when ' A repeats itself,' or what happens in any the least deductive system ; then let him note how much less happens when merely ' A ' ; and then let him name that which is present in the former case but not in the latter, by any name more general than activity that best pleases him. For want of better words this quality will be called in the present volume agency or activity, indifferently. Since new terms seem to result from this activity of propositions, but from terms alone nothing, a superior interest attaches to an idealistic system which, whatever it is in other respects, emphasizes the importance of activity ;—of propositions over terms.

If it were here objected that if activity is so fundamental, nothing can be said of it, the reply might be that we have found the last *fundamentum* to be *being*, of which indeed nothing can be predicated. Within being we have found terms and propositions, and since these are not the *fundamentum* something can be asserted of them, and notably that wherein they differ. A more general word than ' activity ' is doubtless desiderated to denote this difference : yet ' activity ' has here to be used, and it must be remembered that the meaning is, *not* that this difference, this quality of propositions, is, say, ' energy ' or ' will ' or other familiar and special forms of activity, but that all these special activities are at bottom that. Otherwise we should be repeating the idealist's error.

The flaw in Fichte's deduction is as follows. After showing that no science can be anything but a deductive system, Fichte said : " But a science also can *not* have more than one fundamental principle, for else it would result in *many* sciences. The other propositions which a science may contain get certainty only through their connection with the fundamental principle ; and the connection, as we have shown, is this : If the proposition A is true, then the proposition B is also true " ;[1] and so forth. " This fundamental principle is absolutely certain ; that is, it is certain *because* it is certain " (p. 22). It should seem logically sufficient if it is certain. " In undertaking this abstracting reflection we must start from some proposition which everyone will admit without dispute."[2] " As such admitted proposition we take this one, A is A " (p. 65). Agreeably to his doctrine that propositions do not imply the being of their terms, Fichte asserts that this proposition means merely : " *If* A is, *then* A is." But if one tries to discover a meaning here for ' if ' and ' then,' one will see that there is none ; so that so far from ' A is A ' not meaning that A is, it should seem to mean nothing whatsoever else than that A is. It is next said that the only thing ' posited ' in the assertion " is the *absolutely* necessary connection between the two A's. This connection we will call X " (p. 66). Now " X at least is in the Ego, and posited *through* the Ego, for it is the Ego

---

[1] Fichte : " Ueber den Begriff der Wissenschaftslehre." Translation by A. E. Kroeger, London, 1889, p. 15.

[2] Fichte : " Grundlage der ges. Wissenschaftslehre." Translation in the same volume as previous reference, p. 64.

which asserts the above proposition, and so asserts
it by virtue of X as a law, which X or law must, therefore, be given to the Ego ; and, since it is asserted
absolutely, and without further ground, must be given
to the Ego through itself " (p. 66). Truly the ego
asserts X, and ' by virtue of X as a law.' The relation
(of identity), then, *is* a law. But since this law has no
other ground, why, then the ' ego,' of all things, must be
its ground ! This premises that every law must have
a ' ground,' whereas Fichte has himself just asserted
that the fundamental principle " is certain because it
is certain," which must mean, if anything, that it is
certain and for no other reason. But now another
ground is found, and that is the ego. This seems to
contradict his own previous assertion, which had been
correct. It should seem that here as, in logic, a fundamental principle can have no ' ground,' and would
indeed not be fundamental if it had. For if a principle
is first it is first.

Yet in this wise we learn that the fundamental truth
is that the " Ego posits itself within itself." We find
here precisely the same motive, I believe, which we met
once before : just as " independent truth lives and
moves and has its being in the judgements of finite
minds," so the proposition that A is A, " since it is
asserted absolutely, and without further ground, must
be given to the Ego through itself." Yet is any prior
ground needed for the apparent proposition that
' A is A,' and in any case is not the Ego purely irrelevant
to it ? Now from the position so far taken we are not
concerned with the truth of any proposition, but solely
with its *being ;* and we need merely to consider a
proposition or any other of the logical entities, asking

whether there is anything there that is mental. It later appears in the Fichtean philosophy that the Ego is pure will. This philosophy thus finds activity to be a fundamental matter, laying the greatest stress on a property that we seem to have found residing in all propositions : and a feature of which logic, perhaps, up to the present time, has taken too slight account. For the logic of propositions and of classes is curiously reticent on the subject of activity.

The case is not altered for us in those forms of idealism which find the entire universe is the experience of an Absolute mind. As expounded by Royce,[1] for example, this view seems to me quite to resemble Berkeley's theory of the ' perceptions ' of God. Royce speaks of ' four conceptions of being,' but in the course of discussion it becomes clear that he means four conceptions of being *real*. Now certainly some things are that are unreal, as some things are that are untrue, and although I may be sadly astray I should suppose that for philosophy the untrue and unreal would be nearly as interesting as the real and the true ; for philosophy is not a normative science. In any case, I do not for an instant suppose that Royce has meant to discuss in that place ' being ' in the logical sense, in which we here have been meaning it. He does, however, arrive at the conclusion that all being is the mind of the Absolute, including in some wise the entities that are unreal and untrue. Now if the sum total of all that *is*, is an infinite mind, it should seem that we cannot so far transcend our finiteness as to know that fact. We must understand, then, that the sum total of what we *can* know is mind. Our

[1] J. Royce : " The World and the Individual," New York, 1900 and 1901.

own minds? Surely not, else why the Absolute? Nothing else can be meant, then, than that each item of our knowledge is mental in its nature, and not merely mental but Absolute-mental. And this once more is a substantialization of the mind. And I think it is true that every form of idealism makes of mind a universal substance, out of which every single entity that is, is composed. As we saw before, there would be no harm in this, except that the mind that is everything *ipso facto* vanishes. By denoting everything it connotes nothing and denotes nothing special. Yet we are left to face the distinction in the world around us, most clearly forced on us in experimental psychology, between individual minds and physical objects. And further-more, if we leave no room in *being* for the unreal and the untrue, we shall similarly run across a like needful distinction between real and unreal, true and untrue— at least within the individual minds, if not elsewhere in the universe.

Leaving now the question whether everything is mind,—since we have seen that some things really are mind and hence that all things cannot be,—we must ask, on the other hand, whether minds are composed of any other substance. Individual minds clearly are aggregates, and perchance they may consist of entities that are all of one substance. Possibly even one and the same component entity may be in two minds at the same time, as a point can be in two or more lines at once: in other words, perhaps minds can overlap. We defer for a time the questions as to the rela-tion between mind and matter, and the nature of matter.

We have seen that at least some of the entities that

are in our minds are logical concepts, and that among
these there is no question of substances, for they are
all of one substance, neutral stuff, if it must be mentioned
at all. And it is not far-fetched to ask whether perhaps
all the other entities that compose our mental content
are of that selfsame nature. Doubtless many persons
would assent at once, and declare that they are, but
meaning by that that logical concepts are all ' mental '
and hence of one texture with the ideas. This is precisely the reverse of what I mean, and I have tried
repeatedly to show that these logical entities, that are
in minds, to be sure, are no more made of mental stuff
than a man who happens to be in a regiment is made of
regimental stuff. A regiment is made of flesh and
bones (and other things), but flesh and bones could not
be defined as, nor are they, regimental stuff. The
concepts simply *are* just that which they are. Now are
perceptions, ideas, feelings and emotions similarly such
neutral entities ? We may recall now that neutral
entities are either terms or else relations and propositions, and one salient fact about them, in so far as they
enter into individual experiences (though this is really
a fact about experience), is that " their being experienced
makes no difference to them," they remain what they
are. Of course I know that anyone who affirms this
must prepare himself for instant death : the Absolute
will be after him. Yet it is a risk worth taking, for I
know of few more irritating passages in the fabric of
idealism than those that tilt against the ' independent
entities ' ; and they are irritating because there is a
lurking suggestion that they are not candid. The
assertion that " experiencing makes no difference to the
facts " is perverted quite unrecognizably from its

intended meaning, and then overthrown; whereupon the notion of independence is restored, presumably in a highly sanctified sense, and ' independent truths ' and ' transmuted ' entities of every sort are spoken of with the utmost license.[1]

There are two phases to the question of independence, and we may well discuss both here. Firstly, are entities independent of one another; and secondly, whether they are independent of experience. Now at least many entities or terms seem to be generated by the logical activity of propositions: perhaps this is the genesis of all entities whatsoever. And even an idealist may possibly admit that when an entity or ' phase ' or ' distinct moment ' has so come into being, it then *is*. *It*, moreover, is not the coherent ' *living* ' *whole*, but only one phase or term thereof. Now I am not aware that the contention for ' independent entities ' has ever meant, save only in the perversions imputed in idealistic argument, anything else than that these entities do *retain their distinct self-identity* whatsoever their context. It will scarcely be denied, moreover, that other activities can and do weave the several moments of one coherent whole, or weave indeed several such whole systems, into yet another and more highly complicated web; as when in the system of whole numbers certain additional postulates generate out of these the rational fractions. Yet the several numbers, terms or phases, assuredly retain their self-identity through all this further activity. If idealism will deny this, it renounces the old law of self-identity. Now ' independence ' means, I believe, that each distinct

[1] Cf. B. Russell : "On the Nature of Truth," Proceedings of the Aristotelian Society, N.S. vol. vii., 1907, p. 28 : specially pp. 44–9.

' pulsation ' is itself and is no other, so that further
activities may operate on these several pulsations in
some defined serial order. In this sense each entity is
independent of the others.

Precisely this is also meant by the assertion that
" experiencing makes no difference to the facts." The
component items of our universe when taken into the
web of an experience retain their self-identity : new
combinations are formed, but the elements in themselves
are what they previously were. This process can be
beautifully witnessed in miniature when any complex
group is formed of simple entities. In such wise the
' independence ' of entities is truly ' the fundamental
postulate of all logic.' It is not thereby asserted that
an entity A *is* out of all relations ; it *is* of course in
untold relation ; but A *is*, and A alone is neither
spatial, temporal, nor even ordinal, neither subject nor
object of experience. Being experienced, then, makes
no difference to logical concepts. And in the sense just
elucidated, it must be granted at once that being
experienced makes no difference to any of the other
neutral entities that enter our minds as the ' ideas.'
Clearly each perception, each idea, each feeling or
emotion however vague—whatsoever it is, that it is.
Undoubtedly it may stay but a moment, and may be
instantly replaced by another seemingly in its same
place, yet it is itself and is no other. *It* cannot change.
Of course it makes delightfully for philosophic mystery
and equivocation to contend that being experienced
makes all the difference in the world to the facts—that
the facts are changed by being experienced, changed
every time they are experienced, and changed in the
experience of different persons. But " What," says

James,[1] " are the exact facts ? Take the sensation I got from a cloud yesterday and from the snow to-day. The white of the snow and that of the cloud differ in place, time and associates ; they agree in quality. . . . Nevertheless, John Mill denies our right to call the quality the same. He says that *it* essentially differs in every different occasion of its appearance, and that no two phenomena of which it forms part are really identical even as far as *it* goes. Is it not obvious that to maintain this view he must abandon [p. 334] the phenomenal plane altogether ? Phenomenally [and, we may add, logically] considered, the white *per se is* identical with itself wherever found in snow or in cloud, to-day or to-morrow. If any nominalist deny the identity, I ask him to point out the difference. *Ex hypothesi* the qualities are sensibly indistinguishable, and the only difference he can indicate is that of time and place ; but these are not differences in the quality. If one quality be not the same with itself, what meaning has the word ' same ' ? " This consideration is, among other things, the irrefutable basis of psychological atomism. Any item of mental content assuredly maintains its self-identity ; it is a neutral entity, and is in so far independent of experience. This fact may have a bearing on the alleged privacy of ideas, their being in one individual's experience, and in no other.

A further feature of neutral term-entities is their serial properties : they form series, or rather are in series, as the numbers are, and however they may be displaced (for they are independent enough to suffer displacement), yet a certain serial order is often permanently intrinsic

[1] W. James : " The Sentiment of Rationality," Mind, 1879, vol. iv., p. 333.

to them. Is this true of components of a mind ? We may not for the present discuss the perceptions, for these are by definition physical objects in so far as physical objects are mental or are known, and we are not inquiring now into the nature of physical objects. There remain, then, the simple sensations, or in general the secondary qualities, feelings and emotions; concepts being indubitably neutral. Now the secondary qualities, although they seem sometimes to have a fitfulness, an evanescence, and a promiscuity of order that one does not find in the numbers, yet they too have their serial properties which, in spite of all displacements such as the numbers likewise suffer, are obstinate and inviolable in their way like any other logical manifolds. Thus the colours, for instance, form linear series in quite unexpected ways. Reds and yellows merge through the orange tints in a transitive and asymmetrical series; and in this series green quite declines to take a place. Red and green will not unite in series except through grey. And one of these series that is transitive cannot be made intransitive, any more than the circle can be squared or hydrogen changed to oxygen.

In view of these inflexibilities it is remarkable how few attempts have been made to construct an algebra of colours and sounds—not in the æsthetic but in the strictly logical sense. This may be because such an algebra would probably be a very simple one. In any case their classification in series and scales is an inevitable order, and was discovered and not created by any ' merely subjective ' act. How inflexible the secondary qualities can be is very well known to any psychologist who has tried to classify odours. Even the dimensions of the odour system are not known :

but it is at least not one-dimensional. And the would-be classifier finds himself at once to be dealing with as hard realities as a person trying to piece together a disarranged mosaic.

Quite the same is true of all the other secondary qualities, and in general of all sensations. They have an intrinsic serial order which is peculiarly theirs however much, like the numbers, they may be encountered in other arrangements. If this is true of qualitative series, it is even more noticeably so of intensive series. Here the linear order is unmistakable. And the psychologist finds himself inquiring into the qualitative and intensive ' ranges ' of an individual's sensations, or the dimensionality of a special sense, as that of taste, just as the surveyor measures the length of a pond or the geometer examines the dimensionality of space. Thus each group of sensations is a neutral manifold, in which each member has its place : and the difficulty sometimes of discovering what that place is, and the occurrence of elements out of their natural positions, have their precise parallels in any algebra or other logical manifold.

There remain of subjective phenomena that have not been reduced to neutral stuff such peculiarly intimate qualities as pain and pleasure, and the emotions, that are least of all thought to be objective or independent. In the First Dialogue, Berkeley argues that the secondary qualities are ideas, and can reside only in a perceiving mind or spirit because ' the most vehement and intense degree of heat,' for instance, is ' a very great pain '; and so of light and the rest. " And is any unperceiving thing capable of pain or pleasure ? " says Philonous, believing that an affirmative answer is impossible. Of course no psychologist to-day would confuse a high degree of heat or any other sensation with an unpleasurable affection. A loud sound is not pain although it may be accompanied thereby. But most psychologists would still affirm that no 'unperceiving' thing is capable of pain or pleasure.

Their first contention is that no person can experience another's pain or pleasure—this being their prime criterion of the subjective. They will, however, admit that pain is a quality which can exist in a considerable range of intensities: and also, that any one of us can experience a large number of these different intensities. Can no two persons, then, experience the same intensity of pain ?

Yes, but it will be a different pain.

Why ?

Because experienced by different persons.

Can these pains be distinguished, psychologically or otherwise, from one another in so far as they are mere qualities ?

No.

Why, then, are they different ?

Because different persons experience them.

And what makes two persons different ?

They have different experiences, that is, the objects that they experience are different.

Thus by denying the identity of indiscernibles one is constrained to argue in a circle. But if even pain were a unique quality in each of us, these persons would have no right, indeed would be unable, to have a name for it or to communicate with one another concerning it. Furthermore, if being experienced by different persons makes sensations and affections somehow different, everyone's experience is totally and utterly unique, and we find that *all* communication is impossible. The fact is that the uniqueness of sensations and affections in the individual soul is an appendage of the soul-substance theory. When we discuss volition we shall find what the soul is, and that it is a very real and satisfying thing. But the soul or spirit as here meant, that sits in awful isolation and receives its own unique sensations, which nevertheless somehow ' represent ' heaven alone knows what that is outside, is the veriest hocus-pocus. Pains and pleasures are as common to us all as are leagues and fathoms, day and night : and that is enough, in this case, to prove that they are neutral entities.

Such cheap mysticism leaves quite out of account great groups of experiences in which we have to say and believe, and do so in strict accuracy, that the pains and pleasures are not in us, but are in the outer world. A sunny landscape may give a sorrowing person no pleasure at all, yet everyone else will declare that *it* is a pleasant sight. The pleasantness is ' out there ' waiting to be perceived, like the colours of the trees and the acreage of the fields. Yet like these, it may or may not get to the individual experience. Is the onlooker sad and pained at a street brawl involving persons whom he does not know, or is it the situation itself that is sad and painful ? So distinctly objective is the painfulness of such an occasion that the person who fails to perceive it is instantly charged with a dullness of apprehension. When, for instance, the Fighting "Téméraire" was towed in to her last berth at Deptford, it was not the lookers-on but the circumstance, pure and simple, that was fraught with painfulness.

In his " Sense of Beauty " Santayana has mentioned

a large class of cases in æsthetics in which pleasure is
' objectified.' The word is unjust, for these pleasures
never were subjective, and would not have been thought
so to be had it not been for subjectivism and the attendant representative theory of knowledge. But the
fact that these introjections have once more to be
extrajected shows that the truth will sometimes out if
even by a roundabout path. It is literal truth that the
business of poets and artists is to create situations which
in all their objectivity are blithe or the reverse. The
' dulce Galaesi flumen ' was a gladsome nook on the face
of the earth and Horace had, not the imagination but,
the perception to see it. Of course all this is mere
metaphor and simile to those psychologists who have
fixed their gaze on the primitive wits of what they are
pleased to suppose was ' savage man.' For many such
persons anything beyond a string and a stick is the
giddiest hyperbole. But let them adjust their goggles
to the situations described by George Meredith and
Henry James, and then try to work them out in terms
of the pure subjectivity of pleasure and pain. They will
be forced to the most absurd sophistries and evasions.
Pleasure and pain are neutral entities and, both in
theory and practice, are as amenable to communication
and logical handling as are the concepts of acceleration
and π.

The emotions alone remain to be spoken of, and the
treatment is already indicated. All that has been said
of pain and pleasure is true of the emotions. In so far
as we know about them at all they are in the same way
neutral. There is this difference, that many emotions
are so rare and so evanescent that they cannot be
identified in knowledge. Yet if we have them at all,

they *are*, and there is every reason for supposing that if better known they would evince the same serial and other properties as do the more familiar emotions. It is recalled, too, that the dimensionality of the emotions is just now being actively discussed.

In this connection I cannot forbear quoting from an article by James in which he speaks not, to be sure, of the conceptual nature of the mind's contents, but of the impossibility of dividing our world unambiguously into objective and subjective elements. " . . . it is a mistake to say, . . . that anger, love and fear are affections purely of the mind. That, to a great extent at any rate, they are simultaneously affections of the body is proved by the whole literature of the James–Lange theory of emotion. All our pains, moreover, are local, and we are always free to speak of them in objective as well as in subjective terms. We can say that we are aware of a painful place, filling a certain bigness in our organism, or we can say that we are inwardly in a ' state ' of pain. All our adjectives of worth are similarly ambiguous— . . . Is the preciousness of a diamond a quality of the gem ? or is it a feeling in our mind ? Practically we treat it as both or as either, according to the temporary direction of our thought. . . . The various pleasures we receive from an object may count as ' feelings ' when we take them singly, but when they combine in a total richness, we call the result the ' beauty ' of the object, and treat it as an outer attribute which our mind perceives. We discover beauty just as we discover the physical properties of things. Training is needed to make us expert in either line. Single sensations also may be ambiguous. Shall we say an ' agreeable degree of heat,' or an ' agreeable feeling ' occasioned by the degree of heat ? Either will do ; and language would lose most of its æsthetic and rhetorical value were we forbidden to project words primarily connoting our affections upon the objects by which the affections are aroused. The man is really hateful ; the action really mean ; the situation really tragic—all in themselves and quite apart from our opinion. We even go so far as to talk of a weary road, a giddy height, a jocund morning or a sullen sky ; and the term ' indefinite,' while usually applied only to our apprehensions, functions as a fundamental physical qualification of things in Spencer's ' law of evolution,' and doubtless passes with most readers for all right."[1]

James does not say that these predicates are neutral entities, but after we have seen that they are strictly neither mental nor material, a moment's consideration makes it clear that neutral is precisely what they are. It is very instructive, moreover, to have this intermediate region between subject and object, mind and matter, pointed out. For while the distinction between the two is valid, and not to be explained away, it is not a sharp distinction like that between two chemical elements, or like the boundary between two countries. In fact, as we shall see, the regions of mind and matter overlap. Very obviously the purely mathematical and logical entities are inhabitants of both regions. Our algebra and calculus are in our minds, ready to be called and easily dismissed, yet they are also in physical objects, they guarantee the safety of monuments and

---

[1] William James : " The Place of Affectional Facts in a World of Pure Experience," Journal of Philosophy, Psychology, and Scientific Methods, 1906, vol. 2, p. 283.

I

bridges, the success of ships, and the possibility of any reasoned project.

We find then, finally, that while the contents of our minds are not ' mental ' in their nature, these contents are all neutral entities, are all of such stuff as logical and mathematical manifolds are made of.   Complex aggregates are of the substance of their simpler components ;   and not the reverse.   We have in the next chapter to inquire into the composition of matter. Should we find that it, too, is neutral in nature, we shall have deliberately consigned the term ' neutral ' to the royal sinecure of universal predicate.

CHAPTER VII

THE SUBSTANCE OF MATTER

A DISTINGUISHED philosopher said recently, possibly with a touch of impatience, that in the discussions of modern physicists matter evaporates into a set of equations. And certainly every student of physics very soon notes that he has far less in the laboratory to do with matter than in the outside world. From the beginning of his study his attention is directed to stresses, tensions, straight and curvilinear motions, positive and negative accelerations, vibrations, waves, electric charges, capacities and masses. That any of these are physical substances would hardly be asserted by even the stoutest materialist. They are neutral concepts all, and are all dealt with by pretty, mathematical methods. Such a student, however, used to be reassured and convinced that he was really after all studying matter, and not pure mathematics, by the statement of his teacher that the world about him consisted of very small particles of matter (conceived after the analogy of microscopic tennis-balls), and that it was these that possessed the mass, suffered the tensions and motions, and bore the electric charges. He was taught to call them atoms. And some fifty years ago there was very little more for him to learn in this connection. To-day the situation is different.

In his Romanes Lecture[1] Oliver Lodge said : " The mass which is explicable electrically is to a considerable extent understood, but the mass which is merely material (whatever that may mean) is not understood at all. We know more about electricity than about matter ; . . . It is possible, but to me very unlikely, that the electron as we know it contains a material nucleus in addition to its charge." Verily a Berkeley come to judgement ! Now I am neither minded nor competent to review modern discussions of matter, but their general trend is perfectly clear to everyone. The most advanced and competent physicists[2] to-day do not believe for an instant in the microscopic tennis-ball, the minute atom of *matter* which was supposed to be the bearer of natural phenomena. The conceptions of the ' underlying ' or ' ultimate ' entity are very diverse ; we hear now that it is a mass, now an energy unit, now a mathematical point, and again an electric charge or electron. While the notion of an ultimate material substance is as definitely renounced as ever Berkeley desired it to be. According to the definition of Boscovich, the physical atom is a " *geometrical point* in *space,* a sizeless centre of force, having *position, inertia* and *rigidity.*" The reader may decide what one of these is a physical substance. Somewhat similarly Ostwald[3] has

[1] ": Modern Views on Matter " : delivered in the Sheldonian Theatre, June 12, 1903.

[2] I am not referring to the majority of *all* physicists, for this is devoted to other tasks than the study of the ultimate nature of matter. With these men, so far as the subject is considered at all, some traditional view indeed suffices and is not criticized. But I am referring to the majority of those physicists who have made this so-called problem of the ultimate nature of matter their special field.

[3] Wilhelm Ostwald : " Vorlesungen über Naturphilosophie," Leipzig, 1902.

argued that the atom of matter is an energy unit, while the discoveries concerning radio-activity both argue for the breaking down of the supposedly ultimate distinctions of substance between the chemical elements, and seem to show that all atoms are really units of electrical energy. But whatever the details of definition of the ultimate physical element, the most serious students of mathematical physics and chemistry no longer admit any such thing as philosophers and the common run of men suppose that they mean by matter; —in fact, by philosophers frequently written ' Matter.' Indeed, as I understand it, the only capital-letter Materialists to-day, the only educated persons who are still able at all to conceive of the little tennis-balls, are the idealistic philosophers. These considerations are not urged, however, as an *argumentum ad homines*, save in so far as it is logically sound to draw one's opinions on any topic from the persons who by reason of special study are qualified to pronounce. In our present case the only persons qualified are the very ones who would naturally be prejudiced in favour of the strictly ' material ' as opposed to the conceptual or neutral.

Now these very persons, to leave physics for metaphysics, may perhaps be the last to admit that an electron is a concept. " Not a concept," they will say, " but a real thing ";—as if this were an antithesis. Physicists, however, while some of them are experts in the analysis of matter, are not so well qualified to give verdict as to the nature of reality and of concepts. As the botanist analyses the structures of vegetable organisms and finds the chemical compounds of which they are built, but does not analyse them; so the ordinary chemist analyses these compounds down to their elements, but does not analyse these; and so the physical chemist analyses these elemental atoms, as now appears, into minuter components (motions, masses, electrons) which he in turn must leave to the mathematician and logician further to analyse. On the hierarchy of entities according to their degrees of complexity must rest any natural classification of the sciences. And thus while we must learn from the physicist how it is that matter consists only of electrons or other masses, we do not turn to him for information as to the metaphysical status of these, his own last elements. Whither then? Well, obviously to that science which the physicist himself declares to be next more fundamental than his own, mathematical logic. Most of his entities are laws, and these are equations—which are mathematical entities or logical concepts. So, too, are his space, his points, his capacities, his masses and whatsoever else he may declare to be *for him* fundamental and *in his science* not further analysable. These are his ' Given ' which he must ' exhibit ' but not define when he proceeds to deduce his realm from terms and postulates. But that which is the physicist's ' Given ' is the complex realm that the mathematical logician essays to deduce from a yet simpler ' Given.'

Any further argument need scarcely be offered to show that the elements to which the physicist has at length reduced matter are neutral entities. They are the products of such minute analysis, are so strikingly remote from concrete wood and stone, that nearly everyone will grant that they are metaphysically quite of one piece with Euclidean space and the integral calculus, with which they are so intimately bound up.

In the popular mind, probably, the chief objection to the view that matter consists of neutral entities and nothing else, will be the notion that neutral entities can in no wise have that inflexibility and that indestructibility that so signally characterize matter. The neutral concepts, it will be said, are as easily summoned and dismissed in idle fancy as are sensations and ideas—but not so matter. Yet if one bears in mind now, that tangibly seizing or not seizing a physical object is the parallel process to 'thinking' or not thinking of a neutral entity, one will soon discover that the seemingly more pliant entities of logic and mathematics offer the same inexorable resistance to any merely subjective familiarities, as do the concrete masses and forces of the physicist. The former are not a whit less obedient to their own laws. We may think of a circle and a straight line, and desire in fancy to make the straight line cut the circle three times. It will not do so. In order to force it we must bend the line exactly as we should bend a brass rod. To be sure, we need not entertain in thought the circle and the line, just as we need not touch the poles of the Leyden jar : but if we once do, they, like the electric charge, are there in all their hard externality, uncompromising, and unyielding to our wills.

Or again, we build to ourselves a number system by the 'merely subjective act of counting,' someone has impiously said ; but we discover that that number system is infinitely more than we had ever desired or imagined, and that it persists in this unanticipated plenitude. We draw a triangle and then learn that its interior angles equal two right angles. We draw another triangle and yet others, as different from the first as we can, but with the same inevitable result. We are in the same position as a chemist who builds a new salt and finds himself eyewitness to an explosion. But, one may say, we need not draw the triangle. Certainly ; and the chemist need not have mixed his elements. For it is just as easy to keep one's hands away from bottles and test-tubes as it is to keep one's mind away from triangles and postulates :—sometimes far easier. In short, the manipulation of the neutral entities of logic is no more a ' subjective ' act than is the touching of a match to gunpowder.

Nor is it merely that these entities are as inflexible as matter : they are likewise as accessible to all individuals and as enduring in time as any mass or force. One may say with some faint appearance of plausibility that one's emotions cannot be experienced by other persons, but it is perfectly patent that numbers, geometrical figures, and, in short, all the abstract entities of science can be passed around like beetles or postage stamps. And they endure : indeed, there is no means known for destroying them. Certainly the Pythagorean Proposition and the process of long division have seen many generations pass, nations perish, and goodly seacoasts subside beneath the waves.

In a certain sense, indeed, the conceptual nature of those entities to which matter has been reduced is freely admitted ; but it is admitted in a sense so erroneous that the admission gives rise to a new fallacy as monstrous as any that was known to materialism. It is a fallacy for which the Cartesian theory of knowledge by ' representation,' with its duality of *res externæ* and *res cogitantes*, is responsible. The reader is probably all too familiar with the drift of the argument,[1] which is that thought and ' outer reality ' are ever twain, reality being ' represented' to us by thought : even the material scientist has access only to his own thoughts, never directly to matter, and the conceptions of science are only his own subjective constructs devised for convenience [*sic*] in order to ' describe in shorthand ' the outer reality.[2]

This is indeed, although vaguely, the notion of truth as correspondence, and in the words of Joachim, " it is not easy to learn, from the adherents of the correspondence-notion, *what* precisely the ' mental ' factor is, and in what sense it is ' real '; or, again, *what* precisely the ' real ' factor is, and in what sense it is related to consciousness, or to *what* consciousness it is related. Yet without a clear account of both these factors it is obvious that no definite meaning can be attached to the correspondence between them, which is truth."[3] Now we have already seen what the ' mental ' factor is : it is invariably a manifold of neutral entities. And neutral entities are not ' mental ' and not ' subjective.' Clearly the ' real ' factor, too, is not mental and not subjective. Both factors are neutral, both objective, and in the sense already explained both are independent of ourselves.

[1] Yet should he not be, I beg to refer him to Karl Pearson's " Grammar of Science " (London, 1900), a volume in which every known epistemological fallacy is sympathetically expounded.

[2] I feel it to be almost an insult to the reader's intelligence even to mention this ridiculous epistemology, and I should not do so were it not that some such theory seems actually to be entertained by a considerable number of natural scientists in England, America, and Germany to-day. And I certainly beg the pardon of any disaffected reader.

[3] H. H. Joachim : *op. cit.*, p. 20.

Scientists are gravely misled in their philosophizing by the representative theory of knowledge, a theory which we shall consider in the following chapter. But our point is here that in their special field of research, scientists find that physical objects are completely analysable into neutral entities, with no residue left over such as was once called ' Matter.' We may be quite indifferent to the opinion of scientists when they leave their special field of competency, and essay to pronounce on the epistemological status of the neutral concepts. This the logicians can better do. In short, then, ' Matter ' does not exist ; the ' real ' objects about us are composed of neutral stuff.

The objection may here be offered that, contrary to my profession, I have sought to explain away matter. But it is to be remembered that the real objects about us, which can never be explained away, are not ' Matter '; they are just objects, while ' Matter ' is the stuff that philosophy has declared these objects to be made of : it was conceived as the hidden and unattainable bearer of the colours, sounds, smells, motions, energies and masses which alone were the immediate objects of our experience. The discovery that these are neutral entities, each and every one, does not explain them away ; but explains away merely a philosophical vagary. The contention is at this point supported by every one of the arguments that Berkeley urged against the material thing-in-itself. " If any man thinks this detracts from the existence or reality of things, he is far from understanding what hath been premised in the plainest terms I could think of."[1] . . . " I am not for changing things into ideas, but rather ideas into

[1] Berkeley : " Principles of Human Knowledge," Section 36.

things; since those immediate objects of perception, which according to you are only appearances of things, I take to be the real things themselves. . . . We both, therefore, agree in this; that we perceive only sensible forms : but herein we differ, you will have them to be empty appearances, I real beings. In short, you do not trust your senses, I do."[1] In everything that he says concerning matter Berkeley was a thousand times right, and the most competent natural scientists have now come to be quite of his opinion. He was wrong, however, as we have seen in the previous chapter, in his contention that the essence of ideas (and all neutral concepts) lies in their being perceived ;—their *esse* is precisely not *percipi*. ' Matter,' indeed, is not the reality about us, but a philosophical misconception, the in-experienceable substratum supposed to bear the phenomena. None of us ever walked on it, swam in it, or in any wise touched it. *This* ' Matter' exists not. But so far from this argument making things unreal, it is the very condition of their ever being to us quite real, quite themselves. We are relieved at once of the monstrous self-distrust of the present-day amateur scientist-philosopher, who declares that the laws and conceptions of science describe the heaven-knows-what of reality ! But if the concepts do ' describe' reality, then *we* through them know what reality is : while if we ' constructed' the concepts, it is incredible they should ' describe' a reality known only to heaven. Thus would the representative theory of knowledge unseat one's reason. The error is twofold : firstly, no man ever ' constructed' a concept. The mathematician

[1] Berkeley : " The Third Dialogue between Hylas and Philonous." Philonous speaks.

or the theorizing scientist (whether he correctly or incorrectly theorizes) is not an artificer but an explorer in a neutral realm.[1] Secondly, reality is not a thing-in-itself ' behind ' phenomena. The scientist of to-day is not a whit more advanced if he makes of ' reality ' a thing-in-itself such as former generations made of matter. The fact is that both minds and physical objects are and are ' real,' and they are composed of one and the same substance—neutral stuff. Such, I conceive, is the true monism.

In this connection it will not be amiss to consider the programme of natural science laid down by the late Heinrich Hertz ; which if correctly interpreted becomes a most illuminating piece of epistemology. It will be recalled that Hertz, like Kirchhoff, renounced the notion of efficient cause (or Anstoss) and professed merely to ' describe ' physical events. Hertz said that the only necessity that we know is logical necessity ; and this I have already attempted to refer to the ' activity ' of propositions. Now Hertz said : " The process by which we succeed in deducing the future from the past, and so in attaining that foresight which we seek, is always this : we fashion for ourselves mental images or symbols of outer objects, and in such wise that the relations of the images lead by logical necessity to those very same pictures which proceed by natural necessity from the objects which we had imaged. That this ambition shall be possible of fulfilment, certain correspondence must subsist between nature and our thought. Experience teaches us that this requirement can be fulfilled, that

---

[1] He *finds* concepts *in* the mathematical realm, and the natural scientist *finds* concepts in the physical realm. And of conceptual stuff are both mathematical and physical objects composed.

is, that such correspondences do in fact exist. If now we have once succeeded in constructing out of our total previous experience images of the required conformation, we can in a little while develop from them, as if from models, the same consequences which will appear in the outer world after a longer time, or perhaps only after our own physical interference. . . . The images . . . have that *one* real correspondence with the objects which they must have in order to fulfil the stated requirement, but they need have no other correspondence. . . . We have to exclude in the first place whatever images contain among themselves any contradiction with our laws of thought, and so we demand at once that all images be logically consistent, one with another, or, in short, consistent."[1]

Now this is in its essentials a remarkably clear statement of that which the natural scientist actually does : —it is in itself an empirical observation which philosophy is called on not to deny, but to interpret. And it is precisely the issues here raised that the current, dualistic theories are designed to meet. They fail to do so, and therewith fails our current epistemology.

The first salient point of Hertz's programme is his emphasis on a correspondence ; a correspondence that he says is between symbols constructed by the mind and outer objects : and in the current interpretation this becomes at once a correspondence between ' idea ' and ' reality,' or things-in-themselves of the worst sort. Just here lies the error ; and it is one that Hertz himself may possibly have favoured. It is true that there is a correspondence, but we have seen that the mental

[1] Heinrich Hertz : " Die Prinzipien der Mechanik," Leipzig, 1894, Sections 1–2 (Einleitung).

symbols are neutral entities, and that the ' outer objects ' are neutral entities in which lurks no trace of an unanalysed ' Material ' residue. Therefore the correspondence, which truly is, is between *two neutral manifolds*; and not between one manifold which is ' ideal ' and another which is ' material ' or ' real.' Between the two there is a complete identity of substance. It is recalled that in Chapters II and III the possibility of correspondence between logical manifolds was defended, as against certain objections urged by Joachim and others. The main objection was that corresponding systems, if they truly correspond, are identical; whereas if they are identical they cannot be said to correspond. But I there tried to show that identicals can be and are repeated; and that this statement is in no wise self-contradictory. The repetition of identical points, with a difference of position is well-nigh universally admitted; the repetition of identical manifolds, likewise with a difference of position or context, is equally undeniable : and for that matter, equally easy to understand, and just as frequently observed. Two manifolds likewise correspond if they are partially identical, and at the same time one is simpler and the other more complex. The latter then includes the former, but is something more ; the former does not include the latter. Or again, two manifolds may be partly identical while each contains features not in the other, as is the case with one musical theme developed in two or more different manners.

Now precisely such as these last are the correspondences of natural science. A relatively simple manifold (commonly called mental) is partially identical with a highly complicated neutral manifold of ' objects ' (usually called ' material ' or ' real '). But the former manifold is not in truth more mental than the latter, for obviously the mind of the investigator must survey both manifolds alike in order to apprehend their correspondence : and the two are in part identical, both in form and substance, and just in so far as they do correspond are wholly identical. We say then simply, and we are entitled to say, that the correspondences which natural science deals with are correspondences between equally neutral manifolds. The theoretical that is said to correspond (apart from its context in consciousness) to a material manifold is identical with such part of the latter manifold as it is said to correspond to. But the first is not more ' mental ' than the second, nor is the second more ' real ' than the first. Both are neutral ; and their ' reality ' is at this point an irrelevant issue. In discussing Joachim's objection to the statement that truth is correspondence between idea and reality, I did not attempt to defend anything but the possibility of correspondence between partially identical systems. That one-half of the correspondence should be thought to be the ' ideal ' and the other ' real,' seems indeed as absurd as Joachim says. If the correspondence is to *be* at all for us, it is clear that both members must be in the onlooking consciousness and must there enjoy the same ontological status.

The physical world, then, is a neutral manifold which is no more outside of the mind or severed from it by a ' yawning chasm ' than is the number system. It is, however, just as much outside of the mind as is the number system, or any other logical manifold. We have seen that these are not ' subjective '; their substance is not idea. Thus matter is as independent of our minds as is the number system ; but it is also just as immediately accessible to our minds and our knowledge. Both matter and mind consist of the same elemental neutral stuff. In this sense, matter is by no means a thing-in-itself, and we may refer to it precisely as we refer to other relatively distinct universes of discourse, such as Euclidean space or Dedekind's continuum. The physical world is of course the universe of time and space.

While now it is such a neutral universe, it is one admittedly which is remarkably complex, that is, one whose several terms (according to the theory of universals and particulars set forth above) have a very high degree of particularity, or concreteness. Beside it our other neutral manifolds are indeed meagre and abstract. They correspond to it, which is always so much more. From its extreme complexity follow its concreteness and its remarkable importance to ourselves. We shall perhaps see, however, that this physical universe is not the most inclusive, not the most concrete that *is*.

Returning now to the Hertzian programme, we notice, secondly, that the ' mental symbols ' are said to be *constructed by the mind*. This, as we have seen, is the popular view much insisted on by natural scientists who believe that scientific laws are shorthand expressions.[1] merely, of physical events ; and also, I believe, by not a few idealists. We have already seen, however, that these ' mental symbols,' like all other mental contents, are neutral entities ; and we have seen that even the logician discovers but does not construct his realm. Is, then, the natural scientist who aims only to describe physical processes, for Hertz asserted that he

[1] Cf Karl Pearson : " The Grammar of Science."

did not even seek for explanations, a free artificer ? In the chapter on volition I shall try to show that the will is free and that the mind can construct and fabricate. But as the statement was possibly meant by Hertz, and certainly as it is commonly understood, at the present time, it is erroneous.

Now it is to be admitted that the spheres and cart-wheels of the Ptolemaic astronomy smacked decidedly of free artifice and imaginative construction. But at nearly the close of the seventeenth century Newton declared, " *Hypotheses non fingo.*" It was his profession if not quite rigorously his practice. In 1825 Ampère, addressing the Académie Royale, said : " The principal advantage of formulas which are obtained as the direct result of observations numerous enough to be incon-testable, is that they are independent of all hypotheses, whether of such hypotheses as the discoverers of the formulas may have employed in the course of their investigations, or of such as may later come to be in vogue."[1] Most materialists, furthermore, believed that truth was discovered, not constructed. Then in recent years Kirchhoff and Hertz have expressed their distrust not merely of hypotheses, but of all ' explanations,' and declared their own aim to be merely the ' descrip-tion' of physical processes. And the scientific world to-day works very little with hypotheses : the word ' theory ' no longer means an hypothesis deliberately added to the observed facts, but an actually observed law or set of laws from which deductions may be drawn. And these laws are not hypothecated or constructed ' to fit ' the facts, they are found in the facts ; and the

---

[1] In J. C. F. Zöllner's " Prinzipien einer elektrodynamischen Theorie der Materie," Leipzig, 1876, p. 295.

K

process of formulation is one not of construction, but of abstraction, of analysis. In view of this general tendency of science away from the fabrication of hypotheses and from the interpretative mutilation of observed events, it is astonishing that the most impartial description that man can achieve is called a subjective construction of mental images. It may be pertinently asked of science, why it should strain at hypotheses if by principle it can swallow only free constructs and fancies. The fact is that this theory of ' mental constructions ' is the child of idealism which is now put out to service for the support of its parent.

The conscientious scientist, if he dared trust his own perceptions and disregard the ukase of idealism, knows perfectly well that he ' constructs ' nothing ; and that, indeed, his prime concern is precisely not to construct anything. It is his purpose to efface his personal will, and if it were possible he would transcend the limitations of his sense-organs, so as to be an impartial witness of the events. Truly it is his purpose to *abstract* and sometimes to *re*-produce, but this is not to ' construct ' in the sense that our philosophical dualists mean. For there is a distinction presumably between selecting a coat and stitching it ; or between writing an essay and tracing it through tissue-paper. The Latin alphabet and the Arabic numerals are symbols, certainly, but the concepts of science are the true body of the objects. Their ' correspondence ' with this or that feature of the universe of time and space is their identity therewith.

Dualism is ever a compromise. In the palmy days of materialism any man who would not blink the facts of his experience had to make a dualistic reservation ;—

all reality might be matter, but at least there were some unreal things, such as arithmetic and self-respect, that were of some importance. To-day dualism is still, I think, the protest of sane minds under duress, now of idealism : all experience may be idea, but nevertheless there is a reality back of experience, which is not idea, and it is well worth groping for. Both of these compromises are logically fallacious and futile. It is the merit of the revival of logic to have shown that concepts are not mental in their substance, but are neutral ; and of the most advanced scientific investigation of matter to have shown that the material world is a neutral realm with no unanalysed residue of ' Matter.' Both mind and matter are neutral aggregates, and on the basis of such a monism we may hope to deduce a consistent definition of consciousness.

The third important feature of the Hertzian programme is the statement that " we demand at once that all images be logically consistent, one with another, or, in short, consistent." And it seems generally to be assumed that the universe of time and space and the world of ' reality ' (whatever that may mean) exclude discord or contradiction. This assumption must be scrutinized, and it is of such importance to our view that it will be the subject of a later chapter.

In fine, I have tried to show that material objects, like mental objects, are composed of a neutral stuff. The elements of the physical world are neutral entities —propositions and terms—with no residual substance to be called ' Matter.' This is not to explain matter away, any more than Berkeley explained it away. It is, however, to explain away that thing-in-itself called ' Matter ' which has been so extensively advertised as

the fatal defect of realism. Without denying the being
either of mind or of matter we have at length reached
a genuine monism—one fundamental substance. Two
items confirmatory of this monism may here be noted.
The first is that it explains at once the otherwise remarkable and inexplicable parallelism, so plainly asserted
by Hertz, between the ' logical necessity ' governing
the ' images ' and the ' natural necessity ' governing
the outer objects. I know of no one else who has so
openly recognized this parallelism : yet no one can
deny it unless he will accept the doctrine of a pre-
established harmony. The parallelism between logical
and natural necessities must be admitted, but on any
dualistic theory it can be explained only by assuming
ad hoc a pre-established harmony ; while for every
failure of prediction, and such are frequent enough, a
lapse of the pre-established harmony must be likewise
adduced *ad hoc*. Our monism, too, has the failures on
its hands, as we shall shortly see. But the cases of
parallelism, where the logical deductions from the
premises correspond with the actual behaviour of the
physical objects, are now self-explained. The two
so-called ' mental ' and ' real ' systems correspond in so
far as they are identical, and in so far they will of course
run parallel, even down to the remotest deductions.
In other words, causality and logical necessity are one.

Again, and lastly, the community of substance
between mind and matter satisfactorily accounts for
our finding that large realm of entities that are neither
unmistakably the one nor the other. We have already
touched on these briefly and have seen how the vacil-
lating dualistic theory now projects them into space,
now introjects them into mind, and now again ejects

them. Such, very notably, are all the mathematical concepts, which in themselves are clearly neither mental nor physical, and which yet enter into the construction both of minds and of objects. But such most notably of all are the so-called ' secondary qualities.' The physical universe of time and space is itself an abstraction, a system abstracted from the original objects of our experience which assuredly had colours, sounds, odours and all of the secondary qualities. The ' physical universe ' is abstracted from these as truly as the notion of space is in geometry abstracted from time. " Where the motive of the physical sciences," as Perry has said,[1] " is the determining one, and this is very commonly the case, the world gets itself divided into the physical and the psychological realms, the former being [p. 291] employed as the standard and defining world." It is proper, of course, for the physical sciences to choose for their realm the movements of masses in time and space : but it becomes a sheer impertinence when this abstract universe is declared to be more ' real ' or more ' objective ' than the original universe which was all of this together with all of the secondary qualities. And it is monstrous that this division should ever have been recognized in epistemology and psychology. In both sciences it is entirely untenable. Even in physics and chemistry the exclusion of colours, sounds and odours is very imperfectly accomplished. The student of optics is interested in the properties of certain wave-lengths, but he selects for study, say, the ' ultra-violet ' or the ' red ' end of the spectrum : the student of acoustics is analysing the components of

[1] R. B. Perry : " Conceptions and Misconceptions of Consciousness," Psych. Rev., 1904, XI, p. 290.

compound sound-waves, but definable types of compound waves are ' highly disagreeable ' : the synthetic chemist finds that a certain compound is of a ' very muddy appearance ' and so unfit for the dye-house. And the experimenter with radium may find that it affects the skin so ' painfully ' that some square centimeters of new skin are necessary to him. Nevertheless, the world of time and space may be abstracted and the attention may be focussed on its laws. But the concrete objects studied are never merely masses in time and space, they have many more determinations. And their purely artificial division when it creeps into the theory of knowledge, as in the Cartesian psychology, ends in arrant nonsense. For the monism here advocated the secondary qualities enjoy the same ontological status as the primary qualities, and no view but this corresponds with our pure, unsophisticated experience.

CHAPTER VIII

THE NEUTRAL MOSAIC

IT has been shown in the foregoing chapters that the idealistic doctrine that all *being* is idea is no more tenable than the derided materialistic doctrine that all being is matter : and that in fact the inquiry into the substance of all being has been shown by mathematical logic to be a frivolous and meaningless quest. The simple entities, of which in the last analysis all things are composed, have no substance. And if for a moment any substance is predicated of them this predicate instantly comes, by reason of its universal denotation, to connote nothing at all. Yet in philosophy the habit has become so ingrained of dividing the universe into two substances, the primary and secondary qualities, or object and idea, that I have tried in the previous argument to show that all members of the two classes so referred to really consist of simpler entities—akin to the logical and mathematical entities—so that the substance of the members of these two classes (matter and mind) is the same as the substance of these entities. What this is, is found in the last analysis to be an idle or indeed a meaningless inquiry : these entities do not *have* a substance, they *are* a class. Yet owing to the habit of demanding that everything shall have a substance, an almost insurmountable habit of thought, I have resorted to the merely expository convenience of calling this class a stuff. There is a sacrifice in exactness, which can be borne in mind, but an immense gain, I believe, in communicability. And this ' stuff,' being of the class of mathematical and logical concepts, in the narrower sense of this word, might with accuracy be called ' concept-stuff,' save that this term would for many minds carry a misleading hint of subjectivity. And so, as already stated, I have adopted the name ' neutral stuff.' In doing this I fully realize that the term comes thereby to denote everything and hence to connote nothing, but we can spare the term scientifically, for, in fact, nothing is that is not a neutral aggregate. We *need* not, therefore, connote anything by it.

We face now immediately, for the first time, the real object of this book, namely the interpretation of the universe as a purely neutral universe, or, in other words, the deductive showing of how a neutral universe can contain both ' physical ' and ' mental ' objects. It will be seen at once that this point of departure involves no theory of reality, nor of knowledge, no ' sensationalism ' or other veiled form of dualism : that is, it will not deduce its two categories of mind and matter by having implicitly assumed them at the outset. We start, as I believe every epistemological theory should start, on the basis of pure *being ;* and we shall derive the ' knowledge ' relation without assuming it in our premises.

Let us now look at our familiar old universe, from which a few universally admired fallacies still need to be cleared away. The first is that of the representative theory of knowledge, a theory that is largely bolstered up by the doctrine of primary and secondary qualities. By grace of this monstrous notion we are actually brought to believe, in theory, that our firm old universe is a colourless, soundless, smell-less, tasteless and touch-less desert of time, space, masses and energies: the colours, sounds, etc., being secondary qualities sensed within our skulls. Happily in practice, however, reason mostly retains her seat, and we ' act as if ' the secondary qualities were out there ' on the objects.' Indeed, those who theoretically profess the representative theory may safely be challenged to act as if these qualities were *not* out there on the objects. But worse ensues ; for the ' sensations ' of colours, sounds, etc., are them-selves colourless, soundless, and so on, as Berkeley and every psychologist since his time stoutly aver ! Where and what, then, we vainly ask, *are* those familiar and actual qualities, the colours, sounds, odours, tastes and touches ? They are neither on the objects nor in our skulls, nor yet are they in our experiences : but they are there ' represented ' by ' sensations ' which are destitute of every one of those qualities, whose presence in knowledge we began by trying to explain !

Now whatever Berkeley may have said concerning the general pallor of ' sensations,' not he nor yet Locke, but Democritus, probably, originated the distinction of primary and secondary qualities. For Berkeley said, " Let anyone consider those arguments which are thought manifestly to prove that colours and tastes exist only in the mind, and he shall find that they may with equal force be brought to prove the same thing of extension, figure and motion."[1] So he shall, and this

---

[1] " Treatise concerning the Principles of Human Knowledge," Section 15. Cf. also an interesting article by J. Kodis : " Einige empirio-kritische Bemerkungen über die neuere Gehirnphysiologie," Zeitschrift f. Psychol. and Physiol. d. Sinnesorgane, 1900, Bd. 23, S. 194–209.

fact alone proves that the supposed ontological distinction is utterly invalid.

Now on what argument does the distinction of primary and secondary qualities rest ? Firstly, it is said that such qualities as colour, sound and temperature cannot be in the outer world because, for instance, the same body which appears cold to one hand may seem warm to the other. In the secondary realm man is peculiarly the measure of all things. But then, as Berkeley would truly say, extension is also a secondary quality in the mind : for a house does not look quite the same to one eye as to the other ; as the laws of stereoscopic vision show. Nor does a ball feel to be of quite the same size to one hand as to the other. Nor does a fly, though its pace does not change, seem to crawl so rapidly on the palm as on the forehead. Thus this same way of arguing proves that extension, size and motion are as much secondary qualities as are colour and sound.

But it is again said that different persons do not agree on the secondary qualities. To one the sky is blue, to another purple. But neither do they agree in reading the deflections of a needle or in observing the moment of transit of a star. Are such motions, then, mere secondary qualities ?

The real reason why the distinction of primary and secondary has been preserved is merely that the physical sciences have *chosen as their subject-matter* the movements of masses in time and space, and this involves size, shape and motion. Scientists have then had the effrontery to call these qualities, and these alone, external and ' real ' ; while philosophers, strangely enough, have assented. The distinction is accidental and not logical. Physical scientists happen not to be studying the development of language or the survival of species, but they will scarcely assert that philology and the study of evolution are subjective sciences. Yet they could say so quite as reasonably as they say that the classification of colours and sound timbres are subjective occupations.

One who assents to this abandonment of a false distinction will experience considerable relief in thus returning to the naïve view of things. So obvious is it that the tree is green and the cloud grey, that it is amazing for thinking beings to be so bent on denying it. It is common, but ridiculous if one stops to think of it, to hear a teacher say to a class of children that the forest is not green when no one is by to look at it. The leaves will rustle to-morrow and the same sinusoidal vibrations play through the air, but there will be no sound, for the gypsies left to-day. Let such a teacher say either that the trees themselves will not be there to rustle if no perceiving mind is at hand, or else that an absolute God will be there to sustain the trees and that God may be counted on to hear. This last is what Berkeley would have said. The representative doctrine is even more absurd for psychology. The clover is not yellow : *that* is merely my sensation. Yet mine is not a yellow sensation. Oh no, as Berkeley and all psychologists firmly agree ; the sensation is neither yellow nor red, loud nor soft. Where then is the yellow, if the object is not yellow, nor yet the sensation yellow ? " Why, it is a sensation of yellowness. The sensation represents yellow." This is, of course, the most dismal verbiage, and would not be tolerated for an instant were it not for the egregious and well-nigh universal carelessness with which philosophers have handled the concept of representation.

Berkeley did not allow the ordinary distinction between primary and secondary qualities ; but at times, at least, he adopted the representative theory of knowledge, and it is hard to see how he could reconcile this with such reasonable opinions as the following, which he expresses repeatedly :—" That the colours are really in the tulip which I see is manifest ";[1]—" To be plain, it is my opinion that the real things are those very things I see and feel and perceive by my senses. . . . It is likewise my opinion that colours and other sensible qualities are on the objects."[2]   For Berkeley both primary and secondary objects were alike ' ideas ' ; and although he meant by idea a substance (each least particle was ' idea '), and I have sought to disprove this, I hope that the reader will agree with Berkeley in so far as to admit that there is no faintest logical distinction, so far as subjectivity and objectivity, reality and unreality go, between primary and secondary qualities : and that the latter are ' on the objects ' just where and how they naïvely seem to be. We have seen that the total realm of experience is of one texture, composed of diverse elements but of one stuff, and that in order to avoid false implications this may well be called neutral stuff, but cannot be called ' idea.'

As Berkeley said, the same arguments that show the secondary qualities to be in the mind apply equally to the primary ; and for this reason the distinction between

---

[1] " First Dialogue between Hylas and Philonous " (Philonous speaks). Cf. also Wm. Hamilton : " Lectures on Metaphysics and Logic," vol. ii., p. 128.

[2] " Third Dialogue " (Philonous speaks).

primary and secondary, as, for instance, Locke made this distinction, was never anything but a specious argument for the representative theory of knowledge. For as we perceive the secondary qualities so also do we perceive the primary—' solidity, extension, motion or rest, number and figure.' But the soul, according to the doctrine, is not solid or extended, and so can know these primary qualities only by the means of ' ideas ' which are neither extended nor solid. This in the immediate domain of psychology gave rise to the theory of local signs whereby extension was represented in consciousness by ideas which were themselves only *in*-tensive (sensations of movement). The theory of local signs was fully implied in Berkeley's " Essay Toward a New Theory of Vision," and was long afterwards worked out by Steinbuch and Lotze.

Thus, for secondary and primary qualities alike, the representative theory of knowledge asks us to believe that these are ' known ' by means of entities which have neither extension, shape, size, motion, colour, sound, odour, taste nor touch. These marvellous representers constitute the ' subjective ' realm, or ' consciousness.' In short, according to this theory, consciousness or knowledge contains almost none (happily number is conceded) of those properties that are actually in knowledge. I submit, that explanation could not more flagrantly explain away that which it professes to explain. What becomes then, one must ask, of the shapes and qualities that are all about us if in our knowledge these are only shapeless and unqualifiable entities called sensations ? Shapes and qualities cannot *be* for us, if they are not in our knowledge : and it just happens that they very much are, and are for us. " Oh,

but they are represented ! " Indeed, and according to
your theory by shapeless representations of shape,
motionless representations of motion, colourless representations of colour, and odourless representations of
odour ! Whereas the fact is that my knowledge is
neither shapeless, motionless, colourless nor odourless.
Of course, the experience of every waking moment shows
that this pallid herd of sensations and perceptions thus
conjured up by the representative theory constitutes
the life experience of no man. James has stated this
conclusion the most frankly. " I believe that ' consciousness,' when once it has evaporated to this estate
of pure diaphaneity, is on the point of disappearing
altogether. It is the name of a nonentity, and has no
right to a place among first principles."[1] Certes, either
this ' consciousness ' does not exist, or else the world we
know and live in does not exist. I leave it to the sane
mind to choose.

The logic of the situation is simply this, and to logic
it is that we turn :—Nothing can represent a thing but
that thing itself. And if anybody has ever assented
to the representative theory of knowledge it is only
because he has not examined the concept of representation. The theory plays altogether fast and loose with
this concept. Typical and indisputable cases of representation are readily found. A photograph represents
a landscape : a sample represents a web of cloth : a
statesman represents a borough. But the photograph
does not represent the landscape in all respects : it

[1] William James : " Does ' Consciousness ' Exist ? " Journal of
Philosophy, Psychology, and Scientific Methods, 1904, vol. 1, p. 477.
Cf. also the same author's " la Notion de conscience," Archives de
Psychologie, 1905, t. V

leaves out, for instance, the features of colour and size. The photograph of a distant mountain-top gives no clue to the size of the mountain. It represents the landscape in the one respect of contour, and does so by being in that one respect *identical* with the thing it represents. If with a perfectly just lens a photograph were taken of a carefully constructed ellipse, the photograph would have exactly the same shape, but not the same size, as the original. And the photograph does not represent the size : while that the two shapes are identical is proved, because the analytical equation for one will be found identical with that for the other. Only the constants which define the size will be different. The same is true *mutatis mutandis* for a photograph of any the most complicated object. In so far as it truly represents the object, it is just so far identical with it. Likewise the sample of cloth represents the web in so far as it has the exact colour, texture and thickness as the rest of the web. If it has not these identical, it is not a fair sample or a true representation. As to the number of yards, be it noted, the sample does not profess to be a representation. Just so the statesman represents the voters who elected him in so far as he does precisely what a majority of them, in the same situation, would do. If he does not do this he does not truly represent them, although he may do better or worse than they would do.

A representation is always partially identical with that which it represents, and *completely identical* in all those features and respects in which it *is* a representation. In its more strictly logical aspect, every case of representation is a case of partial or complete identity between two systems, or of complete identity (save in point of position) between two simple entities. One can represent one, or red and green can represent red and green : or in systems a triangle can represent a triangle, a curve a curve, a map a country. A magnetic deflection can represent a quantity of electricity, a synoptic museum exhibit can represent an entire flora, and alphabetical symbols can represent thoughts. And in every case, if one will stop to consider, there is in some respect ' correspondence ' or identity between the system representing and that represented. And just *in so far* as there *is* representation, in so far there is complete identity or correspondence. It was mainly in anticipation of this point that in Chapter II the logical possibility of correspondence and of the repetition of identicals was argued for, against the objections of Joachim and others.

The truth of all this comes out with emphasis if we consider the concrete cases in which ' ideas ' are supposed to represent outer objects. To consider first the case of ideas representing objects in space. The idea represents space or a part of space : Is the idea then spatial ? The representative theory declares that it is not. In what manner then, being non-spatial, can it represent space ? The most plausible answer to this would be that it does so as an analytic equation represents an extended curve, or as any symbol represents the thing symbolized. But it is *spatial* space and not a subjective symbol that we started with, as we may see from the concrete case in which a psychological experimenter has before him his apparatus and his experimental subject, both in space. Whatever now may be the nature of the space known to the experimenter, whether it be called idea, symbol, or whatever else, it is the same space that is known to the one experimented on, and vice versa. And it is certain that this same space cannot sift through the sensory apparatus of the experimenter any more than of the subject and lodge an adequate representation within that person's skull. The subject's known space is certainly the same as that of the experimenter, and the pretendedly ' representative ' or ' symbolic ' knowledge of even the mere subject can after all be nothing else than immediate knowledge, must be simply the space that is.

It follows, then, that the experimenter, if he justly conceives the situation, will be brought to admit that the spatial sensations experienced by his subject are themselves extended, and that they have just the size and occupy just the positions of the objects that the subject is said to have experienced. In other words, ideas of space are spatial ideas.

An objection will be made to this from the fact that the spaces that a person knows by means of his various senses are not always the same, by which is meant that they are inconsistent. Visual space does not quite coincide with auditory space, nor this with tactual. Hence the ideas must be thought not to be spatial, but to be symbolic of space, that is, to be but very inadequately representative; representing, say, certain purely ordinal features, but not the extension of space. This is mainly the question of the subjectivity of contradictions, and must in so far be referred to the later discussion of error. We shall then perhaps find that contradictions or errors are as objective as any other of the elements of experience, and that conflicting experiences with regard to space in no wise imply that *knowledge of* space is anything but space.

The term 'symbol,' no less than the term 'representation,' is misleading and usually covers a multitude of sins. It is true, for instance, that an analytic equation represents an extended figure, but only because both equation and figure are instances of order, and it is only the *order* of the latter and not the extension that the former represents. Any geometer knows this, and it is universally admitted that an equation 'represents' *extension* only when the unit used in the terms of the equation is a unit of real extension. It is admitted even of that ordered series that is called the point continuum, that in spite of its infinitude of points it is in its entirety not spatially bigger than the geometrical point, unless the 'points' of the continuum themselves have some finite extension. Anyone who thinks otherwise will need carefully to consider what manner of thing could represent the extent of a centimeter, say, except just another centimeter. Surely a person whose idea of space was itself not actually extended could never know space any more than a blind man, whose ideas of colour are in very truth, for once, symbolic, can ever know colour.

Exactly the same situation exists with regard to the ideas that are supposed to represent time. Time is another kind of extension, and it too cannot be represented by anything that is not temporally extended. Time *order* can indeed be represented by other (identical) orders, whose units are not extended; but the two *orders* are identical, and in point of *extension* the latter does not represent the former. We must conclude, then, and for my part I gladly conclude, that the adequate 'idea' of a minute or of an hour is just a minute or an hour. For some reason the traditional psychology happens to admit that ideas do have extension in time ; the ' time-span,' for instance, has a finite duration that is ordinarily something less than a second ; and many sensations can persist with little or no modification for considerably longer. But this slight concession to truth has never prevented psychology from drawing sharp distinctions, absurdly enough, between ' subjective ' and ' objective ' times ; thus ' subjective time ' sensations are said to persist in ' objective ' time. But such little absurdities give no pause to psychologists of the Cartesian school.

It is to be further asserted that an adequate idea of a year would be just a year long, but it need not be affirmed that a person ever has an adequate idea of a year, any more than he ever has an adequate idea of a thousand miles. It is true in the exact sense that our knowledge of the pre-Christian era, like our knowledge of celestial space, is representative, that is, it is immediate knowledge (identity) so far as it goes, but the correspondence is incomplete. Whatever it is is identical with the time or space represented, but many items of these are certainly not present in the knowledge, and in respect to the omissions knowledge is not representative : in fact, there *is* no knowledge. Our knowledge of remote time and space is chiefly an ordinal knowledge, and anyone who supposes that he has a very adequately representative knowledge of the extension of remote epochs and distances need only consult his consciousness to see that he has nothing of the sort. We cannot represent to ourselves a very great *extension* in either time or space, but we do know, and know immediately, the *order* of some of the events that take place through long intervals of time, and the order in which some objects are arranged

through vast spaces. This fact argues nothing whatsoever in favour of the ' representative ' theory.

We now come to representation of the so-called
secondary qualities, more properly the qualities. Descartes himself, I believe, admitted that these, not being
extended, were truly and immediately in the mind.
The sensations were coloured. And indeed the later
contention of the representative theory is so preposterous that we need consider it no further than to
ask,—What symbol or other device, human or divine,
could represent a colour or a sound except just that
colour or that sound ? Obviously none. Nor can the
representative theory fall back on the notion of ' similarity,' for the concept of similarity is precisely synony-
mous with that of representation. Similarity is partial
identity : and similars are completely identical in those
respects in which they are similar. We must agree
assuredly with Berkeley that the colours and all other
secondary qualities are ' on the objects,' precisely as
to a naïve person they ' appear ' to be.

We have seen that if a sensation or idea represents
anything else, whether this be an object or an absolute
God's idea, it is so far identical therewith. And psychologists must admit that a sensation of red is a red
sensation, and the perception of a landscape is as big as
the landscape ; and by as much as it is smaller, by
just so much it is not a representation. What is more,
they will some time have to admit that the exact idea
of an hour's time would be just an hour long, and of
ten years would be just ten years.

The upshot of all this is that there are no such two
things as knowledge and the object of knowledge, or
thought and the thing thought of.

" Our experience presents no such duplicity as the content of knowledge in contrast with its object ; the content *is* the object."[1] And this is to be affirmed with no sort of private reservations, such as are customary when men assent to a creed. The reason that this is so repugnant to philosophic prejudice is that knowledge, truly, never is complete ; our ideas, therefore, are never completely identical with the objects. Hence we have become wedded, or indeed welded to the phrase—my thought is *of* an object—when we ought to say and mean—my thought is a portion of the object—or better still,—a portion of the object is my thought :—exactly as a portion of the sky is the zenith.

It is, once again, in physiological psychology, that subjectivism and the representative theory framed thereto, will receive their final quietus. However attractive they may be made in the abstract, the concrete situation is as follows. The psychological experimenter has his apparatus of lamps, tuning-forks, and chronoscope, and an observer on whose sensations he is experimenting. Now the experimenter by hypothesis (and in fact) knows his apparatus immediately, and he manipulates it ; whereas the observer (according to the theory) knows only his own ' sensations,' is confined, one is requested to suppose, to transactions within his skull. But after a time the two men exchange places : he who was the experimenter is now suddenly shut up within the range of his ' sensations,' *he* has now only a ' representative ' knowledge of the apparatus ; whereas he who was the observer forthwith enjoys a

[1] Cf. W. James : " Does Consciousness Exist ? " Journal of Philosophy, Psychology, and Scientific Methods, 1904, vol. i., pp. 478 ff.

windfall of omniscience. He now has an immediate experience of everything around him, and is no longer confined to the sensations within his skull. Yet, of course, the mere exchange of activities has not altered the knowing process in either person. The representative theory has become ridiculous ; and yet any experimental psychologist who accepts that theory may confidently be challenged to interpret the situation otherwise. Day by day he sees this little drama repeated. In short, the representative theory of knowledge utterly fails the experimental investigator. In plain fact the experience of both experimenter and observer is at all times immediate. The real objects, and no ' sensations ' thereof, *are* their two experiences. When the observer says that he has a ' sensation ' of so-and-so, he means merely that it is so-and-so *much*, a certain portion, and not another, of the objects that lie about him at that moment, which is in his experience. Because I see one side of an opaque body and not the other, I am not obliged to suppose that such portion as I do see is anything other than that very side itself of the body. It could exactly as well be argued that because an oak tree is not the entire forest, it is only a sensation of the forest. In short, there is no sensation *of* an object. Experience presents no object once as outer and again as inner fact, and no content of knowledge that is other than its object.

Another fallacy that needs to be cleared away is a derivative of the representative theory of knowledge. It is the oft-reiterated dogma that two consciousnesses or minds cannot overlap ; they are said to be mutually exclusive, so that one and the same sensation or idea can never be in two minds, at either the same or different times. We know about one another's minds, as the common phrase is, only through ' inference ' : that is, if another person acts as I act, I infer that he is having the same sensations as I. But clearly I have no right, on this hypothesis, to make such an ' inference,' since we have just been informed that two persons can never have the ' same ' sensations. In short, one is asked, on a certain hypothesis, to ' infer ' what that very hypothesis denies to be possible. Or again, we are said to ' acknowledge ' that our fellows are conscious, and have sensations ' similar ' to our own. Now similarity is partial identity, and this is merely a case of acknowledging what, again, the hypothesis denies. But surely one either believes a fact and believes it inferable, or else one declines, in science at any rate, to ' acknowledge ' it. The ' acknowledgment ' of that which is not only not inferable from, but is even contradictory to, an hypothesis that one has accepted, marks a high degree of scientific sophistication.

The actual error, however, lies in the hypothesis —that minds are mutually exclusive classes : an hypothesis that the plain fact of our human intercommunication distinctly refutes. For any theory that attempts to explain communication between mutually exclusive classes will easily wrest the palm from *quaternio terminorum*. But this view of the isolation of minds from one another, as I have phrased it here, is merely a part of the psychologist's ordinary stock-in-trade. Its more dignified aspect, the one it assumes among idealistic philosophers, is solipsism ; concerning which, as Windelband observes, it is remarkable only that anyone should have gone to the pains of setting forth such a theory for the delectation of his neighbours.

Now the theory either of the uniqueness of one's self, or of the mutual isolation of individual minds, is most convincingly refuted, as it seems to me, merely in its exposition. At best it is nothing but an appendage of idealism and the representative theory of knowledge, and falls with these. No empirical facts support the notion, and countless contradict it, so that in giving up idealism and the representative theory we are relieved from dealing further with an absurdity—the denial of human intercommunication—that could be justly deduced therefrom; and relieved from a serious confusion of our own thought.

The fact is that human beings do communicate, and that is possible only because ideas can be common to two or more men at once. As in the syllogism no conclusion can be derived unless the two premises contain a common and identically the same term, so surely two persons could not communicate unless they could experience identically the same ideas. Personalities, then, once and for all, are not mutually exclusive aggregates. It is also true, of course, that not only ideas but objects as well, can be common to two or more individuals. The landscape that I experience is, if we take certain simple precautions, in all essentials identical with the landscape that you experience. This presents no more logical difficulty than the simple fact that one and the same physical atom can be shaken by a ray of light and by another ray of heat, impelled by the capillary movement of a fluid, swayed by a gust of wind, and belong to the aggregate known as a poplar leaf, all at the same instant of time. This is easily possible. It is no less clear that one and the same village can be in Europe, in Italy, in Lombardy, in civil uproar and in bankruptcy, all at the same time ; or that a man can be a national hero, a socialist, a carpenter, a husband, a pietist, and a villain, at one and the same time. In exactly the same way a certain shade of red can be the quality on a tulip and can be immediately within the experience of a hundred lookers-on at the same time.[1] This, of course, implies that the soul, so called, is extended in space ; and we shall also find that it is extended in time.

Now we have seen that the so-called secondary qualities are no more ' subjective ' than the primary, and that the colours, sounds and odours are just as much on or in the objects as to the naïve intuition they seem to be. Both the primary and secondary qualities, then, and with the logico-mathematical concepts they include everything in our universe, are quite on a par so far as being subjective or objective goes ; so that it is no more just to name both subjective (as does idealism) or both objective (as does materialism) than to name an atom of carbon chemical rather than physical, or the reverse. They form one universal class and are of one stuff : their being is simply neutral being. These entities are undoubtedly the empirio-criticist's ' objects of pure experience,' but we have, I believe, gained over the empirio-criticist in freeing our class of all classes from any least idealistic implication. We have prepared for the deduction of consciousness or mind, for finding among the neutral entities the knowledge relation, without surreptitiously introducing that element into our premises. And such a preparation, I think, was

---

[1] Cf. William James : " How Two Minds can Know One Thing," *Journal of Philosophy, Psychology, and Scientific Methods*, 1905, vol. ii., p. 176.

absolutely indispensable : and it is in this respect, perhaps, that empirio-criticism has not been critically established.

The reader has also been asked to free himself of the notion that knowledge is somehow indirect or representative. And it has been shown that the concept of representation reduces to that of identity. Nothing can represent anything but that thing itself. And if a piece of knowledge ' represents ' a portion of anything, as, say, one side of a stone, it simply is just that side of that stone without any sort of let, impediment, or intermediation. An individual's experience is a greater or lesser fragment of the universal stuff, in exactly such wise as the country of France is a fragment of the face of Europe.

In coming, now, to survey the realm of the neutral entities, the neutral mosaic, we recall that these entities, just as in any logical system, are graded in a strict and inalienable order of complexities. This order suggests the Platonic hierarchy of ideas, except that our first principle is not the Good, any more than it is the True. The first entities are the simple ones, and we may call these the fundamental entities. Precisely what these are, we are, as a race, even yet scarcely in a position to state. Yet we seem vaguely to have made out that the concepts of identity, of difference, of number, and of the negative are more fundamental than most others, are among the relatively simple in the order of complexities. To be more precise, or to affirm that there is one simplest entity or one first principle, would doubtless be to anticipate rather childishly the inevitable development of empirical knowledge, and to invite the surely unindulgent smile of later generations.

But if our human experience has not extended to the

fundamental end, if end there be, of the simple-complex hierarchy, there is a considerable range along this complexity series, with which we may truly pretend to some slight and tentative acquaintance.[1] Firstly the relatively simple entities are, agreeably to our view of the particular and the universal, the relatively universal. Here we find the already long-acknowledged logical and mathematical entities, and those in special that students of *order* are now rather busily discovering. Then come the innumerable algebras—rather elaborated cases of order.

About here, in the simple-to-complex series of neutral beings, must appear the so-called ' secondary ' qualities, more properly, the qualities. This may seem very much forced, but that will be purely by reason of the traditional Locke-Cartesian psychology. I have tried to erase the *tabulæ* in order that we may consider each and every entity for what it just logically *is :* and if we do this we see at once that aside from their actual brute *qualities*, the colours, sounds, odours, *et caetera*, have none but purely ordinal properties. The colours, if we will examine them without prejudice, are not intrinsically even extended : but they are merely a rather simple ordinal system of several dimensions. The concept of intensity here appears.

Then comes geometry : and the system of Euclid, it seems to me, has cast more light than any other piece of knowledge on the structure of the realm of *being*. Somewhere in this region, too, are the various branches of so-called higher mathematics.

---

[1] The reader will see at once that this view of the simple-complex order of being, as indicated by modern logical methods, is an extension and a confirmation of Comte's classification of the sciences. Cf. " Cours de Philosophie positive," tome premier, deuxième leçon.

Space, it has been demonstrated, is a case of order.[1] Yet no order is spatial unless the units ordered, themselves have extension, and extension is rather under suspicion with mathematicians, since it involves ' the element of intuition.' Now undoubtedly the interesting features of extended objects are their purely ordinal features, yet it seems unadvised for the mathematician to balk at extension, and betake himself to psychological considerations in order to justify his aversion. For that matter, points and numbers are ' intuitive,' but the fact is wholly irrelevant : for in this region of the complexity series there is neither perceiver nor perceived—the knowledge relation comes later on. Mathematics seems to be running the risk, undoubtedly owing to the influence of Kant, of doing with extension what physics (and philosophy) have done with the ' secondary quality '—making it ' subjective.' Extension enters at this region of the complexity series, where as yet *is* nothing subjective, and it is, of course, a neutral entity having the same ontological status, the same *being*, as the others.

Extension is either in space or in time, and one must believe that one kind of extended order is temporal, another spatial (the number of dimensions being perhaps a prominent difference). With time appears the concept of motion, although motion seems to depend on purely *mathematical change* (an ordinal change that is neither spatial nor temporal), which is certainly more fundamental, has been involved already in the algebras, and is closely related to the activity of propositions.

[1] And one could desire that another Euclid had as successfully studied time.

Then comes the concept of mass, which is simply the ratio between the acceleration of two entities, and this, added to some of the simpler systems, yields the subject-matter of the science of mechanics. This will undoubtedly seem to many, who care for such a thing, a long step toward ' reality.' We have, however, as yet no such systems as those of the real and the unreal. And the important point now to notice is that the more complex systems are always some of the preceding simpler systems, plus some new determination. As we have seen before, complex entities are always defined in terms of simpler ones : that is, the complex *are* the simpler with an additional determination.[1] In mechanics the seemingly new concepts of mass, energy, force, and work consist of nothing but simple entities in motion, in time and space.

After mechanics comes physics entire. It was pointed out in a previous chapter that in the concrete, physical objects about us there remains no residue unanalysed into neutral components, such as would have to be called ' Matter.' We now have the same fact from another point of view : various concepts in combination *are* matter. It is to be remembered here, too, that this complexity series is not proposed as a classification of human knowledge, as knowledge, but as that intrinsic and inalienable order in which the neutral entities *are*. It is a property of the hierarchy of pure *being*.

The seemingly large number of chemical elements would once have made it look to be a long step from physics to chemistry, but now stereo-chemistry, not to

[1] Certes, the " additional determination " can be supplied in a variety of ways, but their enumeration is not within our present scope.

say the intimations we have recently had of the actual transmutation of certain elements, gives us ample reason for at least suspecting that the several chemical elements are all definable in terms of small masses arranged as units in various geometrical forms. Here, too, is no Material residue. Yet it is to be remembered that the *concrete* physical objects are much more complex, much further along in the complexity series :— as will presently appear.

Somewhat more complicated than the small masses are their larger aggregates, such as clouds, rivers and seas, mountains, plains, continents and planets. These are the objects that form the subject-matter of engineering, geology, geography, physical geography, meteorology and astronomy. This seems a long step toward the concrete and particular : yet it must be remembered that ' England,' for instance, in geography is still but a small fraction of England in its infinite, concrete complexity.

Three places in the series from simple to complex entities, so far, would have looked, not so very long ago, like actual gaps—the transitions from mathematics to space, from space to mechanics (matter), and from physics to chemistry. But we now come to the transition that would once have seemed an even more hopeless breach. It is from inorganic to organic substances, to vegetable and animal life. In spite of the neo-vitalists, however, it is to-day perfectly clear that life is definable in terms of chemical process ; although, confessedly, this definition has not been actually ascertained. Life *is* some sort of chemical process, and nothing further. Here is the region that, from the point of view of human knowledge, is the subject-matter of botany, agriculture and horticulture, of physiological chemistry, and materia medica, of biology, anatomy, physiology, surgery, eugenics, *et caetera;* and of palæontology and many other sciences.

This region of the complexity series is for us a critical place, for here, of course, appears that type of complex entity called consciousness or mind. It is here that I shall undertake to show that, once again, there is no break in the series : that no new substance enters here, and that the consciousness aggregate can be readily and completely defined in terms of the entities that have appeared before. This deductive definition of mind is the subject-matter of the following chapter, and we may provisionally grant a possible gap here in order to complete our hasty sketch of the simple-to-complex order of beings.

Admitting now the presence of minds in the series, we come to those neutral aggregates that have no better name than the names of those sciences that study them—psychology, anthropology, political economy, government, ethnology, history and archæology.

The next striking transition is to the realm of values. I am not concerned to show that here, too, there is no gap in the ontological series. Yet, in a word, it is clear that a value is a still neutral property that is added to some and not to others of those entities that lie in the simpler regions of the ontological series. There is some property, and we express it in a definition, by which all the entities going before are divided in two classes, according as they have or have not a value. Herewith are given the entities that are studied by the normative sciences, æsthetics, logic only in so far as a part of it is indeed a science of truth or of reality and not of *being,* and ethics including, perhaps, theology. The least fundamental, that is the most complicated entities, of such portion of our ontological system as is known to man, seem to be the beautiful, the real and the true (if these are distinguishable) and the good. The common meaning of ' value ' shows that while these elaborated entities are the least fundamental, they are the very most important for us as human beings. It should seem that the term ' fundamental,' and with it possibly our entire intellectual point of view, has been vastly modified since the time when Plato called the Good the most fundamental of the Ideas.

Our survey of the great mosaic in its asymmetrical order of simple-to-complex beings, has necessarily been very brief and schematic : yet it may serve its purpose as being a bird's-eye view of the infinite realm of *being*, which in substance is neutral and not ideal, and as showing fairly nearly the place in the grades of complexity where the mental first appears. Before proceeding in the next chapter to the deductive definition of consciousness we must consider two features of this complexity order.

The first is that very obviously the more complex entities are those which we call more concrete and particular : the simple and fundamental entities are ' abstract.' The more complex an object (or system) is, the more particular are its parts. This bears out the theory of the universal and the particular that was offered in Chapter III. Now, as touched on in Chapter IV, human thinking, and I am now speaking psychologically, never grasps entities of any high degree of particularity, our formal discourse is never complex enough, and our thoughts are never nearly so particular as our inarticulate perceptions, nor these so particular as the objects that our hands can touch. Our mere perceptions, for a reason that will plainly appear in the next chapter, and *a fortiori* our ' abstract ' thoughts, select from the concrete world relatively simple parts. So much, and so much only, *is* our perception and our thought. Thus it happens that every science is in the first instance a process of abstraction (the technical arts abstract to a far less degree), and of this abstraction we have noted one instance that by reason of its false interpretation has borne evil consequences. The natural sciences quite properly select certain entities to study, namely masses moving in time and space, and discard the secondary qualities. But this arbitrary selection ought never to have been confused with the distinction between subjective and objective, with which, as Berkeley said, it has nothing to do. Nor should this selection have been made the foundation for a theory of knowledge or of reality. This error was the germ of idealism.

The other feature of the simple-to-complex neutral series to be considered here is the matter of those ' additional determinations,' which make of simpler entities, such as are more complex. Are these additional determinations actually new concepts present for the first time at a certain place in the series, and thus not definable in terms of simpler neutral entities present in the more fundamental parts of the complexity series ? And it must be admitted at the outset that in certain places entities appear that do not seem to consist of the simpler entities that are more fundamental. The most striking cases of this are those of each one of the qualities. A quality seems to be precisely what it is,

M

and seems not to develope out of any ordinal or other system. Yet one must also admit that qualities form ordinal series (qualitative and intensive) which in many respects resemble series of points. Further, it is clear that given two qualities, as, say, red and yellow, together with appropriate propositions of repetition, and admixture in varying proportions;—a system deductively developes that contains many more distinct qualities than the two originally given. This is true of all the qualities.

Furthermore, the fatuous ontological theory which we have so long entertained regarding the qualities, has prevented their being studied by anyone who would take an intelligent interest in their purely logical properties.[1] We may yet learn that qualities can be defined in terms of entities that are not qualities; that is, according to our earlier glimpse at logic, that they develope deductively into being from systems which at the outset do not contain qualities.[2] Should this appear, it will not be more astonishing than the discoveries of stereo-chemistry in regard to the relations between many substances which at first seemed absolutely distinct from one another; the differences reducing to different arrangements of atomic masses in space.

Another instance of an apparently new entity, not

---

[1] For an interesting and, to my sense, noteworthy effort in this direction I would refer the reader to Franz Brentano's two essays on " Phænomenal Green " in his " Untersuchungen zur Sinnespsychologie," Leipzig, 1907.

[2] A proof of this has indeed been attempted, but, in the sense in which I mean, not successfully. Whether this is sometime realized or not, the fact involves no prejudice to the strictly neutral, and not " subjective," ontological status of the qualities.

developing deductively from more fundamental entities, would at one time have been that of mass. Mass
could be defined in terms of force or of work, or these
in terms of it (as seems to me to be intrinsically simpler),
but in these three concepts, and especially in mass,
something seemed to be involved which did not
grow out of the entities of pure mathematics. Yet
we now recognize mass to be merely the ratio between the accelerations of two entities. And quite
the same could once have been said of the ' vital
spark ': it seemed to be quite distinct from the
entities of the inorganic world. Yet we are now convinced that life can be defined in terms of chemistry
(but not the reverse) : life developes deductively in
certain manifolds.

On the other hand, it is an unmistakable trait of the
developement of human knowledge that the number of
seemingly independent entities is, with every step in
advance, reduced. The tendency is, and has always
been, for those entities, whether mathematical, physical
or ideal, that seem unresolvable into simpler components, to be nevertheless, after all, resolved. Whether
by analysis or by synthesis, the proof is gradually
attained that without the entering in of new entities
the simple developes into the complex. The ancient,
anti-vitalistic fable of the homunculus synthetically
generated, after many failures, in a wise man's crucible,
is an allegory of the growth of human knowledge. The
homunculus, once achieved, would prove that life is
a chemical process and not an independent and irreducible energy. Thus we vaguely make out, not merely
that all *being*, even in its forms so diverse as mind and
matter, consists indeed of one neutral substance (for

that it seems to me is perfectly assured), but also, that these neutral entities are marvellously compacted in a united system such that the simple develope without break or discontinuity into the more and more complex, even down to the infinite diversity of concrete being. This is, I believe, that monism, that " one substance of which mind and matter are the two aspects," regarding which rather Heraclitean hints are put forward in the concluding chapters of recent volumes by Strong and Busse.[1]

The successive closing in of the apparent gaps of the simple-to-complex series of beings brings it more and more within the limits of probability that we shall one day learn that all being is a single, infinite, deductive system in which the entire variety developes deductively from a relatively very small number of fundamental propositions. How small this number is we may hardly conjecture ; for it is a matter of slow empirical ascertainment which must not be rashly anticipated. Yet it seems not absolutely impossible that some day the ideal of Fichte and others should be realized, and that the subject-matter of all our sciences, in fact the entire system of being, should be seen to be one united deductive system. But as we saw before, that thinking of ours that we call deductive, our coherent thinking, does but follow after the intrinsic activity of the neutral entities. They develope of their own motion those portions of any system which we, in our deductive thinking, call the logical consequences. The great fact is, then, that the infinite mosaic of being is neither

[1] C. A. Strong : " Why the Mind has a Body," New York, 1903. L. Busse : " Geist und Körper, Seel und Leib," Leipzig, 1903.

subjective nor objective in substance, but is neutral, that it is ordered, that it developes unceasingly of its own motion, and that as our knowledge advances we have more and more reason to believe that its unity is complete.

CHAPTER IX

THE CONCEPT OF CONSCIOUSNESS

IT was said at the outset of this volume that our aim is a deductive account of consciousness. This means the framing of a set of terms and propositions from which a system is deducible that contains such an entity, or class of entities, as we familiarly know under the name of a consciousness or mind. There can here be no difference of substance between the original terms and the consciousness entity deduced, for the latter consists of the former in some sort of combination. But this consciousness entity, if our deduction is to be correct, must possess all those properties of relation to other things, of volume, of change, of appearance and of disappearance, that we ordinarily call the empirical phenomena of consciousness.

In the last analysis this could be done in the formal manner of mathematical logic : we could start with a class of terms and postulates one, two, three and so forth. But this would be for us now neither a convenient nor a satisfactory way, for it is at present the procedure of a highly abstract science that deals with relatively fundamental entities : whereas we have seen that consciousness, or mind, first appears about midway in the simple-to-complex series of *being,* and is therefore a relatively superficial and particular entity. The procedure indicated for us, therefore, is that adopted by

166

other sciences that treat of relatively complex entities. The science of kinematics (the pure geometry of motion), for instance, treats of entities and complexes that are indubitably of one substance with the entities of pure mathematics, and indeed are in large part just these ; yet it does not deduce these algebraic and geometrical entities *ab initio*, for this would be a gratuitous repetition of mathematics, but starts with the (neutral) systems of algebra and geometry ready-made. Otherwise kinematics would be kinematics *and* geometry, *and* algebra, *and* mathematical logic. Kinetics and chemistry, similarly, take the finished entities of pure mathematics, kinematics and mechanics, and trace the deductive sequences a step further.

For this very reason we shall not start with an abstract class (K) of *simple* entities and postulates one, two and three, regarding them, but we take ready-made, as we are entitled to take, the entities that are next simpler than consciousness in the simple-to-complex order of being and trace the deductive steps to consciousness and mind. Of all the entities in the neutral series that are simpler or more fundamental than minds, it is clearly those that immediately precede in point of simplicity that are the most important for us. These, as we have found in our survey of the neutral hierarchy, are physical objects,—organic and inorganic entities, both living and dead. " Ah, now," as some reader will certainly say, " this whole business is exposed for what it is—a disguised Materialism." But no, I must reply, it is nothing worse than mere materialism. Material objects after all *are*, and it is a sad evasion to deny or to misconstrue their *being* : but I believe that I have fully shown that their ' substance ' is the same as that of all mathematical logical concepts, and that the ' substance ' of both is strictly neutral. I have also tried to show that it is a pardonable point in any theory not to deny the *being* of any of the familiar and indubitable entities of experience. It was partly in order to forestall the charge of ' Materialism ' that the foregoing ontological considerations have been presented. And after all, though we start out with inorganic and organic material objects, their composition out of strictly neutral entities will still not fail to appear from time to time in the discussion.

Now the first step in our deduction of mind is a consideration of several species of entities that would fall under the generic name of ' parts.' An example from pure mathematics, and already mentioned, is the class of prime numbers, a true part of the series of whole numbers that has interesting special properties, and one whose singular distribution through the series has a so-far inscrutable relation to the orderly, linear arrangement of the whole. A similar instance among physical objects would be such portion of any such object as is included in a geometrical plane that intersects the object. Let us suppose that a plane mathematically true but one millimetre thick passes perpendicularly through the roots, trunk and branches of a tree ; and let us suppose all the molecules of chemical substances belonging to the tree and included within the section, to be simply enumerated. It is clear that this collection is an actual part of the tree, and yet one that in itself would contribute very little to the life and developement of the tree. A complete knowledge of it would afford a very inadequate notion of the anatomy and physiology of trees. Yet this would not

be a random collection, for it would include none but
vegetable molecules included within the intersecting
millimetre plane. The plane, with what it includes, is
exactly defined in terms of the entire tree and the
position of the plane. Merely from the point of view of
the vital organization of the tree would this collection
be a random one. The law that defines the lie of the
plane is not among the laws that define the anatomy
and vegetable economy of the tree. Such a collection
may be called a ' cross-section.' Similarly the prime
numbers are a ' cross-section.'

Again, if the plane is a geometrical one of no thickness
and passing horizontally through the trunk, it defines
by its intersection a collection of contours that is a true
portion of the tree, but one that is even less significant
for the total economy of the tree than the collection
previously defined. A complete knowledge of it would
be next to no knowledge of the tree as a whole. It
would be, roughly speaking, merely a circular contour
containing an infinity of minor contours. It is clear
that a part so defined, for it is truly a part of the tree,
reveals the fundamental substance of which the tree
itself is composed : for of course these mere contours
are our fundamental neutral entities. And it is highly
significant for us to note that *when a part of any object
is defined by some law that is independent of the laws that
define the whole object, the part usually intersects the
whole in such a way as to reveal the essentially conceptual
or neutral constitution of that object*—even when this
whole is a material object. This is true also when part
collections are defined by other than geometrical means.
If during a military engagement the velocity of every
projectile that is flying in the air at a certain instant is

enumerated, these velocities form a part collection, for obviously they are an essential feature of the whole physical system at that moment. They are also ' mere ' velocities, that is purely mathematical quantities, neutral in substance, and not physical objects.

But ' part ' collections may be defined in an infinite number of ways, some showing out and some others not showing the neutral constitution of the whole. Thus those men in a congregation at church who are political conservatives, the attractive faces in a railway coach, the students at a university whose given names begin with W, the mauve-coloured postage stamps in a philatelist's album, the particles of matter lying in the plane of the earth's orbit, the words anywhere spoken with honest intent through the course of a day—all these are larger or smaller collections that are true parts of various definite manifolds. For want of a better name we may still use the term ' cross-section ' to designate any part collection that is defined by a law which is unrelated (or but remotely related) to the laws that define the whole in question : in other words, let us call any definable part that is in no wise *organically* related to the whole, a cross-section.

Now the cross-sections so far adduced are not merely insignificant for the whole of which they are a part, but they are also rather insignificant for any system, howsoever inclusive. There are other cross-sections, however, which do have a prime significance in and for some manifold more complex and inclusive than the manifold through which the cross-section is initially made. Thus the sum total of all the whales living in certain given waters is a cross-section of the sea that is significant for the whalers who are trying to locate and gather them in. The various shafts and levels of a mine are a cross-section of the mountain, and of import to the shareholders : and it is the business of the engineer so to direct the workings that this cross-section shall coincide with that other cross-section that is made by the vein of ore. The brute mass of the mountain is twice cross-cut.

Once again, a navigator exploring his course at night with the help of a searchlight, illuminates a considerable expanse of wave and cloud, occasionally the bow and forward mast of his ship, and the hither side of other ships and of buoys, lighthouses, and other objects that lie above the horizon. Now the sum total of all *surfaces* thus illuminated in the course, say, of an entire night is a cross-section of the region in question that has rather interesting characteristics. It is defined, of course, by the contours and surface composition of the region, including such changes as take place in these (specially on the surface of the waves), and by the searchlight and its movements, and by the progress of the ship. The manifold, so defined, however, is neither ship nor searchlight, nor any part of them, but it is a portion (oddly selected) of the region through which the ship is passing. This cross-section, as a manifold, is clearly extended in space, and extended in time as well, since it extends through some watches of the night. It includes also colour qualities. This cross-section, furthermore, is in no sense inside the searchlight, nor are the objects that make up the cross-section in any wise dependent on the searchlight for their substance or their *being*.

Now cross-sections that in many respects resemble the one just described are found in any manifold in which there is organic life. We have heard of late in the field of both animal and vegetable physiology of the concept of *response*. Organisms of either kingdom respond to their environment, and one chapter at least of physiology treats mainly of the influences that elicit response and the mechanism of the process. It is to certain features, and not to others, of its environment that the living organism responds, and the group of things to which it thus reacts constitutes a cross-section manifold that is of prime importance to one who is studying that organism and one that is of the most vital importance, of course, to the organism itself.

The mechanism of response is typically the nervous system, although in studying the irritability of tissue we meet with cases of response that involve no such differentiation of function. Yet even in plants where the subject of response is being actively studied at the moment, we find that in many cases the mechanism of response involves well-differentiated lines of conduction which bear a remarkable analogy to the nerves that are found in animal tissue.[1] "As long as it was still thought," writes Haberlandt, "that the tough cell-membranes of vegetable cells completely separated the neighbouring plasm bodies, the hypothesis of a conduction of excitation from cell to cell through this plasm hung quite in the air. It was therefore the discovery of

[1] The subject of plant response offers many delights to one who is interested in general physiology. The following works are of special interest in connection with the topic here discussed :—
J. C. Bose : " Plant Response as a Means of Physiological Investigation," New York, 1906. G. Haberlandt : " Die Sinnesorgane der Pflanzen," Leipzig, 1904. " Das reizleitende Gewebesystem der Sinnpflanze," Leipzig, 1890 : and " Sinnesorgane im Pflanzenreich zur Perception mechanischer Reize," Leipzig, 1901.

a pioneer, in the fullest sense of that word, when Edward Tangl first demonstrated the existence of delicate plasm threads traversing the cell-walls and bringing adjacent plasm bodies into direct connection with one another. Thus the existence of continuous paths was established, and the comparison was soon to be drawn between connecting threads of protoplasm and the nerve fibrils of animal tissue.[1]

We have always known, of course, that plants ' respond ' in a general way to sunlight, air and water. More recently we have become acquainted with processes that are more appropriately named responses. Roots do not grow downward by chance nor by any pre-established harmony, nor yet by instinct, but they respond mechanically to the attraction of gravitation, nor is this merely due to the general weight of the root, since by a comparable mechanism the stems grow contrarily to gravitation. The roots are positively geotactic or barotropic, while the stems are negatively, and many kinds of branches transversely barotropic. Similarly, and by virtue of a distinct mechanism, the various parts of a plant respond variously to light of different colours and intensities, growing toward or away from such light : they are variously heliotropic. There are similar responses in vegetable organisms to thermal, chemical, and even electrical stimuli, and we are gradually coming to know that these involve a well-differentiated and oftentimes a highly elaborate mechanism of response. Now clearly in the case of a given plant these baro-, helio-, thermo-, chemo-, and galvano-tropisms, these several mechanisms of

[1] G. Haberlandt : " Die Sinnesorgane der Pflanzen," Leipzig, 1904, p. 14.

response, define a certain cross-section of the plant's environment that is comparable with the cross-section defined by the searchlight. The forces to which the plant responds are those components of its environment that are of vital moment, favourably or unfavourably, to it. And these forces, be it noted, to which the plant responds are distinct from the mechanism by which the response is effected; *they are a portion of the environment.*

But even the tropisms are not the most intricate mechanisms of response. Contractile tissue is found in plants that functions, for all practical purposes, like the muscle tissue of animals. Of course, the rapid contractions, such as those of the leaves of the sensitive plant, and many of the Droseras, are the most striking: while we vaguely refer the slower movements, such as the closing and opening of flowers (though these too are sometimes rapid), to generally diffused osmotic processes. But we are learning that a vastly greater number than was ever suspected of plant movements is produced by distinctly differentiated and characteristically located organs of sensitivity, of conduction, and of contraction.

Among innumerable instances given by Haberlandt, we may consider the following. "In the year 1804 Sydenham Edwards discovered the sensitivity of the six little tufts of hair on the upper surface of the leaf of the Venus fly trap, *Dionœa muscipula*. This insectivorous little plant is perhaps, after the *Mimosa pudica*, the most notable contribution to plant physiology that we have had from the New World. On each of the two halves of the leaf, which are provided around the edge with sharp strong teeth, there are three upright tufts of hair and numerous circular digestion glands. When an insect crawls on to the surface of the leaf and touches one of the tufts of hair, the two halves of the leaf clap quickly together, the insect is hemmed in, and the teeth along the edge lock firmly into each other so that all attempt to escape is useless. The insect is killed, digested, and slowly the leaf opens again to lie in wait for other prey."[1] A prerequisite for the successful study of the sense-organs of plants " was the recognition that, just as in the animal so in the vegetable organism, the reception of the stimulus and the response thereto might be separated some distance from each other. As the moth receives the light stimulus with its eyes, and hurries toward the flame by means of its wings, so the tender wheat sprout perceives by means of the tip of its cotyledon sheath the direction from which rays of light are coming, whereon the heliotropic deflection takes place in a deep-lying layer. The discovery of this important fact is one of the many special contributions made by Charles Darwin in the capacity of plant physiologist."[2]

Now here in the separate organs of reception, conduction, and contraction are all the essentials of the reflex-arc that is so important a part of animal physiology. It is exact to name these responses of plants ' reflexes,' and it is clear that they considerably augment the cross-section of the plant's environment that we have seen to be defined by the tropisms. The complete cross-section that is so defined, constitutes all, or very nearly all, of the plant's environment that *for it* has any existence. *For the plant* any other portions of the surrounding world *are not*. Yet the plant remains

[1] *Ibid.*, pp. 10–11. [2] *Ibid.*, pp. 12–13.

itself an organism that is distinct from this effective environment. And it is interesting, finally, to notice that in connection with these effective agencies, this cross-section and the mechanisms that respond thereto, physiologists have come to use the term ' plant-psychology.'

The reader will already have reflected that in animal organisms the phenomena of response define a similar, although in the higher organisms a much more complicated, environmental cross-section. In the lower forms of animal life the tropisms present themselves as all-important, while in higher forms and particularly in vertebrates the tropisms give place more or less completely to reflex movements. The mechanisms of response have been further differentiated and wonderfully co-ordinated and unified in a nervous system. Of this system the anatomical unit is undoubtedly the neuron, while the physiological or functional unit is the reflex-arc. And the reflex-arc in animals is, in its anatomical essentials, not different from the reflex-arc in plants. These essentials are an irritable end-organ that receives the stimulus, and is called a sense-organ or *receptor :* a differentiated fibre that conducts the excitation, or *conductor :* and a contractile tissue that transforms this nervous excitation into movement, or an *effector.* These three members are well differentiated in plants.

Now the physiology of the animal nervous system may be divided into three parts :—the physiology of waste and repair in neurones : the physical-chemistry of nerve conduction ; and the physiology of reflex-arcs. To the retarding influence of psychological theory, physiology owes the fact that until now the capital importance of reflex-arcs has not been recognized, nor these arcs fairly studied. So far as reflex-arcs that involve the cerebral cortex go, the Cartesian psychology has in large measure successfully imposed its caveat on the physiologist, who modestly betook himself to posterior regions. There might be, one feared, a Soul in the pineal gland or elsewhere, that was directing affairs from that end ; and if disturbed it might fly away to lodge a complaint in high places. Little by little this preposterous tabu has lost in sanctity, although it still exerts some unhappy influence. The alienist is even to-day in doubt with his hysterical patient whether to administer bromide of soda and other medicaments or a good hearty walloping ; ' physick ' being good for the body, but discipline for the soul. Yet for the most part the physiologist has come to feel that he may now examine the cerebral cortex, and even the pineal gland, without apprehending an un-canny surprise.

Psychology of this sort has in another way prejudiced the free study of reflex processes. It divided the nervous system into two parts, one including the afferent portion of all reflex-arcs that involve the cerebral cortex, the other including the efferent remainder. To put it bluntly, this mythical division was necessary in order to preserve a ' seat for the soul.'[1] But the functional units of the nervous system are not afferent and efferent nerves ; they are reflex-arcs of longer or shorter extent. In every case they begin with a receptor, pass through some part of the central nervous system, and terminate

---

[1] Cf. the discussions of parallelism in any comprehensive psychological treatise, for instance, W. Wundt's " Physiologische Psychologie," in any of its editions.

N

in an effector.[1] And *physi*ologists do not find that in passing through the cerebral cortex, nervous currents are diminished by a leakage into the unseen psychical world, or augmented by any ' volitional' influxes therefrom. They move through the mazes of the hemispheres no more mysteriously than through the lowest spinal level. Yet what a hocus-pocus has been intercalated here by the psychological theories of parallelism and interactionism !

In the case of vegetable organisms we found that the sum total of entities in the surrounding physical system to which a plant responds, forms an intricate and in some respects an interesting cross-section of such physical system. And from the point of view of the plant, clearly, this effective environment is all the environment that it has : and this environment is distinct from its own organic structure. We saw furthermore, even in our earliest cross-sections, in inorganic manifolds, that the cross-section often so cut the manifold as to reveal the conceptual or neutral nature of physical objects : the *velocities* of all flying projectiles, and the section of a tree cut by a mathematical plane, were such cross-sections. They are true parts of the projectiles and the tree, respectively, yet they are not ponderable physical bodies : they are certain neutral components of these bodies. The same is *a fortiori* true of the cross-sections defined by plant responses. The leaflet bends toward a ray of light (a ' physical' energy, if you will), but it responds more rapidly to a more intense ray, and to a very weak ray will not respond at all. It therefore responds not merely

[1] Cf. C. S. Sherrington : " The Integrative Action of the Nervous System," London, 1906.

to light, but also to intensity. In responding differently to different grades of intensity, it defines *grades* of *intensity* as well as light energy, as components of its effective environmental cross-section. Now whatever light may be, *grades of intensity* are not physical objects. It is self-evident that they are the fundamental, neutral substances. The response of the plant has so cross-cut its physical environment as to select from the physical objects certain of their obviously neutral constituents. These and these alone belong to the plant's cross-section. And these grades of intensity are not *in* the plant, certainly no farther in than the surface of the leaves. In a similar way plants respond in all their tropisms very specifically to *direction* ' as such '; and direction is a neutral entity. It too is not *in* the plant. And if we were thus to study plant response in detail, we should find that very few indeed of the factors to which the plant responds are such entities as would ordinarily be said to have ' physical ' existence : although both the plant and its environment are plain, physical objects. The plant's cross-section is as neutral a manifold as any purely mathematical system : yet this cross-section, we have seen, is all that there *is* by way of environment for the plant. It is therefore not a stretching of the facts, but an inevitable concession to reason and to common sense, to say that the plant lives and moves in a purely neutral realm. Though the plant organism remains a physical object, its effective environment, indeed *its* sole environment, is a metaphysical manifold. This manner in which a cross-section is defined by response, I may say at once, is my definition of the knowing process.

Let us turn once more to the animal kingdom. If the

response of plants is predominantly not to physical objects but to certain of their neutral components, the same holds increasingly true of animal response as we pass up the series to the highest animal forms. In order to ascertain what entities belong to the cross-section of any given animal, one has only to discover what entities (whether physical objects or their neutral components) the animal responds to with a *specific* reaction, that is a reaction which is definably distinct from its reaction to any other entity whatsoever.[1] To this end the Baconian canons of induction [*sic*] seem almost expressly to have been framed. Does a certain colour quality belong to the effective environment of a mouse ? Let him be presented with this quality, as the canon prescribes, in all its intensities : and then let the same intensities be presented in conjunction with the other colour qualities. If he always reacts when the quality under investigation is present, in such a way as he never reacts when it is absent, we have one proof that the given colour *is* in that cross-section to which the mouse responds. And so on through the other four canons of induction. But clearly the specific reactions of the mouse are relatively limited in number, and if merely his turning toward or away from the quality under investigation is investigated, no other reactive sign being observable in his behaviour, the quest may be as fruitless as to try to find whether the mouse will react specifically to a neat demonstration of the Pythagorean proposition. But the failure to observe a specific reaction to a certain quality can never constitute a proof that such a reaction does not take

[1] Cf. Otto Wiener : " Die Erweiterung unserer Sinne," Leipzig, 1900.

place, until one has under observation every separate reflex-arc in the mouse's body, and sees that there is not *one* of these which responds always when the colour is present, and never when it is absent. But then the proof is indeed perfect, and such proof is in principle always possible, although confessedly our means of observing nervous response in animals are at the present time of the most summary and casual order. Almost the least effector whose contraction we are able to study is an entire skeletal or visceral muscle : and many of these are accessible to observation only in rough groups, and many others not at all. This is very far indeed from our being able to analyse the specificalness of response, of being able, that is, to ascertain exactly and completely the make-up of an animal organism's effective environmental cross-section. In this connection in human psychology, of course, the language reaction is a tremendous aid ; for language tremendously augments the number of specific responses that are easily observable. Thus the mathematician when expressly stimulated by a material triangle of any form reacts with the word ' triangle ' under nearly all circumstances, which shows that in his cross-section, and quite apart from any accidental visible qualities and any materials out of which the triangle may be constructed, there is the neutral entity—a plane surface bounded by three straight lines.

Now we have seen on the purely epistemological side, in our preceding chapters, that consciousness or mind is not inside the skull nor secreted anywhere within the nervous system ; but that all the objects that one perceives, including the so-called ' secondary qualities,' are ' out there ' just where and as they seem to be. We

have seen, too, from the physiological side, that the
nervous system is a strictly physical system of neurones
and reflex-arcs, in which no trace is found of an entity
that could resemble the soul. Yet we do know beyond
any peradventure, and have known ever since the days
of Democritus, that the human consciousness, mind, or
soul in some way or other depends on the human
nervous system. But it is not within the nervous system,
as logic, epistemology and physiology combined do
plainly demonstrate. The solution of this difficulty
must now be clear. We have seen that the phenomenon
of *response* defines a cross-section of the environment
without, which is a neutral manifold. Now this neutral
cross-section outside of the nervous system, and composed of the neutral elements of physical and non-
physical objects to which the nervous system is responding by some specific response,—this neutral cross-
section, I submit, coincides exactly with the list of
objects of which we say that we are conscious. This
neutral cross-section as defined by the specific reaction
of reflex-arcs is the psychic realm :—it is the manifold
of our sensations, perceptions and ideas :—it is consciousness.

In the following chapter we shall consider this
psychic cross-section in greater detail, and shall consider
specially some apparent difficulties that seem to make
this deductive definition of mind inadequate or incompatible with the empirical requirements. But in
closing I wish to point out that the manifold of mind,
of idea, has been found by deduction. The knowing
process has been reached deductively : we have found
the psychic cross-section, the conscious manifold, by a
series of necessary deductive steps in a system where

neither knowing process nor conscious entity was postulated. The knowing process is one form of the response process. All *being,* once again, is fundamentally neither mind nor matter, but one neutral substance. Certain relatively simple combinations of the neutral entities are the logico-mathematical terms and systems ; certain more complicated aggregates are physical bodies in their spatial and temporal relations ; while the yet more complicated aggregates defined by the response relation are the manifolds that are known as mental. But the deductive chain that we found in our simple-to-complex order of being, our neutral mosaic, is unbroken. I believe that these considerations close up the supposed gap between organic life and conscious life : the knowing process is deducible from the life-process of response.

Since now we have arrived at consciousness or mind without implying it under *any* disguise, in our premises, I shall henceforth feel free to use these terms. I shall call the environmental cross-section the ' psychic cross-section,' or ' consciousness,' or ' mind,' and later on ' soul ' (for we shall discover the soul herein) : and the individual members of this cross-section I shall call ' sensations,' ' perceptions,' ' ideas,' *et caetera,* just as one calls the units of a physical manifold ' atoms.' But their substance remains always neutral ; for it takes the *entire* cross-section to constitute a mind, and its individual components are no more made of mental substance than they are of cross-section substance, or no more than physical objects, as we have previously seen, are made of physical substance or ' Matter.'

In fine, the consciousness that depends on any given

living organism is the sum total of all neutral entities to which that living organism responds, and it is the system of these entities in just such and such quantity and just such spatial and temporal arrangement as the environment and the responses themselves define.

CHAPTER X

THE EMPIRICAL PROPERTIES OF CONSCIOUSNESS

WE have just seen why the body has a mind, and it is now in place to inquire what are the empirical properties of consciousness, in order to learn whether the definition thereof just given implies, that is will deductively yield, the essential features of mind as they are empirically observed. For it must be that mankind was not without some reason biased from almost the very beginning of reflection in favour of subjectivism, as indeed a study of the ancient philosophers proves ; and it must be that there were really phenomena of pretty common experience that led to the framing of the concept of mind, as distinct from matter. If our definition of mind is correct, it must account for all these features that mind is empirically found to have.

The very earliest motive that led to the notion of consciousness can hardly have been other than the simple observation, verified a thousand times each day, that the individual's world is closely dependent on the individual's sense organs.[1] It was necessary only to close one's eyes in order to learn that one's world at that

[1] Cf. G. Galloway : " On the Distinction of Inner and Outer Experience," Mind, 1903, vol. 28, p. 61.

moment became greatly and instantaneously diminished. One's experience then was clearly not simply the outer objects entire, since it shifted and varied as they could hardly be thought to do. After the notion of mind or consciousness had been once so derived, thus dependent on the sense organs, it may have seemed natural on some accounts to suppose that it had its abode within the body

The probable correctness of this conjecture is borne out by the theory of perception devised by Democritus and his contemporaries. Mind consisted of atoms like all the outer objects, but of the smoothest and finest atoms which by reason of their lightness were always being carried away from the surfaces of all substances and circulated in the air. Thus they readily entered the eyes, ears, nose, mouth and pores of the body; and thence were carried through the veins and arteries to the heart, which, being the point to which all tubes conducted, could be nothing else than the seat of consciousness. These finest atoms were just like the coarser ones outside in colour and other essential properties, so that the individual had within him very good, impartial samples of the outer objects. This was sensation and perception. Very interesting indeed are some of the minuter workings out of this delightfully straightforward theory.

Quite in line with all this, seemingly, were the observable facts of memory, sleep, and death. Memory was the case in which old residues, atoms that had collected in the heart and remained, were stirred by some means or other, and thus they revived perceptions that had been already experienced. In sleep the sense-organs and circulatory tubes were closed so that no new atoms could enter; and those already within settled down to quiescence. When the sleep had gone on for a due length of time, the fires within the body rekindled themselves and caused the pores and channels of perception to reopen. Death was the same phenomenon, except that here the bodily fires were quite extinguished, never again to rekindle themselves.

Whether the doctrine of the shades or the souls after death involved at first more than this theory of perception, it is difficult to say. There may have been some notion of an inner spirit resident in the heart, that received and manipulated the inflowing atoms, much like the Cartesian soul sitting in her pineal gland. Yet this is unlikely, at least in the time of Democritus and for some time afterward, for the shades lived on in the outer shapes they had had on earth. For in the poets, and specially in Homer, the shades were instantly recognizable by their friends and even the characters of sex were not wholly in abeyance. And it is certain that the bodies of the dead were handed over to the god of death with great care and observance of prescribed rites. Thus quite possibly Pluto took over to his nether realm the very bodies of the dead. It seems even conceivable that the burial fires were supposed to rekindle the vital fires within the body as it passed down to the company of the shades.

But aside from theory and religion, the facts observed are that consciousness, prior to death, depends in a remarkable way on the human body and specially the nerves and the sense-organs, and that in memory (as likewise in imagination and dreams) consciousness contains other things than are to be found at that same

moment in the concrete, physical world without. Our
theory of consciousness must make room for these two
indisputable groups of fact ;—some sort of dependence
on the sense-organs (in sensation and perception), and
some sort of independence of them (in memory,
imagination, and dream-life), and some sort of inter-
mittence of consciousness (during sleep). The conditions of consciousness after death have hardly been
empirically observed. The death of the body is a
purely physiological matter that does not concern us ;
and since no one yet knows what becomes of the mind
after death, we are responsible for no explanations on
this score. But consciousness certainly is dependent on
the body, and is capable of memory, imagination and
dreams.

Another motive leading to the notion of the subjective
was undoubtedly the fact of error. Men agreed fairly
well as to the existence of rivers, mountains, and temples:
but there were other matters on which they by no means
agreed. The social practices of the gods, and the
ultimate substance of the cosmos, whether earth, air or
water, were important subjects of dispute ; although
it was allowed that the cosmos could not really consist
of one and at the same time of three substances,
" Opinion " then was not the same as reality. Whether
this fact was noted before the dependence of mind on
the senses is perhaps uncertain ; but probably it was
not, since the latter is a rather more striking phenomenon, and so would have been the earlier to excite
reflection. Although it is true that before Democritus
had framed his theory of perception, Protagoras and
his friends had plunged into their epistemological
debauch, with the watchword : " Man is the measure of

all things." It was, of course, the vulgar herd, that is everybody who was not a philosopher, that was peculiarly liable to false opinions. The upshot is the admission to the realm of *being*, of ' erroneous opinion.'

Of course, the fact that opinions differed and that some must be wrong, would not have led to the supposition that opinions belong to a subjective realm, had it not at the same time been tacitly or openly held that the objective world could contain no errors, contradictions, or untruths. And this latter opinion seems to have prevailed without notable exceptions down to our own time. False opinions and illusions must be subjective phenomena because there is no room for them in the ' real,' ' objective ' world. Nevertheless, as we have seen in an earlier chapter, errors, like any other discoverable entities, are certainly a part of the neutral realm of *being*. This consequence may be gladly accepted : and it will be discussed at some length. The empirical fact is, that men's opinions are often erroneous.

The next notable fact of experience that seems to imply a subjective world distinct from the concrete and objective one is the fact of volition. Here one does not at once think of other persons : their movements may seem not different in kind from the movements of waterdrops or crabs. But within one's self one is aware of something not strikingly visible elsewhere :—one is conscious of purposes. A person living quite alone would probably never come to say that his perceptions were subjective, he might well believe that his dreams and fancies were a part of some other objective realm, and he might not have occasion to reflect on the fact of his own death, *ex post facto :* but he probably would believe that his desires and purposes were peculiar to himself.

As in the case of error, I must hold that volitions have being in the neutral realm, and are there as conceptual entities where as yet there are no minds or consciousnesses. This too is an admission that may be gladly made and dealt with in due course.

There may be other empirical motives that seem to argue for a subjective substance, but I know of but one more, the unity of consciousness ; unless perhaps another is the pure act of thinking. This, however, is partly to be accounted for under imagination and memory, and partly under volition. In so far as thought is other than these, as may well be contended, it presents neither difficulty nor very special interest to us. For from the point of view already enunciated pure thought, if it does not ' correspond ' to an outer fact (sensation, perception, and memory), nor yet contains volitional elements, is nothing but the passage through the conscious cross-section of our familiar neutral entities in more or less connected groups. The same is true of reflective thought and of judgement, two important heads that I shall not omit to discuss. Where no ' truthful correspondence ' to an ' outer ' something is involved, and no trace of volition, the mere entry and exit of ideas and their greater or less connectedness alone remain to be accounted for. The conditions of entry and exit of ideas are of course the same as for sensations or for imagined entities : while the connectedness, so far as there is any, is undoubtedly subject to the same conditions as the connectedness of all other sorts of mental content, and ultimately to those of the connectedness of consciousness as a whole.

And this is the last of our empirical features of consciousness, the features that seem to speak for a separate subjective substance, and which in denying this last, one must still account for. The unity of consciousness has been, it seems to me, greatly overemphasized ; yet some degree of unity there undoubtedly is, and it must be explained.

We find, then, that the realm of being presents to us, in fact, collective entities that have been called consciousness or minds,—our psychic cross-sections of the preceding chapter ; and that these involve the phenomena of sensation, perception, memory, imagination (and dreams) ; of error, volition, and some degree of unity. The definition of consciousness as a cross-section, that group of entities to which a given organism responds, must give a reasonable account of all of these : an epistemological account in the first place. After that I shall attempt some little discussion of the physiological aspect of these same phenomena, that is, the mechanism of response.

The principal phenomena for which the theory is to be held responsible, or, as some will say, the difficulties which it must surmount, are now, I believe, stated. And I might proceed at once to a discussion of them, were it not needful first to point out a fallacy that has permeated almost all psychological discussion ; and it is one that, unless it is avoided, will reduce any account of consciousness to confusion. We must carefully distinguish, namely, between the presence in consciousness of any entity, simple or complex, and the presence there of a reflective process relating to this entity. Thus an item A may be for a longer or shorter time in consciousness, but there may or may not be a

reflective process, say a judgement, on A to affirm that
it is or has been ' present,' or whatsoever other predicate
might be affirmed. The striking of the hours may be
audible in my consciousness, although I may only
considerably later, or not at all, further reflect that
" the clock has struck," or that " it is time for luncheon."
Yet almost invariably, in such a case, the sound of the
clock is said not to have been in consciousness. But
for this statement there is no warrant, unless one will
assert that every element in consciousness has or ' can
have ' a conscious reflective judgement affirming the
said element to have been present. The ' can have '
we may reject, since in the absence of such a reflective
judgement, no one shall know what could have been :
' can ' and ' may ' mean nothing here. But now if
every element in consciousness has a conscious reflective
judgement based on it, this ' conscious ' judgement,
since it is now an element in consciousness, has attached
to it another judgement to make it conscious, and this in
order to be conscious yet another, and so on for ever.
And this, be it noted, for every least feature of which
we are conscious. Of course, this is a pure myth, and a
preposterous one. Our minds are not knitted up in any
such regressions, and the few actual cases approaching
such a thing are cases of a grave malady. The fundamental fact is that elements either are or are not
in the consciousness cross-section ; and if they are
then they are, and they need no further endorsement from reflection. It is true that they sometimes have it, but such cases instead of being the
most usual, as the theorists would have us imagine,
are in the vanishingly small minority. Of how many
entities could we be conscious if we stopped to

reflect, even *once* on each entity, that it was in consciousness ?

These elements which decline to participate in the reflective regressions of the dilettante in psychology, form actually the great bulk of consciousness. They may be of the highest degree of vividness (as, for the merest instance, in states of confusion, bewilderment and ecstasy), or they may be very little vivid, and these compose the conscious states that James has brought into notice as the ' fringe.' Whether vivid or not, these straight components of consciousness, unscored by the ego's countermark, have been for the most part accorded only the most grudging scientific recognition under the term ' feeling ' or ' sentience,' or ' bare consciousness ' : and their significance for cognition has not been justly acknowledged. A few quotations will illustrate their present curious status with psychologists. They are ignored theoretically (however much they may be ' discussed ') by all writers who define the mental in terms of immediacy ; as Dewey in the quotation above cited, or Wundt in the following :—" The distinctive characters of the psychic are subjective in their nature : they are known to us only from the content of our own consciousness."[1] With reference more direct Sherrington says : " The processes apsychic, or so indefinitely psychic as to baffle introspection, at root of those amenable to introspection, must by their coalescence " *et caetera.*[2] The elements which are so indefinitely

[1] W. Wundt : " Grundzüge der physiologischen Psychologie, 5te Auflage, erster Band," Leipzig, 1902, S. 19. It would be a nice matter to discover whether the redundancies in this purely circular definition number three or four.

[2] Charles S. Sherrington : " The Integrative Action of the Nervous System," New York, 1906, p. 379.

psychic as to approach the apsychic, take their stand, certainly, among the ineffables. Again, McDougall, although he recognizes " the fact that it is not only the clear, vivid affections of consciousness with which the science has to deal, but that it must take account of other processes also, processes less easily recognized by direct introspection, and in fact usually only discoverable indirectly by inference,"[1] and although he finds that ' some of our leading writers ' . . . " are still hampered by the definition of their science, as that of conscious processes,"[2] nevertheless he regrets " their reluctance to recognize frankly the importance of the part played in the mind by nerve processes that have no immediate conscious correlates " . . .[2] But surely the ' definition ' of psychology as the science of conscious processes is, so far as it goes, unimpeachable, and McDougall finds it hampering simply because for ' conscious ' he (and the others who are hampered) understand ' reflectively conscious.' That he so understands the word is clear from the last phrase quoted : for nerve processes, which actually have *no conscious correlates* (such are the metabolic), do not play an important part in the mind : but those are indeed important which have no *reflective* conscious correlates.

Judd, one of a very few, acknowledges the importance in and for consciousness of the states that elude reflection : thus he says, " The inclusiveness of a percept is ordinarily much larger than the descriptive analysis of percepts by introspection would admit."[3] But in most

[1] William McDougall : " A Contribution towards an Improvement in Psychological Method (I)," Mind, 1898, N.S. vol. vii., p. 15.
[2] *Ibid.*, p. 16.
[3] Charles H. Judd : Yale Psychological Studies, N.S. vol. i., 1907, p. 419.

of the discussions mind and consciousness are assumed
to be limited to that which is accessible to reflection,
which can be revived and commented on introspectively.
This erroneous point of view is almost universally
adopted in experimental psychology, where most experiments, even on the senses, are so arranged that the
subject of the experiment is required not only to receive
a sensation or perception, but then further to *say* that
he has had it and also to try to *describe* it in all detail ;—
to 'introspect' as it is called. The experimenter thus
learns, not the conditions of sensation and perception,
but these conditions as complicated by the faculty of
reflection—a much more complicated process. But
how, one asks, since one must learn what was perceived
by the subject, can one avoid this complication ?
And I should say that one can avoid it by exhausting,
firstly, the entire experimental field in which no processes
of reflection are involved. Certainly many facts are
thus accessible, and these are bound to be the least
ambiguous and least hazardous data on which to found
experimental psychology. We have such a case in the
field of reaction-time. But one physiological response
is demanded of the subject, he reacts. If he can further
reflect on his own reaction, he may afford suggestions
as to the shaping of further experiment : but it should be
remembered always that what he can *say* about his
consciousness during the reaction undoubtedly omits
something, and more unfortunately may add something,
to the experience that was actually his. Whenever a
subject is asked to say anything he is asked to reflect :
and the process is much complicated. In short, the
boasted advantage of human over animal psychology,
the fact that the subject can introspect, is rather a

positive drawback if it leads us to forget that the introspection about an item in consciousness is not the
original response that conditioned the entry to consciousness of that item.

But the field of reaction-times will not carry us very
far. The solution lies elsewhere. We ordinarily say
that our physical organism performs many nervous
responses of which we are ' not conscious ' ; in fact, it is
more or less classically assumed that a response involving
tracts not higher than the cerebellum is ' unconscious.'
Let us grant this proposition and note its consequences.
We find that these subconscious centres perform
' automatic ' activities that are of a ' highly intelligent
nature ' : such are walking, swimming, dressing, and so
forth. Further, that many of these activities, so highly
' intelligent ' are, when first performed or until fully
learned, also highly conscious. Hence we must suppose
either that these subconscious centres are sometimes,
say ' at first,' conscious centres ; or else, that very
complicated co-ordinations of response are ' at first '
performed by cerebral arcs and ' later on ' performed
by arcs of the lower levels which *ex hypothesi* were
not involved while the co-ordination was being (consciously) learned. This conception of a co-ordination
being established at one reflex level, and then transferred to a lower without needing there to be relearned, is certainly hard to grasp. It is as if one
person were to learn French and then to hand over
the gift bodily to someone else. On the assumption of subconscious nervous responses, however, we
must accept one of these alternatives :—either these
subconscious centres are ' at first ' conscious centres,
in which case we must define the moment when

' at first ' gives way to ' later on ' ; or else complicated correlations are established by frequent repetition in the cerebrum and then transferred to lower
levels.

A third alternative has been suggested :[1] it is that
automatic movements are unconscious, because in these
the nervous impulse meets with little or no resistance ;
and that consciousness depends on the ' difficulty,'
or the resistance, encountered by the impulse. Now
this resistance becomes often very high, apparently,
and then consciousness should increase accordingly in
vividness ; until when the resistance is so great that the
nervous impulse cannot traverse its arc at all (as seems
to happen in cases of inhibition), consciousness should
reach its highest degree of vividness : and since where
the nervous current is blocked there is no response, we
should then be most acutely conscious of that toward
which the body is most apathetic, by which it is least
moved ! But we are conscious, after all, of that to which
the nervous system does respond, not of that to which it
makes no response ; our bodies are least moved by
precisely that of which we take the least cognizance,
of which we are least aware ; and therefore this view is
precisely the reverse of that which the very most
fundamental fact of all requires. I shall revert to this
point later on.

In order to escape from this embarrassing dilemma, we
must reconsider the assumption of subconscious nervous
process. I call it an assumption because the notion
rests, so far as I can discover, on a naïve argument well

[1] William McDougall : " A Contribution towards an Improvement in Psychological Method," Mind, 1898, N.S. vol. vii., pp. 15,
159, and 364.

instanced in the following words of Ziehen.[1] Having cited the cases of automatic piano-playing, walking and so forth, he says :—" We have no reason for assuming [here] a parallel psychical process. Introspection, which is after all the only thing that can establish the existence of a psychic event, speaks for the opposed view." Such is the argument almost everywhere ; and at first sight it seems too obvious to challenge scrutiny. But on second thought, could any argument be feebler ? For what is introspection ? It is firstly memory and secondly judgement. For introspection to affirm a content of consciousness, that content must be recalled and then, further, judged upon. In other words, the content must be not merely recalled, but self-consciously recalled. Now no one will dare to say that every item which comes to consciousness can be recalled (frequently, indeed, it is not even recognized on its reappearance), and even less can all items that are recalled be made the basis of a coherent, introspective judgement. I need but remind the reader of that large section of consciousness that James has called the " fringe," as an instance of consciousness unmistakable yet almost entirely unamenable to introspective judgement, in large part even to recall. This fringe is a universally accepted but persistently neglected feature of consciousness. But more than this, many of the elements that have seemed to occupy the very focus of attention regularly fade away without possibility of recall. Anyone who has been subject in a tachistoscopic experiment will have a lively appreciation of this ; shapes and colours that are vividly seen during

[1] Theodor Ziehen : " Leitfaden der Physiologischen Psychologie," Jena, 1896, p. 10.

the momentary exposure, and are then even *judged* as being seen, vanish utterly and leave nothing behind save that *judgement* of their having been seen. They defy recall, and introspective comment, yet they *were* vividly present. Now concerning such items introspection declares, for instance, that " *Several other* shapes and colours were clearly there which I cannot recall " ; and yet no one will say that the immediate experience was one of " several other shapes and colours." Of course, at the moment certain particular shapes and colours were in consciousness ; but what these were introspection cannot specify. In a similar way one often knows in the morning that one has had in the night a dream, a vivid, detailed and dramatically animated dream perhaps. Yet will anyone say that the matutinal memory and introspection adequately reveal even to the dreamer himself the events that befell in his consciousness ? These facts prove that introspection is not competent to " establish the existence of a psychic event." In the cases of the fringe of consciousness, the tachistoscopic experiment, and countless other experiences, introspection reveals just enough to demonstrate its own inadequacy. We know that there are countless elements in consciousness which introspection cannot recount. It is thoroughly fallacious then, however prevalent the habit, to confuse the content of consciousness with such small part of that content as subsequent reflection is able to vouch for.

It is therefore a plain empirical fact that consciousness often attends on nervous responses where introspection is unable to bear it witness. There may be strictly unconscious nervous processes (aside from the metabolic, *et caetera*), but I believe that we have at the present time no facts to indicate them. We need not, then, assume such processes, nor accept either alternative of the dilemma to which that assumption led us : that is, we need believe neither that lower centres are ' at first ' conscious and ' later on ' not, nor yet that co-ordinated activities are learned by the cerebrum and are performed (after they have become habitual) by other and lower centres. If the statement that " the cerebrum is the seat of consciousness " means anything, it means that the cerebrum is the seat of *reflective* consciousness, or of introspection ; although even this is far from being assured. And certainly the failure of introspection is no ground for assuming that there are any actually unconscious nervous responses.

Experimental psychology, then, should relinquish its fetish of introspection, at least until a great deal has been learned about the simpler conscious processes which introspection wots not of. Reaction-time experiments, as I have said, do not by principle involve this fallacy. But the greater region lies here all unexplored, by psychologists : it is those lower responses of the nervous system which psychology has hitherto been pleased to call ' unconscious ' reflexes and automatisms, that a sound scientific instinct should select as being the simplest and hence the elementary processes of consciousness, out of which the more complicated processes are compounded,—even at last the self-reflective. Under the happy guidance of the introspective, soul-substance view psychologists have left this field entirely to the physiologists ; who have investigated it industriously and who are consequently the ones who have made the most important contributions that have been made to the question of the immediate correlation of mind and body. For a few instances, the reader will recall Weber, Hermann, Helmholtz, and, of to-day, Mach, Exner, Hering, von Kries, Nagel and Sherrington.

Now I have no desire to put into consciousness more than is there; and I know that a number of readers will accuse me of introducing a mass of elements that no one was 'ever conscious of.' What I do, however, is merely to insist that the process of reflection is distinct from the processes of perception and of sensation. And however much this distinction may be ignored in ' introspective,' it cannot be ignored in physiological psychology. It is not true that I am unconscious of everything save that which my subsequent reflection is able to bring up again and analyse. If this has bearings on experimental procedure, it has quite as important bearings on epistemological theory.

To revert once more to the experimentalist, if he cannot find an interest in studying those nervous responses that have erroneously been called unconscious, so that he must work with processes that are complicated by introspection, let him do one of two things. Either let him reduce introspection to its lowest terms, even then quite complicated enough, and so shape his experiments that the subject responds only with a ' yes ' or a ' no,' meaning that the sensation is present or absent, or with a ' Greater,' ' Less,' or ' Equal,' meaning that a sensation-difference is present and is positive or negative, or is absent. Or else let him use introspection as he will, only never forgetting that he is studying not consciousness but self-consciousness (including memory and judgement), and always taking this grave

complication into account. How he will ' take account '
of it I leave to his superior ingenuity.

This fallacy of confusing immediate with reflective
consciousness has borne its fruits elsewhere than in
experimental psychology. It is responsible, so far as I
can see, for that mysterious and luxurious jungle of the
Subconscious, of which the finest flower is the Unconscious Conscious :—or is it the Conscious Unconscious ? The literature of these precious specula-
tions takes up a goodly space on the bookshelves, yet
does not, I fancy, long detain any reader whose mental
powers are in danger of impairment from this or any
other line of thought. We find the subconscious
flourishing, however, in psychopathology ; where, for
instance, one may read that, " By the subconscious is
meant all mental or psycho-physiological processes of
which the individual is not directly conscious " ; [1] by
which, I suppose, are vaguely intended conscious processes which elude the individual's introspection and
reflection. The doctrine of the subconscious seems to
be generally held in psychiatry, and is thought in
particular to help towards an understanding of multiple
personality. The merit of such a view is that it affirms
a consciousness dependent on many, if not all, nervous
processes where the introspective psychology denies it. [2]
Its demerit is that it makes this consciousness an utterly
distinct thing from the self-reflecting consciousness of
the ' person himself.' In other words, the view implies

----

[1] Boris Sidis : " Studies in Psychopathology," Boston, 1907,
p. 3. (Reprinted from the Boston Medical and Surgical Journal,
1907, vol. 156.)

[2] Morton Prince's term " co-conscious," for the subsidiary
consciousness (whether one or many) in cases of multiple personality,
seems to me impeccable.

a doctrine of the unity of the normal personality that seems, to me at least, to be erroneous. The unity of consciousness is not to be demonstrated by first selecting out of the total mass that part which has a reflective unity, and then ignoring the larger mass that does not so cohere. Besides, we shall later see that this reflective unity is anyhow not the true unity of personality.

The confusion that I have here dwelt on, of holding that that alone is in consciousness which is available for introspection, has a somewhat odd position in psychology. For although introspection seems to be almost universally admitted as the one sure criterion of consciousness, yet conscious states that elude introspection were long ago pointed out and were given the general head of ‘ sentience,’ ‘ sensibility,’ or ‘ feeling ’—by various authors. Thus G. H. Lewes, for instance, particularly insisted on this portion of consciousness : “ Everyone could testify,” he said, “ to the fact that many processes normally go on without being accompanied by consciousness, in the special meaning of the term. Reflex actions,—such as winking, breathing, swallowing,—notoriously produced by stimulation of sensitive surfaces, take place without our ‘ feeling ’ them, or being ‘ conscious ’ of them. Hence it is concluded that the Reflex mechanism suffices without the intervention of Sensibility. I altogether dispute the conclusion.”[1] “ The grounds of this conclusion are, first, the unpsychological assumption that the unconscious state is out of the sphere of Sentience ; and

[1] George Henry Lewes : “ The Physical Basis of Mind,” London, 1877, p. 191 : cf. also p. 413. The volume contains a deal of sound psychology, and still deserves to be read more than I imagine that it now is being read.

secondly, the unphysiological assumption that the Brain is the only portion of the nervous system which has the property of Sensibility."[1]   " Pain, pleasure, hope and terror, are special modes of Sensibility, dependent on particular neural combinations. The organs comprised in the anterior half of the animal furnish the main conditions for these special modes, whereas the organs comprised in the posterior half furnish few or none of those—they contain none of the special Senses, and they are without the chief combining centre, the brain. But since we know that a large amount of normal Sensation is wholly without the special characters of pain, pleasure, hope, or terror, we need not hesitate to assign Sensation to the spinal cord because these characters are absent."[2] These and similar contentions[3] have been rather generally admitted ; and yet the term ' consciousness ' has been none the less generally restricted to self-consciousness. Thus even Lewes speaks of ' sensibility ' *and* ' consciousness in the restricted sense,' and Morgan[4] of ' sentiency ' and ' effective consciousness.'

The lack of a convenient term for effective consciousness, or in general for self-consciousness, co-ordinate with sentience, the two being subordinate divisions of consciousness, seems to have brought it about that sentiency, or sensibility or ' feeling,' after a brief preliminary acknowledgement, is usually ignored : and psychology is called the ' introspective science of con-

[1] *Ibid.*, p. 362.

[2] *Ibid.*, p. 491.

[3] Cf., for instance, so different an authority as E. Pflüger : " Die sensorischen Functionen des Rückenmarks," Berlin, 1853.

[4] C. Lloyd Morgan : " Animal Behaviour," London, 1900, pp. 42–3.

sciousness ';—a contradiction in terms. For if psychology is the science of consciousness (of all consciousness) it cannot be called introspective. And clearly a
definition of consciousness must, as the definition
offered in the foregoing chapter does, include ' mere
sentiency.'

If now introspection is not a criterion of the
psychic, since we are on this point, even less valid
are some criteria that are proposed in animal psychology.
The commonest are perhaps ' docility,'[1] ' associative
memory,'[2] and even ' intelligence.'[3] This last, unfortunately, demands another criterion for its own
determination ; and yields, besides, the immediate conclusion that the unintelligent man is unconscious. As
to ' associative memory ' its chief promoter has said that
"For the present, we can say that if an animal can learn
. . . it must possess associative memory."[4] So that
this criterion reduces to ' docility ' ; and concerning
this latter Yerkes has very pertinently remarked that
it "is a characteristic of protoplasm."[5]

Indeed it should be obvious that the *definition* of
consciousness is its only possible criterion. If consciousness is that cross-section of the realm of *being* to which
the organism specifically responds, then the criterion of
consciousness is the specific response ; and the animal

---

[1] A. Bethe : Pflüger's Archiv. für d. ges. Physiol., 1898, Bd. 70,
S. 15 ff.

[2] J. Loeb : *Ibid.*, 1895, Bd. 56, S. 247 ff.

[3] W. Preyer : Mittheilungen aus der zoolog. Station zu Neapel,
Bd. 7, S. 96.

[4] J. Loeb : "Comparative Physiology of the Brain and Comparative Psychology," New York, 1900, p. 218.

[5] Robert M. Yerkes : "Animal Psychology and Criteria of the
Psychic," Journ. of Phil., Psychol., and Scientific Methods, 1905,
vol. 2, p. 145.

or the plant, like the human being, is conscious of that
to which it specifically responds. But, it may be asked,
if a plant turns toward the sun, is it to be thought
conscious of the great luminary so far away ? Or, if a
dog runs away from a labour-union demonstration, is it
conscious of the aims of the proletariat ? Scarcely, I
should say. The plant turns toward the sun, but
similarly turns toward other sources of heat and light,
and indeed toward quite other stimuli. The plant does
not, therefore, respond specifically to the sun : and in
order to learn what that is to which it is specifically
responding, and of which it is conscious, one must
ascertain the one element or property that is common
to all the stimuli that elicit that particular response.
This can be discovered, as I said before, by means of the
canons of induction. It is that common element and no
others, to which the response is specifically made, and
of which the plant is conscious. So too the animal that
flies a riot flees also from other noises : and it will
respond to sounds in as many different ways as there
are sound differences in its possible range of experience.
If it should be said, on the contrary, that a man often
responds similarly to two things which he is conscious are
different, I would reply that the nervous system, like
the rest of matter, cannot in fact respond alike to
different stimuli. If it seems so to respond alike, it
is really to something that is common to the two stimuli
which seem different.

The true criterion of consciousness is not introspection, but specific responsiveness, and from this it follows
that no (neural) responses are unconscious, or subconscious, unless this is meant as sub-selfconscious.
Not every item within the conscious manifold, not even

a majority of the items, is attested as so being by an additional and superimposed process of introspection or reflection. Any term or proposition of the hierarchy of *being* may be included in the conscious cross-section, and so may be conscious, without being amenable to recall or to introspective judgement. And psychology is the science of the psychic cross-section, and not merely the science of introspection.

CHAPTER XI

SENSATION AND PERCEPTION IN THE CONSCIOUS CROSS-SECTION

OUR view of consciousness as a cross-section of the infinite realm of being and a cross-section that is defined by the responses of a nervous organism, must yield certain deductions. It must follow from the theory that the psychic cross-section has all the empirical properties of consciousness. In the last chapter we surveyed these briefly and shall now consider them in turn.

The first property seemed to be the functions of sensation and perception. And we saw that it was noted very early that these depend strictly on the physical organism, or, as we know now, on the nervous system. This empirical fact of dependence on the nervous system is amply recognized by our definition that such elements of the neutral realm of being as the nervous system responds to, and only such, are elements in consciousness. It may be said, indeed, that the definition goes further than the purely empirical facts warrant : and in the strictest sense I think that it does. We rest well assured that all of sensation and perception, and most if not all of imagination, memory, volition and judgement, depend on responses of the nervous system. But as regards volition and several other of the ' higher processes ' the actual proof is hardly complete, although the indications are strong. Nevertheless the evidence is almost overwhelming that consciousness does depend absolutely on nervous response : firstly, because almost every new investigation argues that way ; and secondly, because there are no authentic instances of a conscious process that surely did not depend on nervous response. Our theory, then, as is ever the case with theories, reaches further than the empirical facts and remains in so far to be verified. I know now of no facts that refute it.

But sensation and perception are something in themselves, aside from that which conditions them, and here is a distinction which from now on we must draw sharply. Just as the projectile that is launched by whatever means traverses a trajectory that is something in and for itself, so the manifold of consciousness, howsoever selected, is something in and for itself. The mariner's search-light is the nervous system, and the totality of objects that are illuminated is the cross-section, or consciousness. Thus ' empirical ' or descriptive psychology, or I may say the psychology of selves, is rightly distinguished from physiological psychology. This volume is primarily an essay in epistemology and empirical psychology : and if the final chapter is on physiology, that is in order to draw still more sharply the distinction. If then we consider sensation and perception in and for themselves, we find that they involve the entrance into consciousness of neutral entities, their remaining there for a time, and their departure : and also the mooted problem of their ' true correspondence ' to ' reality.'

In regard to the entry, manence, and exit of sensations

P

and perceptions there is no difficulty. The conscious cross-section is a manifold that moves in time and space as would the contents of a township if its boundaries were defined anew from moment to moment, or as the collection of all particles on which the sun casts shadows, or as the objects that the search-light illuminates. Changes certainly go on in the neutral realm of being, and there are countless collections which preserve their collective identity while their contents fluctuate. Such a collective entity is consciousness. In sensation the neutral qualities, the so-called ' secondary qualities,' come and go as more or less unrelated elements : while in perception they enter and depart in groups—smaller or larger. Doubtless few, if any, qualities (sensations) enter consciousness absolutely single : they too seem to come and go in larger or smaller masses. But I believe that the term sensation is usually applied to them so long as the mass of qualities that enter together has within itself little or no logical structure or unity, no internal relationship : while in perception the groups have some logical coherence. The line is not sharply drawn and need not be. Thus a blur of colours, a vague noise, or an undefinable change in one's mood, if too little organized or coherent to *mean* anything, is a case of sensation or of the sensing of a group of sensations (for I take it that ' meaning ' is always some form of logical unity, and of this more will be said later). While if qualities come in more coherent groups they constitute perceptions.

I have already pointed out that consciousness is extended in both space and time :—in space as spatial objects are extended, consciousness being actually such parts of the objects as are perceived, i.e. such parts as

are consciousness ; and in time as a quarter-hour, a
day, or a week, is extended. The measure of its extension is an empirical matter. Consciousness also, of
course, changes in time and moves about in space. A
convenient picture of this extendedness and movement
in space, and an admissible analogy, is an imaginary
contour moving over a country-side. Thus if one were
to superimpose a sheet with a hole in it on a map and
then move the sheet continually about, the sum of the
places disclosed by the hole would be, like consciousness,
a manifold having spatial extent and at the same time
moving in space. But the hole in the sheet must vary
in both size and shape as it moves. A picture of the
extendedness and movement of consciousness in time
is more difficult to find useless by an illustration from
consciousness itself ; so inverately do we infinitesi-
malize time. But if a mechanism is supposed, such
that at *any* instant it possesses energy enough to continue running for three minutes, clearly the *possibilities*
of the mechanism at any moment are a three-minute
series of successive movements. But by hypothesis
the energy is ever renewed, so that the temporal succession of possibilities constitutes a manifold both extended
in time and progressing in time. Again in any endo-
thermic reaction, the compound possesses enough heat,
at any one instant, to carry on the reaction for a finite
length of time, but the reaction itself liberates heat
and so the capacity for a definite continuance of reaction
is maintained. The length of time, at any instant, for
which the heat *then present* will sustain the reaction,
corresponds to the span, or temporal extent, of consciousness ; and the illustration is better in that this
finite length of possible continuance varies from moment

to moment, as does the span of consciousness. If
the heat that is being liberated is cut off at any moment
by some other means, the reaction capacity of that
moment works out its little span, and winds up the
whole process. The temporal succession of possibilities
from moment to moment is a manifold that is both
extended in time and progressive with time. The
entities contained in any one span, are *together* in
consciousness but not simultaneous.

I have spoken as if time and space were the only
dimensions of the conscious manifold, and this may
be the case so far as sensation and perception are concerned : but I think we shall later see that its dimensionality is of a considerably higher order.

Now sensations and perceptions seem not merely to
enter and depart from consciousness, but while there
they are said to *change :* a red colour is said to turn
yellow, a small object to grow large. But since red is
not yellow, it is scarcely true of the red that *it* becomes
yellow. We speak of *it* as changing, because the
qualities that successively supersede one another,
generally in a given position, are similar each to the
next. Now similarity is partial identity, and hence
the successive colours have something in common
as well as something of difference. Therefore the red
that seemed to be a simple quality is not simple but
compound. But, it will be objected, the red *is* only
what it seems to be in immediate consciousness. I must
reply that the red is precisely what it is ; it has its
being as have lozenges and butterflies : nor can ' immediate consciousness ' lightly assign predicates (such
as ' simple ') to red or the other secondary qualities
with more facility or with more authority than it can

sum up the truth about seed germination or fossil remains.

Red and the other qualities, as I have tried at the outset to show, are not made of immediate consciousness stuff, but primarily they simply *are :* and it is only subsequently, logically speaking, that consciousness is they. If red *is* complex although it seems simple, so also do coal-tar, water and air seem simple ; but are not. But, once more, the red in question is surely in consciousness and whatever else it may really be in the hierarchy of being, so much of it as *is* in consciousness, is just and only what it is in consciousness ; and that is simple red. Red it is, I quite agree, but the quality red and the judgement that it is simple are quite different things. " But the judgement that it is simple, is also immediately given." So it is, and is also given with air and water : and the judgement is untrue. In anticipation of the chapter on error, I ask the reader to bear in mind that not the quality red, but the *judgement about it,* is in error.

It may still be objected that the red as it is in consciousness is not complex ; and that which is not complex is simple : therefore the conscious red is simple. I admit that the red is given in consciousness and that introspection cannot say that it is complex ; that introspection does say that it is not-complex, and hence that it is simple. But introspection is often wrong.

This is a fatuous assertion, no doubt, but let us examine the good old doctrine that introspection cannot be wrong. Its most common form is that consciousness ' knows ' its own immediate content. This is not held to mean, of course, that it is its immediate content, but that consciousness can be ' aware of,' can *judge* about its own immediate content, can retain, analyse, and describe it. This involves such a wealth of untruth that one is embarrassed how to proceed. Can consciousness retain its content ? If one will close one's eyes for a moment, one shall see for how long consciousness can retain visual sensations ; and the data of the other senses evaporate as quickly. Consciousness can retain its sensory content about as long as the incandescent filament retains its glow. A memory-image, bereft of the intensity and the original qualities that are ordinarily confounded with the ' reality coefficient ' and immediacy, lingers for a little, in its turn immediate ; but the attention rapidly flags and fails. A present stimulus almost infallibly erases every trace. And then can consciousness analyse ? Can it analyse the fringe,—the peripheral field of vision, the mingling undercurrent of sounds, the odours that resemble one another, the diffuse organic sensations ? Can it analyse anything except, after long education, by acquiring a faculty for perceiving components, which faculty actually prevents sensing of the whole ? Retention aside, one has only to refer to one's first experience with the microscope, in order to know how helpless consciousness is to analyse its content save where familiarity has made the *separate parts* the actual object of perception *instead of* the whole. At first one focuses on the several depths of a microscopic preparation, up and down, and can make nothing out of it. Where analysis has to depend on retention or recall, the case is doubly hopeless. And lastly, can consciousness describe ? If it can analyse and if language favours, it can sometimes name. I do not of course deny that enough retention and analysis go on to make us somewhat rational : but I do insist that the statement

that " consciousness knows its own immediate content "
is a wild exaggeration.

The doctrine of the introspective infallibility of the
' immediate ' consciousness is even remotely plausible
only when one unwarrantably singles out a case, where
an unchanging object is presented fixedly to the senses,
where distractions are absent, the attention good, every
other conceivable condition auspicious, and where the
object presented is already so familiar that the components of the experience could be readily named before-
hand. ' Retention ' then seems good because the object
abides and the actually feeble faculty of retention is not
required ; analysis seems rapid because it is habitual ;
and the experience can be ' described ' because the
names are already in current usage. Of course it is only
the ' *immediate* ' consciousness that can thus be intro-
spected on : by which is tacitly meant the consciousness not of immediate, but of intense present stimuli
in the focus of attention. For what consciousness is
there, after all, which is not immediate ? Whatever one
experiences, one experiences immediately, and one
experiences no more than one's consciousness. And
since one cannot analyse or describe even a memory
image without reviving it in immediate consciousness,
the reputed infallibility of ' immediate ' introspection
becomes infallibility of introspection as a whole. Then
too, according to the representative theory of knowledge, every judgement is really introspective, so that no
erroneous opinion would be humanly possible. This
compares interestingly with the contempt of the ancient
Greeks for human opinion. And with no error in the
objective world, whatever the representative theory may
suppose that to be, and none in the subjective, we ought

to find ourselves heartily in sympathy with a religious institution called Christian Science.

The fact is that "consciousness *knows* its own immediate content" by no means. The original content of consciousness and later introspective judgements about that content are to be distinguished. We have already seen something of the incompetency of introspection as a criterion of consciousness, and the same incompetency appears again here. Psychology, even human psychology, is by no means a science of introspection.

Now as a colour red, to resume, changes to yellow, *it* does so because it is not simple. A series of qualities is experienced, each of which resembles and is partly identical with the qualities before and after it. As the series proceeds the amount of one component decreases and of the other increases. That some colour qualities, at least, are not simple can be ' immediately ' experienced by most persons. A yellowish green looks, for many persons, like both green and yellow ; purple looks both red and blue ; and similarly for many of the other colour qualities of the spectrum.

The same is true beyond a doubt for all of the senses. Introspection is not competent to pronounce on the simplicity of any of the sensory qualities. As one colour changes into another through grades of resemblance, so every quality whatsoever varies in intensity. It is admitted that quality and intensity are distinct ; but the conclusion is not drawn, and it should be, that a sensation having both properties is not simple. Münsterberg has pointed this out.[1] The so-called simple sensory

[1] H. Münsterberg : " Psychological Atomism," Psychological Review, 1900, VII, p. 8.

quality is after all not simple ; it is comparable with a molecule of which the component atoms remain to be discovered. It may be a difficult matter, but it is certainly the direction in which psychology must go. I insisted before that consciousness and self-consciousness are distinct ; that undoubtedly self-conscious processes, those that are amenable to introspection, are in a minority : and that experimental psychology should study simple reflexes of which the self takes no introspective cognizance, that is, the simpler responses that are merely conscious. It is probable that these sub-introspective states are simpler than the introspective, they should then shed more light on the nature of the psychic atom than do the introspective states. The way in which these states can be studied, notwithstanding that introspection remains silent about them, appears from our definition of consciousness. That entity is in consciousness to which the nervous system responds with a specific reaction. Here not merely the nature of the stimulus is in question, but the peculiarities of the reaction. What, namely, excites just that particular nervous arc, and no other ? Under the happy guidance of rationalism, and by the light of introspection, psychology has built its superstructure without foundation. It should commence afresh now to study the simplest psychic processes, the simplest nervous responses, and the psychic atom.

These atoms will, of course, be neutral entities, like all the components of consciousness and like all entities in the realm of being. It may be contended that since we know some simple logical entities, so that these are in consciousness, the psychic atom cannot be more complicated than the logical atom. Probably not, as we now know the logical elements, but we do not know that even these are really simple : and indeed some difficulties connected with their likeness and difference suggest that they are not simple. And it may well be that non-simplicity of the psychic atom will bar the way to our ever knowing the absolutely simple neutral elements. Nevertheless, it is not *intro*spection, but a different effort of judgement that has given us such logical elements as we do know, and the conscious atom is certainly simpler than the least element that introspection can discern.

Thus the observation that sensations change, one quality seeming to become another that resembles it, points to a variety of parts within the quality that to introspection seems simple ; these simpler parts not resembling one another but being combined in varying proportions, and the parts or psychic atoms themselves, so far as we know, not changing. And I have no doubt that for the present purposes of psychology, this atomic explanation is sufficient. Nevertheless there certainly is such a thing as logical change. There is change or activity in the neutral realm, and this must also be involved in any object, such as consciousness, that is made up out of the neutral entities. But unfortunately we know almost nothing about logical change, and I see no means at the present time for surmising what function this change may have in consciousness. If logicians can ever be persuaded that universes of discourse are not necessarily static, we may some day know something about this.

We have now seen how our definition of consciousness accounts for sensation and perception, in so far as these processes involve the entrance and exit of neutral entities, and their changes while passing through consciousness. The remaining matter to be considered is that of ' true correspondence between sensations and perceptions and their objects.' Now in an earlier chapter I attempted to defend, against Joachim and others, the notion of correspondence between manifolds, as a fact of logic. But this was not with a view to introducing correspondence here. And it must be obvious that under the definition of consciousness here offered, sensation and perception do not involve correspondence at all, true or untrue. If, as Aristotle said, ' thought and its object are one,' so are sensations and perceptions one with their ' objects.' In fact, there are not sensations or perceptions *and* their objects. There are objects, and when these are included in the manifold called consciousness they are called sensations and perceptions. Correspondence in this connection is involved only for a dualism such as the representative theory of knowledge, which in its fantastic efforts to account for truth and untruth has hatched out the doctrinal monstrosity of Inside and Outside, with true and untrue correspondences between them. Truth and error are a different issue which I shall deal with in a later chapter. Sensations and perceptions are objects in the hierarchy of *being*, and they are in the psychic cross-section when the nervous system specifically responds to them.

But, it will be objected, some sensations and perceptions do not correspond to any objects that are ' out there,' and how can the nervous system which is out there in time and space respond to anything that is not out there ? By ' out there,' however, the objector means the special universe of masses in time and space ; and declines, through unwillingness or inability, to join

me in considering the neutral realm of being. If by
' out there ' he consents to mean this general realm of
all that is, I freely assert that the most erroneous possible
sensations and perceptions *are* out there. And if then
he arrives at the actual issue by asking, How can the
nervous system, which is admittedly a mass in time and
space, respond to anything that is not a mass in time
and space ? I reply that it does so precisely as it responds to warmth and cold, sound and silence, light and
the absence of light, motion and the cessation of motion,
harmony and confusion, or to a geometrical square or
circle, to a position in space, to the multiplication table,
to the price of a commodity, to the prospective value of
unseen mineral deposits, to a weather prognostication,
to a business proposition, to beauty and ugliness, to
loyalty and treachery, to sense and nonsense. None of
these are masses in time or space, and but two of them
are energies, yet the nervous system responds specifically
to them all. And whether they happen to be true or
false is a totally different issue.

The logician, at least, knows that all of these are
' objective ' entities. Yet if anyone chooses to insist
that some of them are ' ideas,' the evidence is otherwise
abundant that all masses in time and space whatsoever
never respond merely to other masses : they are
affected by accelerations, directions and innumerable
other ' attendant circumstances ' which are not masses
and are not ideas. It is pleasant to testify that masses
moving in time and space are masses in time and space ;
but the so-called physical world which is conceived as a
sharply demarcated universe of masses moving in time
and space is not so cut off from the general realm of
being. The student of physics is sometimes disappointed

that on entering the laboratory he studies almost anything except matter : he learns of force, energy and
work, magnitude, motion, acceleration, inertia and
momentum, and above all law ; he is busy with algebra,
geometry, calculus, and the theory of functions ; while
the matter that constitutes the physical world " has
evaporated in a set of equations." And in order to
behold Matter treated with respect he must repair
to the athletic field or, even better, to the halls of
philosophy. The fact is that the masses moving in
time and space are a less important part of the ' physical
world ' than the mathematics of their motions. Masses
are subject to equations and laws rather than to other
masses. The particle of matter responds to the *direction*
and *velocity* of the mass that strikes it, and indeed to the
differentials of the velocity ; though direction, velocity
and differentials are no masses. And throughout the
world of physics and chemistry mathematical entities
are the determining factors. Yet philosophers assure
us that these strictly determining factors are not in the
physical world at all, but are merely in our skulls, and
so forth. Happily logicians and some natural scientists
know better. But our point here is, that since inorganic
masses are determined in their movements by directions,
velocities and accelerations, in short, by equations and
laws, since inorganic masses respond to such neutral
mathematical entities which are not themselves masses
in time and space, it is not only not astonishing but is
to be expected, that the animal nervous system will
respond likewise specifically to similar neutral entities,
and even to such as are far more complicated.

Thus the question of ' true correspondence ' resolves
itself into two questions, that of truth, and that of

correspondence. The latter presents no question for the theory of consciousness here presented, because according to it sensations and perceptions *are* the objects. And if the object is more than the sensation or perception, it is because the nervous system is responding to some components only of the object : but such components are at one and the same time, and without any sort of reduplication, a part of the object and a part of the consciousness. Object and consciousness intersect each other, and their cross-section is the sensation or perception. The question of truth or error is a thing apart, which we shall consider for itself. But we must next proceed to some further empirical properties of consciousness.

CHAPTER XII

MEMORY, IMAGINATION, AND THOUGHT

FOR a theory that declares that knowledge and the object of knowledge are identical, I believe that the knowledge of events that are past, and for that matter of those that are future, is accounted a serious obstacle. We have to meet this question in coming now to memory : and indeed the way in which past events can be in present knowledge is the only feature of memory which, on the epistemological side, need concern us. For in other respects the activity of the mind in memory is not different from other activities of neutral entities (now to be called sensations, perceptions, and ideas) within the psychic cross-section. The issues, for instance, of truthfulness and of unity are the same in memory as in perception.

An epistemological account of memory must be based in part on some theory of time, with which the former will stand or fall. But what is the correct theory of time ? According to Russell[1] there are two theories of time, the absolute and the relative. In the former, " we have two classes of entities, (1) those which *are* positions, (2) those which *have* positions."[2] Events are

---

[1] Bertrand Russell : " Is Position in Time and Space Absolute or Relative ? " Mind, 1901, N.S. vol. 10, p. 293.

[2] *Ibid.*, p. 294.

temporal by virtue of having, or being correlated with, successive moments or time positions. In the relational theory no *single* entity *is* a position : but time is purely the ordered series of events. The former is Russell's theory, but the latter is probably the one more commonly held. The former or absolute theory seems to make two important assertions : the first, that there are a specifically time element (the ' absolute moment ') and a specifically time relation (before—after) ; the second, that each of these absolute moments *is* by itself a position. In both these respects this theory differs from the relative theory.

Now with the former assertion we need be very little concerned ; there may or may not be specific time entities. But the latter assertion, that each ' absolute moment ' is in and for itself a position (for this appears to be what Russell means), seems to me quite erroneous. For how can any single entity be a position ? Undoubtedly a series of entities, such as Russell's moments, can be a series of positions ; but each entity is not by itself a position ; it acquires its position only by its relations to the other members of the series. This is what, and all that, we mean by the common phrase that x " has a position " in the series ; we surely do not mean that there is any single entity that *is* a position, either in space or time. Neither any single ' moment,' nor any separate group of ' moments,' taken as a whole, could either be or have a position. But if the ' moments ' have position by virtue of their relations to the other ' moments ' in series, cannot events similarly have position by virtue of their ordinal relations to one another ; indeed, must they not inevitably do so ? If this is the case, events are temporal events by virtue of their order, and the time skeleton of ' absolute moments ' with which events must be correlated is superfluous and perhaps fictitious. I am not denying here that time order is a certain variety of logical order ; but I would emphasize only that *position* within this order depends on the relations of any element to the other elements :—and in the end, to *all* of the other elements. For surely any group of elements, however large, loses its position if taken out of its series. Nor has any series as a whole, even if it be an infinite series, position unless it be as a whole included in some other series or system. In short, it seems to me that the very essence of position is relativity.

But, says Russell, the relational theory is met " by the following difficulty. Whatever can, in ordinary language, recur or persist, is not an event ; but it is difficult to find anything logically incapable of recurrence or persistence, except by including temporal position in the definition. When we think of the things that occur in time—pleasure, toothache, sunshine, etc.—we find that all of them persist and recur. . . . Perhaps it may be said that the whole state of the universe has the required uniqueness : we may be told that it is logically impossible for the universe to be twice in the same state. But let us examine this opinion. In the first place it receives no countenance from science, which, though it admits such recurrence to be improbable, regards it as by no means impossible." (I had fancied that the second law of thermodynamics asserts just this impossibility.) " In the second place, the present state of the universe is a complex, of which it is admitted that every part may recur. But if every part may recur, it seems to follow that the whole may recur." (It seems

Q

improbable that it should, but if it did why should that confuse the relative theory of time ?) "In the third place, this theory when developed so as to meet the second objection, becomes really indistinguishable from that of absolute position. There is no longer an un-analysable relation of simultaneity : there are series of states of the universe, each of which, as a whole and only as a whole, has to each other a simple relation of before and after ; an event is any part of a state of the universe, and is simultaneous with any other part of the same state, simultaneity meaning merely the being parts of some one state ; before and after do not hold between events directly, but only by correlation. Thus the theory in question, except for the fact that *at* is no longer simple, is merely the absolute theory with states of the whole universe identified with moments."[1] Quite so as to the ' merely,' the relative theory is merely the absolute theory with ' absolute moments,' which at least look to be fictitious, replaced by ' states of the whole universe,' which are actual. But it is not true that "before and after do not hold between events directly, but only by correlation." They hold both by correlation *and* directly. Any sequence of events, if ordered in a certain way, contains the relations of before and after : but every such sequence in concrete exist-ence, is correlated with every other. Every such sequence is temporal and so is the correlated whole. If before and after did not hold between events directly, in their ordinal series, it would not hold between them in their correlation. And if the various series were not correlated there would be no meaning to simultaneity or ' the being parts of some *one* state.'

[1] B. Russell : *Ibid.*, pp. 295–6.

The events in their ordered series may be as alike as one will; or the series may be merely of qualities, and these as alike as one will; or indeed the ' whole state of the universe ' may recur, and as often as one will :— yet in the entire correlation of series every event or quality is unique and particular by virtue of its relations to all of the others. Any entity can recur, and the ' required uniqueness,' as Russell seems not to see, resides not in the entity (term or event) itself, but only therein together with all its relations to the rest of the series as well. It was in view of this issue that I stated in Chapter III (see also p. 24) a theory of the particular and the universal. And this is precisely and solely the issue on which I venture to disagree with Russell. He seems to hold that uniqueness (of position) can reside in a single entity, and since all qualities and events are often repeated the required uniqueness of every moment of time must be the postulated uniqueness of an ' absolute ' time moment. But, as I have tried to show, the quality or event is universal when it is alone; and it is particular or unique when it is in series, either with other qualities or events, or with other repetitions of itself.

Russell further says, in summing up his argument against positions as relative :—" When a collection of items are capable of serial arrangement, but some among them occur in several positions in the series, then the terms in question form a series which is not independent, but is obtained by some many-many or one-many relation which each of them has to one or more terms of some independent series."[1] Since Russell states that in the sentence just quoted his argument is divested

[1] *Ibid.*, p. 297.

of all temporal reference, one must suppose that any even logical serial arrangement in which a term occurs in several positions, is a dependent series. How is it, then, with the Class K of elements a, b, c, — — — ; that is, with a typically simple ordinal series? These elements are assumed to be alike or similar, as, for instance, a series of points. Is the series then dependent? It is so according to the sentence above quoted from Russell; and one would admit that it is dependent on a formula of repetition: but this is not the sort of dependence that Russell means. I presume, although I do not feel sure, that Russell means that the series of similar terms, a, b, c, — —, is dependent on an independent series of terms that 'are positions.' But such a series cannot any more be independent, since if each term is a position, the next term is like the one preceding, it too is only a position. If each of these positions is not exactly like the others, it is only by virtue of its different relations to all the other positions in series; but this is a property of each element in any and every ordered series, and is enjoyed in common with the elements of Class K, or the points of a point series. I cannot see, then, how Russell's series of absolute moments (or points) that 'are positions,' is a particle better than the series of events, or even of qualities, on which the relational theory is based. Assuredly each absolute moment is like the others except in its position; but it does not acquire position by being *called* a position, but purely by its relations to the other absolute moments: precisely as do events, qualities or simple logical elements in any ordered series.

Again, although Russell seems to deny that events or qualities are repeated, except " by some many-many

or one-many relation which each of them has to one or
more terms of some independent series," he finds no
difficulty in the notion of a *relation* being repeated in
just such a way. For in his " Principles of Mathematics "
(vol. i., p. 51) he writes, " I conclude, then, that [p. 52]
the relation affirmed between A and B in the proposition
' A differs from B ' is the general relation of difference,
and is precisely and numerically the same as the relation
affirmed between C and D in ' C differs from D.' And
this doctrine must be held, for the same reasons, to be
true of all other relations : relations do not have instances, but are strictly the same in all propositions in
which they occur."[1] I cannot conceive what Russell
means by ' instances,' since in his very illustration two
cases are given which would ordinarily be called instances of the ' general ' relation of difference. At any
rate such cases are precisely what I have meant by
' instances ' in speaking of the universal and the particular. Now if ' precisely and numerically the same '
relation can thus recur (in what I call different instances),
I can see no reason why ' strictly the same ' qualities
and terms cannot recur in independent series : for with
relations, as with these, the same logical problem is
involved—that of identity and difference. Whatever
difficulties are here involved with regard to the repetition of qualities and terms are surely involved with the
repetition of relations.

It seems to me, then, that the absolute theory of
time is to be rejected : neither qualities nor events get
position by being attached to " a term that is a position "—pure nominalism, so far as I can see. Qualities

[1] Cf. H. H. Joachim : " The Nature of Truth," Oxford, 1906,
p. 47.

and events have position in time precisely as the
' absolute moments ' might have, through their relations
to the other qualities or events or ' moments ' in their
series. Both qualities and events are in ordered series,
and these series are correlated ; and it is owing to these
two facts that we are able to speak of ' before ' and
' after ' and of the ' present ' state of the universe. The
repetition of an event or quality does not prejudice the
particularity of each of the repetitions. Now quite the
same argument holds against Russell's ' absolute points '
of space.

Indeed the problem presented by the present knowledge of events that are past is very closely analogous
to another, that of the knowledge of places that are
spatially remote from the knower. Such knowledge is
usually of the distant place as this latter was at some
past time ; so that two issues are involved at once.
The knowledge of remote time and the knowledge of
remote space are two problems, yet closely analogous.
Since the latter is frequently involved with memory, it
may be discussed at this point ; and this the more because the problem of remote space seems ordinarily to
present fewer difficulties, and its solution will facilitate
the understanding of the present knowledge of past time.
Geometry, as well as a peculiarity of our senses, has
made us more familiar with space than with time. To
what extent, then, do we indeed know places that are
far distant ? Above all, how far is their position a part
of our knowledge ? If one considers one's knowledge of
a particular locality that is spatially so remote as to be
out of sight, one finds that it consists of some broad
characters of that locality—a few general features—
embroidered with more or less detail. Thus one's know-

ledge of a Continental town that one has visited as a
tourist will ordinarily consist of fragmentary glimpses of
a cathedral, a square, or market-place, some picturesque
street corner, a few of the more salient impressions of
the picture gallery, and perhaps some details of the
hostelry where one stopped ; and the spatial relations
of these items to one another will be more or less definite ;
—yet in very different degrees, I suspect, in different
persons.

But now how far does this knowledge-mass of the
distant town itself have position ; either here where
the knower is, or there where the actual town is ? It is
held to be incontestable, on the one hand, that such a
knowledge-mass is here where the knower is ; and is
indeed within his skull. But on the other hand a
realistic theory of knowledge, such as is our present one,
is held as bound to assert that this knowledge-mass is
yonder, in the known locality ; for position is a part
of the knowledge, so that if all knowledge is immediate
and not representative, any knowledge that includes
position must itself be just where the object that is
known is. This is the supposed *reductio ad absurdum*
of the realist : he must accept two incompatible assertions. But for my part I cannot see how the realist
has ever allowed himself for a moment to accept *either*
member of the absurd pair. He is betrayed into such
acceptance, I believe, only by a misapprehension as to
what position logically is.

Now I have tried to make it clear that no term, and
no system of terms as a whole, has within itself position.
Position consists in the relations of the term or system
to other terms *outside* it : and ultimately to *all* of the
outside terms that are related to it. And if the term or

system has no relations to terms that are external to
itself, it has no position. Now the knowledge-mass which
we have been considering, identical with a part of
some remote locality, has *within itself* and as that
separate little mass of knowledge, *no* position : it is
neither here in the nervous system of the knower, nor
yet there at the place in space of the locality known.
And we shall see that this is empirically true if we consider more carefully the knowledge-mass itself. The
assertion is ungrounded that one's knowledge of a
Continental town has in itself spatial position : in
itself it is nothing but the fragmentary features of
church, street and hostelry that it is, internally extended spatially, without doubt, but so far possessing
no position; as positionless, in fact, as one's knowledge-
mass of Utopia or Alice's Land Behind the Looking-
Glass. And the same is true of the actual town :
within itself it is spatially extended, but it includes no
position. It is, however, outside of itself, related to the
entire remainder of space, and for this reason it has
spatial position. But the knowledge-mass does not
enjoy all these relations, for space is continuous and
knowledge is not. How far, then, has the knowledge-
mass, identical with part of the town, position that is
spatial or other, by virtue of relations to elements that
are external but related to itself ?

As an empirical fact all spatial relation that it has,
seems to consist in its relations to whatever one can
recall of neighbouring localities that one has visited, to
points on a map that one recalls or looks at, and it consists further in sundry items of knowledge such as the
rail and boat lines that one would need to take in order
to arrive there. Not all of such latter items, I should say,

would help to confer strictly spatial position ; a position in knowledge, rather, of another sort. But the main points are that the position which our knowledge-mass of a distant locality has, is not internal to itself but, like the position of the locality itself, resides in relations to entities outside. The position of the town consists in its relations to the rest of space : the position of the knowledge-mass that is logically identical with a part of the town, in its relations to the rest of one's knowledge. For it is clear that whenever in two systems elements occur that are common to both, the position of such a common (identical) element in *either* system consists in the relations of such element to the other elements of *that* system, and not to those of the other system. It is in precisely the same way that the position of the point of intersection of two lines depends, in *either* line, on the relations of the point of intersection to the other points of *that* line.

As to the question whether one's knowledge-mass of a distant town is " here where the knower is," or there where the actual town is, such knowledge is clearly in neither position. Emphatically it is not " here where the knower is," by which is always ultimately meant where the knower's cerebral lobes are. No knowledge whatsoever is secreted in cerebral lobes. And the knowledge-mass is also not there where the actual town is, for the expression ' knowledge-mass ' means that portion of the actual town that is also in the conscious cross-section of some knower, and means it as a member of such conscious manifold. Its position, then, is its position in that manifold, and this is just whatsoever its relations to the rest of *that* manifold, the conscious cross-section, make it. Thus the little group of neutral

entities which is the intersection of the ' actual town '
and of ' actual space ' with the recalling consciousness,
and which, while remaining identically itself, is a member
of both systems, has two positions,—one in the spatial
manifold and one in the conscious or knowledge manifold. Such I conceive to be the realist's answer to the
supposedly damaging question whether the piece of
knowledge is ' here where the knower is ' [*sic*] or out
there where the known object is.

Nor is it anything strange or novel, for an entity to
have two positions, and indeed many more. The web
of *being* presents an infinite tissue of intersecting
systems, wherein every point of intersection has as many
positions as there are systems which there intersect ;—
a position in each system. Copious illustration of this
is found in arithmetic and geometry. A quadratic
equation and the whole numbers are two systems, yet
when the number 7 is one root of such an equation the
peaceable mathematician is not challenged to state *the*
position of the number 7, whether here in the number
system or out there in the equation. In fact, the rôle
which the several members of the whole-number
system play in arithmetic is an excellent and familiar
example of identical entities enjoying an infinity of
positions. Of course Hegelians deny this and assert
that the 7 which is a root is not the 7 of the number
system, for with Hegelians everything is anything save
that which it is. Yet the unlettered realist continues to
rely on 7 remaining 7 in whatever position it is found,
and in this he has the at least decent authorization of
the mathematician. The several moments or emphases
of the vital whole or Absolute appear identically and
vitally to cohere in many lesser systems. Again, in

geometry, a point situated at the intersection of howsoever many figures, has a position in each figure :
and although a position which is to all intents and
purposes absolute can be defined for this point by
means of co-ordinates, this can be done only when
all of the intersecting figures are defined from the
same co-ordinates, and when these latter therefore
constitute a single spatial system that embraces all
of the intersecting figures. Or once again, if one and
the same entity can have but one position, does it
mean anything to say that Napoleon was great as a
soldier, mediocre as a patron of art, and small as a
stature ? It does mean something : the man attained
different positions of excellence in different systematic
spheres.

It may be asserted that every entity has but one
position, for there is always some one, more comprehensive system that embraces all the lesser ones in which
the positions seem to be different, and that defines these
positions as one. Such is the case, as I have already
indicated, in geometry : the point that has different
positions in different intersecting figures, has after all
but one position in that system of co-ordinates that includes all the intersecting figures. And indeed it may
be that there is always such a more inclusive system in
which such diversities are combined. Yet, in the first
place, we are far from knowing this in most cases of intersecting systems ; and in the second place, such combination (or reconciliation, if one will) makes it no less
true that in the lesser systems severally, and from the
point of view of each, the points of intersection still
occupy different positions. And most notably of all,
it seems to me, in the case of the intersections of the

time and space system with any individual's knowledge
system we have practically no clue toward understanding that more comprehensive system, which should include both, and so define, possibly, one position and only
one for every entity. And if we were able to apprehend
such greater system, the act of cognition would still
have to be discussed in the terms of two intersecting
systems—that of the known and that of the knower :
and the entity cognized would necessarily, from this
point of view of cognition, still have its two positions
in two systems. This view of cognition as the intersection of two systems, that of the known with that
of the knower, while the intersecting region has a
position in *each* system, in no wise reintroduces us
to a representative theory of knowledge, nor prejudices a literal interpretation of Aristotle's dictum—
" Thought and its object are one." The entities at
any intersections are of course simply identical with
themselves.

Returning now to the knowledge of distant spatial
objects, we must consider more closely the position of
their cross-sections, i.e. of whatever of them is known,
in the knowledge system. The section of the distant
object that is the knowledge-mass has relations to other
portions of the same knowledge system or consciousness,
and by virtue of these relations has a position in that
system—a position which it would be simply meaningless to assert as identical with its position in space. Yet
some of the relations of this cross-section to other
regions in which the two systems (of space and of
knowledge) *again* intersect can be, and in fact variously
are, identical in the two systems. And of course it is
only by virtue of such identical relations that our

knowledge of space is practically workable. The more frequently the knowledge system intersects with space, that is the more the person explores and studies space, the more of these identical relations or partial identities of position there will be. And this process is clearly one in which the knowledge system more and more approximates to identity with the spatial system : an infinite knowledge of space would thus be space itself. The knowledge system which is said to ' represent ' space does so only just in so far as it is identical therewith. Such partial identity is illustrated by the accurate map, which owing to its small size can be got to consciousness at a glance ; as the field that it pictures cannot be, owing to our physiological limitations. But the true map is a scheme of spatial relations that is identical with relations that exist, along with much else, in the greater region that is mapped. Thus the consciousness that embraces a map of a country once visited readily sets in fairly accurate spatial relations the various experiences of the visit that may still survive in memory. And empirically it is of course true that we have little idea of the spatial relations of distant places other than those that are contained in maps. The relations on the map are identical with those on the continent mapped : and the knowledge system that includes a map is in important respects identical with the actual space that is mapped.

If the reader here feels that I have decried the representative theory of knowledge and now after all resort to it, I would remind him that I objected to that theory because it has come to the absurd *impasse* of declaring that the idea which represents is not even like the thing which is represented. The idea of space, it says, is not spatial, the idea of shape is shapeless, of loudness is not loud, of colour is not coloured, and so forth.   From this it will not recede, and from this it cannot go on to any statement that is either useful or true.   It has quite forgotten the only meaning that ' representation ' has, which is partial identity.   If the idea of red actually represents red, it must be a red idea : and if the idea of space represents space it must be spatial, that is, it must be a system of relations that are identical with such relations of space as it aims to represent.   Such is the case with a true map ; where indeed the true magnitude is not represented.   But space is much besides magnitude.   As I before said, the representative theory of knowledge is totally invalid and nonsensical because it has no conception of what representation truly is.   On the other hand I have tried to defend, specially in opposition to Joachim, the ' correspondence of systems,'—a conception that appears to involve the repetition of identicals.   And this, as I before argued in connection with the particular and the universal, presents difficulties.   But they are difficulties for logic and not for epistemology.   We do experience repetitions and correspondences, and they play an important part in cognition.   What they may turn out to be fundamentally it is not for the epistemologist to inquire, but for the logician whose sphere of study is a far more fundamental one.   By virtue of the fact that the knowledge system, defined by the responses of a nervous system, trans-sects the system known, at various and sundry places, it results that the two systems are partially identical : yet they are still two because they are not wholly identical.   These two systems therefore partially correspond, and each repre-

sents, if one will, the other; but only in so far as
the two *are* identical. I am unable to see that anything in these statements resembles or is even compatible with the so-called representative theory of
knowledge.

Now it is only because the human nervous system
defines the cross-section, that the knowledge of remote
places is so fragmentary. The nervous system cannot
respond at one time to the details of a continent. But
the case of the space more immediately surrounding the
body, is somewhat different. Here that invaluable
' distance-receptor,' the eye, facilitates a response to
any and all points of a fairly large continuous extent of
space. In this near-lying region the knowledge-mass so
nearly approximates an identity with space itself that
the two systems, the knowing and the known, are
virtually one. We apprehend the limited region before
our eyes almost as adequately as an infinite consciousness would apprehend all space. Our knowledge of this
limited range of space is to all intents and purposes so
much of space itself, and the notion that the knowledge
is only a representation of space becomes by so much
the more fanciful; and becomes indeed as the representative theory interprets the situation, quite ridiculous. Yet even here the identity is not complete, the
incompleteness lying largely in certain facts of perspec-
tive. So that the relations between space and the conscious cross-section are similar to the relations studied
by so-called projective geometry. It will be noted,
however, that our present theory has no room for the
whole rigmarole about the ' *projection* of subjective
sensations into outer or real space.' And from our
present point of view the dreary discussions of both

genetic and nativistic theories of space-perception alike become misconceived and futile.

Now precisely as the knowledge-mass of a distant region has *by itself* some spatial extent but no position, but derives the latter from its relations to other knowledge-masses, so the cross-section of near-lying space is by itself extended but is not placed. We call it ' here ' to be sure, and ' refer ' (as we say) our knowledge of other places to this, yet clearly this ' here ' has no position except by a counter reference to other places. The practical ' here ' is not a position but a focus at which our knowledge of space is most minute and adequate ; so that many persons who travel about but little find no ' here ' save when they are ' here at home.' And at best the ' here ' is no more in itself a position than any one of the many ' theres,' but all alike have position by virtue of their relations to one another.

Thus one mind's total knowledge of space, both as perceived now and as remembered, is a system that is in part identical with ' real ' space, but is discontinuous, fragmentary, and for no considerable extent quite identical. It compares with ' real ' space somewhat as the system of prime numbers with the system of whole numbers. The former would inadequately represent the whole numbers although partly identical with them ; and as in knowledge, the former represent the latter at all, only in so far as they *are* identical with these latter. Yet the fragmentariness of the former system as compared with the latter, does not prevent many identities of relation between the corresponding systems. The number 13 is less than 23 and more than 7 in the primes as in the whole numbers : just as

London is south of Edinburgh and north of Paris both in one's knowledge and in space.

But now although one's cross-section of space as compared with space as a whole is fragmentary, one's knowledge contains a vast number of items that are not spatial: logic, algebra, physics, chemistry, zoology, economics, politics and art either involve space not at all, or involve along with space large additional systems. So that one's knowledge as a whole is a system of more dimensions than the three of space, and one which as compared with space cannot, perhaps, be called wholly diminutive. The system of space as compared with one's whole system of knowledge, one's whole mind, is perhaps in its turn fragmentary. The two systems, merely, occasionally intersect. I have tried to show before, in connection with the ' primary and secondary qualities,' that space and time are the merest fragment of the great realm of being. They are merely two ordered systems (one of three and the other of one, dimension or order) in a realm that contains unthinkably more ordered series, and thus vastly many more dimensions. As Münsterberg has said,[1] " The dimensions of reality are infinite and their multitude is the less to be grasped in that our will-attitude is generally not directed toward some least isolated entity, as say a point, but toward a rich manifold of things with ever new forms, magnitudes, lines, angles, and curves ; the dimensions of mathematics nowhere attain to prominence in this living reality." And knowledge or mind, partakes of this greater dimensionality. If now there occur here and there in the knowledge system entities of the spatial

---

[1] Hugo Münsterberg : "Grundzüge der Psychologie," Leipzig, 1900, S. 237.

R

system, where the two systems intersect, it follows that in knowledge these spatial entities will have many relations that they do not have in space. Just as in the intersection of botany and commercial forestry the pitch-bearing properties of certain trees have relations to commercial value in the latter sphere that the same properties have not at all in botany ; so the fact that Bermuda is in the sub-tropics has relations in the knowledge system of the inquiring invalid that it has not at all in the science of geography. And important among these non-spatial relations of the spatial objects included in one's knowledge are relations to one's volition ; relations obviously which in the spatial system they have not at all. In some consciousnesses Monaco is a place on the Riviera, spatially, but its practically more significant position is among the places which one has resolved never to visit again. And so one's total knowledge of space, however well or ill mapped out spatially in consciousness, is charted again by relations to one's various life purposes. In some discussions this fact is indeed adequately mentioned, if not over-emphasized, but in others (specially in some discussions of the cognition of space) it seems to me to have been forgotten. I mention the point merely as a reminder that the ' absolute position ' of spatial objects, besides being unattainable in knowledge, would be, if attained, by no means so practically important a species of position as is sometimes intimated.

From this consideration of the cognition of near-lying and distant spatial objects we may return to our subject of memory, with the discussion well advanced. For the relation of the knowledge system to time is precisely what it is to space ; although this view seems opposed by common opinion. As Münsterberg says,[1] " This seems to be a prejudice of philosophy, even of the critical : the temporal phenomena of the psychic life have no right to a treatment different from that of the spatial : the problems develop in a way that is thoroughly parallel." The difference commonly alleged is that ideas are not in space but are in time, are successive in ' real ' time. I quite agree to this last, and object only to the assertion of a different state of things with regard to space—that ideas are not in ' real ' space. The admission that ideas are in time, however, is made under a curious proviso : the time of an idea is not the idea of a stretch of time, nor is the idea of succession a succession of ideas. No indeed, the representative theory would never countenance anything so obviously true. Rather, ideas succeed one another in ' real time,' as do physical events, but the time ' represented ' [*sic*] by these really succeeding ideas, if I grasp the profound thought, is not ' real ' but ' subjective ' time. The philosopher is of course cognizant of ' real ' time, but the knower whose cognition he attempts to explain is limited to ' subjective ' time. This is not full enough :—the philosopher should not stop with this other person's inferior grade of cognition, but, essaying the graciously autobiographic, should tell us how he himself comes to know about ' real ' time.

Now in the case of memory, the cognition of past time, we have no more to deal with ' absolute positions ' than in the case of space : and all that I said about absolute positions holds, I believe, equally of such ' positions ' whether in space or in time. The cognition of the past, moreover, is not different, in its fundamental principles,

---

[1] H. Münsterberg : *op. cit.*, S. 247.

from the cognition of the future, nor, indeed, of the present. Here as before there is the temporal system that is cognized, in this case an asymmetrical transitive series of one dimension. And this the cognitive system intersects. The recollection of a past event, the knowledge-mass as we before called it, has some temporal extension, but in and of itself, again, no position : thus if one recalls the way in which a certain person on an occasion carried himself in the saddle, the knowledge-mass is a temporal sequence, like a rhythm or melody, and partly identical with the person's actual movements as he rode ; but *in itself* it has no position in time (or out of time, for that matter). These it has, as in the case of space, from its relations to other items of knowledge. And in so far as it has temporal position in knowledge, it has it by being *before* or *after*, in the cognitive system, other knowledge-masses of ' real ' events. Here, as in space, the knowledge-masses of time are discontinuous, fragmentary, somewhat fortuitously distributed intersections of the time system ;—discontinuous and fragmentary, that is, as compared with the latter system. But the fact does not prevent the cross-sections, identical as they are with some features of the events, having in the knowledge system the identical relations of *before* and *after* that the events themselves have in the (past) time. In one's knowledge as in ' real ' time, Cæsar caused a bridge to be built *before* he crossed the Rhine.

In the consideration of space we were confronted by the question, Is the knowledge-mass that is identical with the distant object, here in the skull or there in the object ? Both alternatives were rejected, and the supposedly embarrassing nature of the question was shown to rest on a misconception of the plurality of positions that the entities at the intersection of systems, have in these several systems. We now meet a parallel question in regard to the position in time of knowledge of the past :—Is the knowledge now in the present or then in the past ? This question, too, is supposed to be embarrassing, since if the knowledge is identical with the event it must be past, whereas the knowing obviously goes on now ; at least so it is said. The answer to this is parallel with that to the other question. The event has a position in the time system, and one which from our point of view is past, but the knowledge-mass which is partially identical with that past event has its position in the knowledge system, by virtue of its relations to other portions of knowledge, and this position so far as it is temporal and the knowledge-mass is rightly ordered is also past :—past in the knowledge system. We do not, then, recollect the past now ? Assuredly not if ' now ' means now in time[1] as I presume it is intended to mean. And if anyone finds this absurd, I would ask him whether in his system of knowledge, and quite regardless of ' real ' time, the idea of Noah building his ark has a position before, at, or after the idea of Cæsar building his bridge ; has this latter idea a position before, at, or after his idea of Michelangelo planning the dome of St. Peter's ; and has this idea a position before, at, or after his idea of the present moment ? But, he may answer, they are all now in the present moment : Well, do the relations before and after hold between these ideas ?

---

[1] For there is a so-called ' now ' of volition. By relations to the will, entities are ordered as ' past ' and ' future,' but such position is not genuinely temporal.

Yes, the ideas are arranged before and after, yet they are all simultaneous and now.

But the words have lost their meaning when events which are ' before ' and ' after ' are also ' simultaneous.' Besides, will you assert that they are mathematically simultaneous, coexistent in an infinitesimal point of time : do they not obviously occupy at least the ' specious ' present, which is a brief duration of time ?

They are not mathematically simultaneous, but they are still *now* in the specious present.

How do you know this ?

Because I am now thinking of these ideas, and my nervous system is now going through the processes necessary to such thought.

Let us examine these two theses. The latter is of a piece with the spatial introjection. I hope that I have sufficiently shown that knowledge is not ' here in the skull.' For the nervous system selects the entities that shall compose consciousness by responding specifically to them ; and by means of its distance-receptors (eyes, ears, *et caetera*) it responds to entities at a distance. So too by a different mechanism it responds to events that are past. If the auditory stimulus of the name of a person who is dead causes a given nervous system to contract the tear-glands and so produce tears, it is by no means the mere acoustical energy transmitted to the ear that has done this ; but a highly peculiar arrangement of nervous arcs that were so organized by past events, it is so-to-say ' stored stimuli,'[1] which only this peculiar configuration of acoustic energies could now set in action. This particular stimulation of

---

[1] C. S. Sherrington : "Integrative Action of the Nervous System," p. 352.

sensory neurones of the first order (starting from the organs of Corti) succeeds in stimulating neurones of secondary, tertiary, and further orders, as no other acoustic configuration could have stimulated them. The present lachrymal response is not such as a like auditory stimulation would have elicited early in the individual's life, but is profoundly modified by changes in nervous structure brought about by many past stimuli. The present response is then not solely a function of the present stimulus but of past stimuli as well; it is, and will ever continue to be, a revived response to past stimuli. It may be argued, by-the-way, that the lachrymal response is not a specific response, since other present stimuli will elicit tears. This is true, but tears are not the whole of the present response ; the nervous currents, of course, reverberate considerably through the nervous system producing a complicated activity of response of which the lachrymal is a small part. The *total* response, and nothing less, is the *specific response*. In short, then, the mechanism of docility is quite as exactly a means of effecting responses to stimuli that are distant in time, as the ' distance-receptors ' with various co-operating structures are a means of response to stimuli that are distant in space. In neither case does our present theory make the slightest concession to the introjection of conscious experience into the nervous system ' here and now.' The argument, therefore, that one's thought is here and now, because one's nervous system is active here and now, is not valid.

The other argument is that my ideas of the past *are now* because " I am thinking now." And undoubtedly the ' I ' is thinking, but is it strictly ' now ' ? Certainly

if the now-thinking I is not able, when it is willing, to
' get into the past,' its present volition is futile. Knowledge-masses of past events, and those of future events,
have indeed relations to the will, that the identical
sections of events, positioned in the time and not the
knowledge system, do not have. Similarly I pointed
out that the conscious cross-sections of space have in the
knowledge system, by reason of its higher dimensionality, various relations, and especially to the will, that
the same entities do not have in the space system. And
the ' I,' although variously related in the knowledge
system to spatial entities, is itself not one of these, and is
therefore not *spatially* positioned in this system ; it is
not here in the skull. Similarly the ' I ' is related in
the knowledge system to temporal entities, but itself is
not one of these and has no *temporal* position in the
system.

The more ample account of the ' I ' must be deferred
to the chapter on Volition, but by way of elucidation I
will here note four points. Firstly, the ' I ' is not thinking at the instantaneous present, because that logical
variable of the time order known as the mathematically
present moment is an infinitesimal time-point to which
consciousness is never reduced : it is temporally
extended in the specious present. " The present is not
sharp like the edge of a knife, but broad as a saddle on
which we sit looking out on time in both directions."[1]
So that this ' now ' of the ego is no mathematical
present, but is already partially past. Secondly, that
kernel of the conscious manifold that is called the ' I,' I
conceive to be a purpose or group of purposes : the true
kernel of ourself is our will, and in the last analysis only

[1] W. James : " Principles of Psychology," vol. 1, p. 609.

the less fluctuating part of this. Now a purpose defines and generates a series, and if the latter is a temporal series it is temporally extended : but the generating purpose is not the generated series and is doubtless neither temporally extended nor temporally positioned. Thirdly, and more concretely, the argument that " I am thinking now " is a reflective act, and is distinct from the conscious cross-section of the past, from the thought that I say I am thinking ; and if temporarily positioned at all is subsequent to the conscious review of the past. As I have intimated, ' I ' must stop thinking that ' I am thinking now ' if ' I ' am to become conscious of the past. And lastly, since the dimensionality of the knowledge system is greater than that of time and space together, the position of the ' I ' in that whole system is not to be defined by the reference ' now ' to a single (the temporal) dimension : any more than in a three-dimensioned system of geometry a point is defined by two co-ordinates, nor an event in the physical world by reference to the one dimension of time. If the ' I,' along with infinite other relations that give it position in consciousness, were also really ' now,' this fact would still not define its position. In fine, the knowledge of a past event is identical with a part of that event, and with just such part as there is knowledge thereof. As Perry has said,[1] " That which represents the event *is* the event, wholly or in part, and together with something

---

[1] Ralph Barton Perry : " The Knowledge of Past Events," *Journal of Philosophy, Psychology, and Scientific Methods*, 1906, vol. iii., p. 625. Perry bases his very clear and careful discussion on the ' absolute theory ' of position in space and time, but I do not think that his solution of the problem, for I believe that it is a solution, really rests on that theory. I am in part indebted to him for my view of the matter as given above.

else [meaning its ' aspects,' or what I have termed its ' relations ']. Since the term representation seems to imply substitution, it is better to avoid it altogether, and to say simply that the event or part of it is a constituent of the manifold of cognition. This enables us properly to understand substitution when it is actually made for [p. 626] purposes of formulation, calculation or record. To my mind it is an incontestable truth that such substitution is possible only when based upon and attested by direct knowledge. Thus I may in a book employ the sentence, ' Columbus discovered America ' in place of the event itself ; and this printed symbol as a visible entity may occupy a time quite other than that of the event for which it is substituted. But there would be neither sense nor use in this substitution did I not distinguish the symbol and what I mean by it as two different entities. The symbolic representation of the past involves, then, a knowledge of the past which is represented, and cannot itself afford us any solution of the problem as to how in the last resort that past itself is known. To this question I can see but one answer, to the effect that it is known directly through itself constituting a part of the manifold which we call knowledge."

The scheme of cross-sections of the past is, of course, like that of distant space, detached, fragmentary, and as compared with the continuous whole of past time, is arbitrarily selected. The gaps, from this point of view, in the knowledge system have led to the notion, referred to above by Perry, that past time is ' known symbolically.' One's knowledge, for instance, of the fifth century B.C. may consist merely of a few items about Pericles and Phidias and Socrates, and these are said to symbolize in our minds that century of time. But, clearly, it is said, this is the merest symbol, for when one comes to think of all the minutes and hours and all the countless events that went to make that century, one sees that one's knowledge is hopelessly inadequate, and therefore symbolic. If anything which is inadequate and partial is a ' symbol ' this view is correct ; but the word ordinarily means something more precise. Yet even the symbol does not represent or stand for anything except it have some identities with the thing : as algebraic formulæ may be said to symbolize geometrical relations, for there are identities between the two, and as language symbolizes meanings because there are certain identities between the two manifolds. Like any other representation the symbol can stand for its object only because it is partially identical therewith. Thus symbols themselves, if they truly correspond to what they symbolize, are direct and immediate knowledge— just so far as the correspondence (identity) goes. *In this sense* I see no objection to saying that gossip relating to Pericles ' symbolizes ' or ' represents ' in some cases a past epoch, but this does not prejudice the fact that symbolic knowledge is immediate knowledge, and identical with its object. This is also not the sense in which symbolic representation is meant by the representative theory of knowledge. In this matter of symbolism we again, of course, have a glimpse of the logical problem of the repetition of identicals.

The knowledge-mass of a small extent of time ' present ' or ' just past ' (like the knowledge-mass of near-lying space) is so much more adequate, is identical with the time-system in so many more respects, that 'subjective time' approximates 'real time.' [1]   For a short extent the two systems, of time and knowledge, have a fairly useful identity.   And the 'present moment' of consciousness appears always to be a finite duration of time, the specious present.

Agreeably to current notions of time and reality, it is usually asserted that one does not experience the future : at best one may imagine it : for the future is 'not yet real.'   If this rests on the assertion that one experiences nothing but the real, its footing is insecure, since undeniably one experiences very much that is unreal—the whole gamut of erroneous opinion.   And imagination too is certainly included under experience. Now while ideas of the future may be a trifle more liable to error than ideas of the present or past, the fact must be duly recognized that we do have reliable knowledge of the future.   We know much about the tides and the planets, the future course of atmospheric disturbances, the trend of commercial and political forces ; and we can *predict* with at least as much certainty the future success or failure of certain enterprises, as we can *recall* many past events.   Knowledge of the future seems to me to have been greatly minimized in most psychological discussions at least, and I believe that it is quite equal in importance and little if at all inferior in reliability (which is here not to the point, however), to knowledge of the past.   All that I have said of this holds, I believe, *mutatis mutandis*, of knowledge of the future.   The epistemological prin-

----

[1] I persist in using quotation marks about 'real time,' not because I do not agree that the time system *is*, but because the predicate real or unreal has no application to it at this level of discourse.   Reality is higher up in the simple-complex order of being.

ciples are identical; and while the nervous mechanism of response to the future is different, this is not to our present purpose. If most persons know more of the past than of the future, it is chiefly because they do not take the trouble to look at the future.

I have but one more point in regard to the knowledge of time. This is the ' past,' ' present ' and ' future ' of volition. Concerning the physical world Münsterberg says,[1] " This ordered world of objects is valid for us as willing subjects, through whose presence the temporal-spatial arises in a quite different sense. It is only from the point of view of the subject that there is a ' past,' ' present,' or ' future '; the manifold of objects has its temporal form, but this is independent of whether the whole is thought as past or future. The subject, however, requires precisely this time structure, and makes it by a threefold direction of the empirical apperception. . . . memory surveys that which is not further accessible to our volition, perception embraces that on which our will actually operates, and expectation, finally, is directed to that part of reality for which the will of the subject is still to be prepared." This is the ' past,' ' present ' and ' future ' of volition.[2] It is the further specification of position that temporal cross-sections in knowledge have, as I mentioned above, by virtue of their relations to the will. But these relations to the will add nothing to the *temporal* ordering of the knowledge-masses ; and the further definition of position that they supply is not position in the time dimension. One may

[1] H. Münsterberg : " Grundzüge der Psychologie," S. 235.
[2] Nevertheless there seems to be a truly temporal ' now ' of the time system—a proper logical variable that can assume the position of any moment—a variable ' Schnitt ' in a continuous series. And it is of some mathematical and scientific importance.

query, furthermore, without feeling certain, whether the so-called ' past,' ' present ' and ' future ' of volition are really more than two classes :—those entities on which the will does not operate and those on which it does. It would have advantage, in regard to the knowledge cross-sections of temporal events, not to confuse their time relations of before and after with their non-temporal relations to the will. The will does after all operate on the past ; and often is inert toward the future : the will of the archæologist is actively bent on the temporal past, and of the moral degenerate is dead to the future.

This completes our discussion of memory, and the knowledge of distant space and remote time. I have tried to show that in both these cases knowledge is a cross-section of the realm of *being*, and so far as it *is* at all, is identical with the so-called ' object ' of knowledge. It remains to consider briefly experiences of the order of imagination, fancy, reverie and dreams. Everything seems to be included under this general head which is not actively believed in and which is also not veridical. Their truthfulness or error must be reserved for the general discussion of error, but imaginary ideas certainly *are* in the great realm of being, if they *are* at all, even in experience. They are, therefore, cross-sections of the realm of being, quite as much as sensations and perceptions. And this is equally true whether they stand to the will in the relation of being accredited or not accredited. Their position in consciousness, entrance into the specious presence and exit therefrom, is determined by the responses of the nervous system precisely as in the case of perception of any entities near or remote in space or time. It may be objected that the nervous system cannot respond to that which is not in the physical world, and of course no one denies this ;—the nervous system is nothing but a physical mechanism acted on by physical forces. But just as in the sciences of physics and chemistry these physical entities are seen on analysis to be aggregates of logical or neutral entities, so that physical processes are simply not describable as a movement of *material* particles but are strictly mathematical manifolds,—so too in physiology the responses of the nervous system require, if they are to be studied with any minuteness, a similar analysis that reveals the neutral constitution of the nervous system and of the forces that act on and within it. It is the sheerest thoughtlessness,—while physics shows the material world to consist of lines, motions, accelerations, potentialities, equations, and mathematical points having position inertia and rigidity, *et caetera*, and no residue by way of Matter,—to insist that physiology becomes metaphysical and ' subjective ' if it analyses further than the ' fine and smooth ' Material globules of a Democritean atomism. The nervous system responds to much that is not ' in the physical world ' in the Democritean sense which is intended by our objector, and its processes are of a mathematical and neutral structure, just as much as the path of a ray of light is a function of densities, temperatures, magnetic deflections, and indices of refraction—neutral entities, all, and unidentifiable with any, even the smoothest atoms of Democritus. I tried to show very briefly how the nervous system responds to entities that are remote in time. And in the case of imaginary ideas, if the nervous response is that which is specific to *red*, to a *triangle*, or to a *favourable omen*, then these entities are

in the field of cognition : and they need not to be found
tangibly assailing the person who experiences them, any
more than the first derivative of a formula of motion is
found sitting upon the cannon-ball whose acceleration
is changing.   The notion that nervous responses ' as
such ' are merely functions of, and completely describable as responses to, some ectodermal impact, derives
solely from a materialism which, so far as I know,
survives only in the mind of the hod-carrier, and, by a
beautiful working of the law of compensation, in the
mind of the idealistic philosopher.

It is, I suppose, in this field of imaginary ideas that
the psychological introjection has its great stronghold.
These ideas are thought to be characteristically untrue,
although in fact the predicate of truth or untruth often
in no wise applies to them, and since the ' outer world '
is supposed to contain no untruth, these ideas must pertain wholly to the inner.   And whatever, for dualistic
theory, the inner world may be as a conscious manifold,
it must in its quality of dependence on the nervous
organism, be a ' by-product ' of nerve activity, and
must be located where it is produced, that is, within the
nervous system.   In such wise, I imagine, the notion of
introjection was first launched.   From this it is an easy
step to the assertion that true ideas of sensation and
perception, which any unbiased person would declare
to be ' out there,' since they are very similar in quality
and form to the imaginary, are likewise within the
nervous system—a by-product.   The ' introjection '
thus accomplished has entailed a painful task on
nativists and geneticists, who have laboured frantically
to effect ' projection ' for all those imprisoned ideas
that are ' true ideas,' but still to secure detention for all

the ' untrue.' And it is the signal merit of Avenarius
to have shown that it was only a misguided introjection
that made projection necessary. He did away with
both ; as, after him, the theory here presented does.

But as long as it is taken for granted that the realm
which is styled (equally erroneously) ' physical,' ' outer,'
and ' real ' is *all true,* the ' vital conscious quality '
(as one hears it called) of vivid dreams, hallucinations,
and lively fancies seems only to be accounted for, their
being at all, by assigning them to some little nut-
shell in this ' outer world,' so that they may be in some
sense ' real,' real ' by-products,' in spite of being both
unreal and untrue. Thus safely quarantined well within
the skull they cannot be examined closely enough to
jeopardize the ' real, outer ' space that holds the skull
nor infect it seriously with their unreality. And the
account which I have given above will doubtless be
objected to on the score of not explaining the ' vital
conscious quality ' of remembered and of imaginary
ideas. Had I but admitted them to be a by-product of
nervous activity in the cerebrum, they would of course
then have their ' vital conscious quality '; then they
would be something ' real,' so that if they were distilled
from the skull in sufficient quantity they could be weighed
or poured out on the floor. But I have asserted these
ideas to be mere vague nuclei of neutral entities,
denizens at large of my ridiculous realm of being, non-
vital, unreal, untrue, and un-everything else save un-
being. In leaving this topic I will say only that reality
and unreality, truth and untruth, are, in our present
manifold and in the respects under debate, nothing to
the point. *Being* is the present issue. And if the words
that I have used lack the ' vital conscious quality '

s

of the rainbow and the nightmare, this is a common defect of printed symbols.   But the *meanings* I have intended are just those things that we meet every day— both small and large, vague and clear, faint and glaring, soft and harsh, pleasant and agonizing, living and dead.

CHAPTER XIII

ERROR

It has been one of the specious advantages of the representative theory of knowledge, that it satisfied the craving for a real and reliable world, such as the 'outer' or 'physical' one, by sequestering all error and untruth in a place apart, the 'subjective' world. It is remarkable that this view has been found attractive and serviceable notwithstanding the fact that at the same time it provides that all that any person can experience or know is his own subjective world—the very stronghold of error. Of course it avails nothing that there is somewhere a real and true realm if it is for ever and completely shut out from the 'subjective.' We shall examine in due course the comforting although unknowable 'truth' of this 'outer' world, but I wish first to point out that errors in the realm of consciousness are discovered chiefly in two places—in one's own past knowledge and in the past or present knowledge of other persons. Concerning the former I cannot do better than to quote from an article by Perry.[1]

[p. 284.] "While primitive experience is entirely free from any general idea of the dependence of objects

---

[1] Ralph B. Perry : "Conceptions and Misconceptions of Consciousness," The Psychological Review, 1904, XI, p. 282. I must especially commend to the reader this entire article.

upon the knowing of them, there are certain accepted cases in which an experience is definitely recognized as *my experience.* . . . [p. 285.] Such a belief must arise very early in connection with discredited or illusory experiences. . . . Experience is constantly correcting itself and discrediting its earlier content. Observation and identification is a process of self-correction. The surviving judgement is the last of a series of discarded judgements which were once as living as itself. They are not the object A, but ' what I thought,' ' the way it seemed to me then,' my mistake or confusion. . . . [p. 286.] In this wise the corrected and replaced experience, in contradiction to the corrective experience, is viewed as merely *my experience,* a term of my blindness and struggle. . . . [p. 287.] The most unequivocal instance is the dream. This is a definite type of invalid experience, recognized as such from the standpoint of a valid corrective experience. Were there only dreaming, there would be no dreaming. Either I must myself awake or have my illusions observed by another, who both knows them and knows beyond them. The waking and the dreaming differ in that the former not only succeeds the latter, but includes and replaces it; while the latter on the other hand knows nothing of the former. . . . [p. 268.] Introspection is retrospective attention to an experience which I now surround and surmount."

Error is discovered in another person's knowledge when one's own knowledge includes that of another and similarly surrounds and surmounts it ; one's own knowledge-mass is for a limited region inclusive of that of another and contains, besides, some mark to indicate where the other's knowledge ends. Of course the same entities can be in the cross-sections of two or more persons, and if the cross-section of one is large enough to include that of another, or even if it happens to extend at any point beyond where the other's terminates, and if this fact is also a part of the first person's knowledge, he is surveying on a small scale the process of cognition. If thus one person hears a cry for help and hurries to the rescue, his knowledge is surrounded and corrected by that of another who has heard the same cry and also seen that it proceeded from a group of merely mischievous and thoughtless children.

But the surrounding and surmounting of one's own or another's knowledge is not necessarily a *corrective* experience of it. I may know to-day that the river near the house rises and falls with the tide, and to-morrow may know that its tidal variation is two feet : then this latter knowledge confirms and amplifies the earlier. The teacher is one who, day by day, confirms and amplifies the less extended knowledge of his pupils. That the more inclusive experience shall correct the more limited it must contain something incompatible therewith, must in some respects contradict and nullify it. And it is the nature of this contradiction[1] that just now concerns us.

In the first chapter we saw that the units of *being*, ultimate so far as we now see, are propositions and terms ; that every proposition contains one or more terms ; and that by a sort of logical activity inherent in propositions they generate, along with other proposi-

---

[1] By ' contradiction ' here and subsequently, I mean *contradiction* proper, and not *contrariety* as well ; although I am referring to a factor that is to an extent, I believe, involved in contrariety, and to which I am not aware that a specific name has been assigned.

tions, series or systems of terms in relation. The tracing out of this generation by thought is termed deduction. Now we also saw that in selecting a set of propositions to generate a system, the logician takes only such as he supposes to be consistent; though he also insists, if possible, that they shall be independent. Many propositions are seen at once to be incompatible, but in other cases the logician cannot tell. In such a case he undertakes to find a system of *terms in relation* which ' satisfies ' all of the propositions, and if he finds that such a system ' exists,'[1] as he says, he is satisfied that the propositions are not contradictory. The significant point here is that a system of *terms* in relation, which ' satisfies ' the propositions, can be neither found nor ' constructed ' if the propositions are contradictory,— because it does not ' exist.' Thus the exhibition of a system of terms in relation is *the* test of consistency.[2] Doubtless the system of terms that ' satisfies ' a set of propositions is one that the latter generate. And the term ' existence ' seems to have been adopted in agreement with general opinion that everything which exists is consistent, or true. The question now arises, whether the ' existence ' of the satisfying system of terms in relation, means anything else than the *being* of that system. If the logician can exhibit the system of terms, then it ' exists,' as he says; and certainly it *is*. He asserts that a contradictory system of terms in relation cannot (i.e. does not) ' exist.' Is it perhaps true that it cannot *be*, or that it *is* not ? Russell has said that a proposition

[1] It seems to me that this logical ' existence ' offers a promising field of study.

[2] Cf. Harold Chapman Brown : " The Problem of Method in Mathematics and Philosophy," Essays in Honour of William James, New York, 1908, p. 425.

of the form ' A is not ' is either meaningless or false :
and the proposition that ' A contradictory system of
terms is not,' while not being false, may be meaningless
because the words ' contradictory system of terms ' are
meaningless. Words of course may slip their moorings
and *be* as printer's ink when their authorized meanings,
in the attempted combination, are ' meaningless.'

Now everyone admits that ' physical ' objects, which
of course are terms, are never contradictory. But has
anyone ever experienced a system of even the most
' ideal ' *terms* that is contradictory ? Is it not clear,
indeed, that the test of consistency itself implies the
assertion that no even ' ideal ' *system of terms* is or can
be contradictory ? since the systems adduced by the
logician as tests of consistency are (as ordinarily understood) of the most immaterial structure,—numbers,
points and other logical simples. He adduces in system
such simple terms that their purely neutral nature is
unmistakable. If then by the very test of consistency
itself, there is no contradiction where there is a system
of terms, even of the most ' ideal ' and ' subjective '
sort, it follows that a contradictory system of terms *is*
not. And it seems evasive and unnecessary to substitute
' exists ' for *is*. In short, the words ' contradictory
system of terms ' are meaningless. And in fact, to take
an example, what would the system of two terms A
and B be, if it satisfied the conditions A is over B and B
is over A ? Clearly enough the point that is both over
and under another point at one and the same instant is
downright *unthinkable*. And try as long as one will, to
think a system of terms that shall satisfy two or more
propositions that are contradictory, one will find any
such system to be unthinkable. Now of course the

unthinkable is the meaningless, and thus empirically we find that the words ' contradictory system of terms ' are meaningless.   The logician ought not to accredit ' existence ' with the guarantee for consistency when this guarantee lies in *being* itself.

But where ?   Is there indeed no inconsistency, no error ?   Of course with such an intent the ' higher synthesis ' is offered and warranted to be a universal solvent for any and all error.   It is a nostrum : and the higher synthesis that can digest propositions of the form, for instance, A is B and A is not B, will be found to do so by artfully providing two meanings for either A or B. Certainly contradiction is, and is not to be explained away.   The difficulty with our purely verbal and meaningless phrase ' contradictory system of terms ' lies in the attempt to combine contradiction with *terms ;* contradiction and *propositions* subsist together, in *being* at least, well enough.   And here it is worth noting that I have been able to carry on the discussion only by using a meaningless verbal phrase on the one hand, and on the other by adducing intelligible but contradictory *propositions* and then asking the reader to think if possible the system of *terms* that satisfies them—the system that *is* not.   And this is the main point :— propositions are often enough contradictory, terms never are.   This truth will perhaps serve as a clue to the general problem of error.

Every case of error or untruth is a case of contradictory propositions : and a single proposition is neither true nor false.   If truisms such as ' A is A ' are adduced as single and true propositions, I would suggest that the words are in propositional form but that the *meaning* is simply ' A ' ; and much the same I take to be the case

with all truisms. But now a set of contradictory propositions need not be utterly contradictory ; it may
generate a considerable system of terms in relation
before the contradiction is at all manifest, as is shown
by the fact that the logician often proceeds for some
time in the deduction of a system of terms in relation
from a set of postulates, until at some point the propositions *meet* in contradiction. Nor is it through any
error of deduction that the contradiction was not
earlier. Something of a system is generated, but there
comes a point where the system stops short. Thus, in a
simple case, if one undertakes to construct a geometrical
figure such that (1) it shall be composed of equilateral
triangles of uniform size, (2) the triangles shall join so
that there are neither gaps within the figure nor indentation of the periphery, and (3) the figure shall have seven
sides : the triangles are taken and placed adjacent to
satisfy (1) and (2) until with six triangles a perfect
hexagon is produced. But the addition of another
triangle in order to satisfy (3) gives, to be sure, seven
sides but does not satisfy (2) in that the periphery is
now twice indented. The three postulates are contradictory. At first glance, perhaps, it looks as if nowhere
in the deduction did all three of the postulates contribute to the process : thus the perfect hexagon satisfies
(1) and (2), and the heptalateral made of seven triangles
satisfies (1) and (3). It is true, of course, that all *three*
postulates are *nowhere satisfied* in the system of triangles
(terms), but nevertheless all three contribute to the
generative process : for if we say, for the hexagon, that
(3) contributed nothing, we find that (1) and (2) are
satisfied as well by a rhombus composed of two triangles
touching on one side, as by the perfect hexagon of six

triangles : and it is (3) which prevents the generative process from stopping with the rhombus ; and once more (3) steps in when four triangles have been combined into a large equilateral triangle (satisfying (1) and (2)) and requires more triangles to be added. Or if, again, we say, for the other case, that (1) and (3) are alone the active generators and that (2) plays no part, we find that (1) and (3) are satisfied by the seven-sided figure composed of five triangles arranged so that a sixth, *if added*, would make a perfect hexagon. But this seven-sided figure contains an indentation of the periphery, and so (2) steps in here and requires more triangles to be added. And of course (1) is active in either case. In short, all three of the postulates contribute toward the generation of an ' existent ' system of terms, for although the propositions are contradictory this contradiction is *local* in the generated system. It is the familiar and typical situation in which something is proposed, and the question remains—' Can it be done ? '

Now this argument confessedly rests on the initial requirement to ' *construct* ' a figure to satisfy (1), (2), and (3). And the logician whose interest is fixed on the static phases of logic would reject the whole consideration, declaring that, " the simple logical fact is that a heptagon without gaps or indentations of the periphery and composed of equilaterals of uniform size does not exist." But then he must explain in what this curious existence differs from *being*, and if, as I have tried to show, it does not differ, he may reasonably be asked how anything *is* not, which is readily defined by perfectly intelligible propositions. To this no answer will be forthcoming from any static logic. But we have found a clue to the situation by recognizing the activity of propositions by which they generate explicit, static systems of terms.

By way of further illustration let us consider, once more, the game of chess, which is essentially, of course, a logical universe in which the rules of the game are postulates, and the moves of the men on the board are an explicit system of terms in relation, which is generated by the rules.

In order to avoid the personally directive aspect of the game, let us mean by it the thirty-two men with their several rules of move, the other rules of the game, and also all the moves in all their possible permutations that the premises logically permit of. For the player of chess does actually nothing as he proceeds but reject logically possible moves. The game is a most elaborate deductive system. Now every one of the possible move sequences, that is, every one of the infinite number of 'games' that could be played, terminates in mate, which is a contradiction between the legal moves of one king and of some member of the opposite side. But prior to this a greater or lesser number of other collisions has taken place, and since chess has no conception of elastic rebound as has mechanics, every such contradiction means the annihilation of a member from the system. Yet the move sequences go on for some time before any contradiction appears, and proceed with unimpaired logical precision thereafter. So that here is a strictly deductive logical system, a true universe of discourse, that holds *in potentia* a very large number of contradictions.

It seems to me to be specially significant, that contradiction is often localized : there is a 'gap' in the explicit system of terms, and yet the propositions continue to generate further terms, just as they did before the explicit point of contradiction was reached. In view of this it seems somewhat arbitrary of the logician to limit his interest to sets of propositions which shall nowhere meet in contradiction. Rather it should seem worth while to study the structure of systems at and around those points where the postulates implicitly define contradiction. In the first chapter I called attention to the ' activity ' of propositions, and suggested that logic has hitherto inclined unduly toward the static, and neglected even the general concept of activity. It may be that some day symbolic logic will come to play more of its games after the pattern of the game of chess. We have found, in fine, that the explicit contradiction in a system of terms in relation *is* not ; and is indeed meaningless and *unthinkable :* whereas contradictory propositions *are,* and are active in producing systems of terms although mutilated or imperfect ones, if I may use the word. We have now to examine the reputed difference between the ' subjective ' and the ' objective ' realms whereby the latter is said to be thoroughly consistent while the former contains all of error that there is.

We have seen that erroneous opinions in men's minds were among the reasons that caused ancient philosophers to divide the realm of experience into the two classes of phenomena, the ' objective ' and the ' subjective.' Erroneous opinions were of course subjective, and the generalization seems to have been arrived at very early, that of course the ' objective ' world contained no inconsistencies. This thesis concerning the ' outer ' world, which must at first have been regarded tentatively as being of the nature of an hypothesis, seems steadily to have gained ground until it is now regarded as unassailable. That 'reality excludes discord' is thought to be a well-confirmed fact.

But now it follows from our definition of consciousness, that opinions, whether right or wrong, pertain to the same neutral realm as material objects, and that a human mind is one kind of neutral aggregate (a cross-section) just as a material object is another kind. Nor does there appear any reason, when these two realms are thus monistically viewed, whereby errors should occur exclusively among the neutral aggregates that are minds. Errors are, as we have just seen, a feature of the neutral realm at large, logically prior to its division into subjects and objects, and are presumably, there-fore, to be found in both the so-called 'subjective' and 'objective' phenomena alike. Since this is directly contrary to the accepted belief in regard to the physical world we must examine this latter belief at some length.

Now what sort of errors do we empirically find in the subjective world ? We say that we have been in error when we find that a distant gleam of light, seen over the water, is not the light-house that we at first supposed, but a setting star. We are in error if we suppose a man ingenuous whom we later find to be disingenuous. Or we have been in error when we have committed a deed which we later find to be in its consequence at variance with our true intentions. Certainly our conscious life abounds in errors. Our past experiences are continually being 'corrected,' as Perry has said,[1] and the corrected

[1] R. B. Perry : " Conceptions and Misconceptions of Conscious-ness," The Psychological Review, 1904, vol. xi., pp. 282–96.

portion of our past is that which we account ' subjective '
par excellence. It cannot be that the distant gleam both
was a light-house and also was not a light-house, but
was a star. The former proposition, then, was ' merely
an idea,' while the latter, unless it in turn becomes
corrected, is a true idea, that is, a ' fact '; for ' objectivity ' excludes contradiction and only one, at best,
of the propositions asserted of the distant light can be
' objectively ' valid. The essence of the erroneous
experience is that one portion of it is either contradictory, or else contrary, to another portion. And this is
true whether the error be one of perception, of judgement, or of a moral motive. The discrepancy is most
frequently one of contraries—both experiences cannot
be true—but since this means that one of the experiences
is found to be untrue, the supposed truth of this experience is contradicted, and so it is exact to say that
every case of error is a case of contradiction. Errors
of experience are, then, precisely as we should expect,
not explicit contradictions in a system of terms, but
they are the being together in knowledge of contradictory *propositions* ;—X is a light-house, X is a star.
And these errors, errors implicit in propositions, we
have just found to *be* in the conceptual or neutral realm
logically prior to the division into subjects and objects.
The X that is lighthouse-star (mere words) is never
experienced, for happily even the ' subjective ' realm
does not contain the unthinkable.

Of course, now the ' objective ' realm will not contain
explicit errors in terms, since these simply *are* not
anywhere. But it remains to see whether the ' objective ' is thoroughly consistent, as is so universally
alleged ; whether it does not contain, precisely like the

'subjective,' contradictory propositions. My thesis is that the physical or so-called 'outer' or 'real' world is through and through contradictory. In order to see whether this is true, let us revert to the Hertzian programme of mechanics. This was to construct images of the objects whose movements are to be studied, which shall 'resemble' those objects in respect to mass, size, position, rate and direction of motion, and so forth. Then to see if the behaviour of the images, deduced by *logical necessity* from the premised masses and motions, *coincides* with the actual behaviour of the objects under *natural necessity*. If the coincidence is complete the mechanical description is so far finished : if not, the constructed images are to be corrected.

We have seen what the 'resemblance' that Hertz mentions is : it is partial identity. And indeed in Hertz's words it turns out to be 'complete coincidence' in all respects of mass and motion. In short, the images constructed are identical with the concrete objects in respect to mass, space, and time, but lack merely various other particularizing properties such as colour, odour, texture, and *position* in space and time. The images form a partially universalized system which is as essentially identical with a certain portion of the concrete objects being studied, as the engineer's designs are identical with the concrete, particular ship or trestle that is constructed in accordance with them. It is further obvious that the constructed images form a logically deductive system, a universe of discourse in which any change that occurs is subject purely to logical necessity. We may conclude, then, that the so-called natural necessity is no more nor less than logical necessity ; called natural necessity if the objects are particular, logical necessity if they are partially or wholly universal.

Now if the logical motions of the images coincide with the observed motions of the objects, the images are valid ; if not they must be corrected. And there are possibly physicists, and philosophers, who would declare that the images which have to be revised are mere epiphenomena of the skull, while those not needing revision are ' objective ' truths. But it is to be noticed that revision is indicated not when the images are found to be mutually contradictory, but when they are found to be in contradiction with the objects. A contradiction between the image and the corresponding object will supposedly be the physicist's error, not a contradiction *within* the system of constructed images. The contradiction is one of correspondence. It is gratuitously assumed, however, that if there *is* a contradiction *within the constructed system*, this system will also be found discrepant with the real objects. Is this true ?

It often happens that such a constructed system contains two masses moving toward each other along a straight line : this corresponds to the situation of two concrete objects that are about to collide. So long as the two masses have not met, there is no contradiction, but when they do meet does not the motion of one mass contradict that of the other ? And there is a point where one or both motions will disappear :—which is precisely the logical mark of contradiction. And such negation is equally true if the masses are concrete objects in collision. But it will be said that no motion is really negated, since in real objects the kinetic energy passes over into thermal, so that none is lost. It is true that no *energy* has been lost, but two oppositely directed motions have most assuredly been lost. Motion and energy are not identical, and it was not said that the initial energies contradicted each other. The two original motions, however, eventually contradicted each other and one, or in some circumstances both, of these are lost. When two spherical objects collide it is at a point, and instantly thereon all the possible lines drawn through that point and contained within the masses are converted into so many levers at various angles of inclination, so that of course the result is not sheer stoppage of motion. Such complicated situations lead the physicist to the concept of elasticity, which is indispensable in mechanics. And it may be that elasticity is such a concept as ensures the logical impossibility of *energies* ever meeting, in three dimensions, so that they shall contradict one another. This is certainly so if the doctrine of the conservation of energy is true. But two actual concrete velocities can contradict each other, and a part of the swifter and the whole of the slower (if the two masses are equal) are lost. Anyone who will deny that these two velocities are a real part of the objective world, will be led through an interesting train of thought. Mayhap velocity, though not energy, is ' subjective ' ! In short, the objective world does contain contradictions. And it is hard to see why it is so persistently denied that the collision of physical objects is a case of objective contradiction. To be sure the unthinkable does not happen among the objects, nor yet indeed does anyone subjectively think it : no single particle of matter moves in opposite directions at once, and this is also meaningless. The contradiction is, of course, between propositions ; which are in the present case expressed as

T

equations of motion. We saw that in the Hertzian programme natural necessity is curiously 'paralleled' by logical necessity, natural process by deductive process : and our previous consideration of the neutral realm of being explains why this is so. Both physical objects and ideas are composed of the same neutral entities, and both physical and mental activity are derived from an activity of these neutral entities—the generative activity of propositions. The laws of nature are not 'convenient constructions' devised by man, but they are an integral part of nature and the source of its activity ; they are the neutral elements called propositions. And if one finds in these, whether expressed as subject and predicate or in equational form, nothing but a social shorthand, one is mistaking for their meaning and essence a feature that is utterly insignificant.

It may seem of the least possible consequence to the physical scientist that such contradictions as that just adduced *are* in the physical world : a direction of motion that is lost owing to contradiction is of no more importance than the extinct outlines of an evening's fireworks, or the shapes that come and go in a kaleidoscope, or the turmoil of the sea,—so long as no least fraction of mass and energy is lost. Be this as it may, it is only the superficial view that the laws of nature, the generating propositions, are no actual part of nature, and that the latter is only a system of masses in relation ' existent ' (and static) at the infinitesimal ' present moment '—only this superficial view gives any warrant to the belief that nature is consistent. A similar exclusiveness of attention to static logical systems gives rise to a similar belief that there can be no contradictions in logic itself

because, as is true, there *are* no explicit contradictions
in the systems of terms that propositions generate.
But motion has to be acknowledged as an integral part
of nature, and in functions there has to be acknowledged
an *independent variable,* and these can be expressed only
in such a way as involves frequent propositional contradictions. Thus all phenomena of *interference* are
cases of contradiction between propositions. At the
point of interference the vibratory motions imparted
to the ether or to molecules are contradictory to one
another, and at that point the wave-motion ceases;
and energy is said to have assumed the form of tension.
All counterbalancings, as in cantilevers and Gothic
vaultings, are contradictory forces in equilibrium.
All collisions between bodies, all interference between
energies, all processes of warming and cooling, of
electrically charging and discharging, of starting and
stopping, of combining and separating, are processes
of which one undoes the other. And they cannot be
defined by the scientist except in propositions which
manifestly contradict one another. All nature is so full
of these mutually negative processes that we are moved
to admiration when a few forces co-operate long enough
to form what we call an organism ; and even then *decay*
sets in forthwith. We call nature everywhere consistent, and yet we admit that life is a mystery while
death is none : it is none, because the antagonism of
contradictory forces is the familiar phenomenon, while
co-operation of forces is relatively infrequent. Those
theologians who once admired the wondrous works of
God were discomfited ever and anon when an impartial
observer called attention to the incidents less admirable.
This doctrine of beneficence has given place to an equally

fatuous one of the smooth consistency of natural process. Nature is a seething chaos of contradiction.

If it is objected that there is no contradiction when a magnet holds a piece of iron from falling by gravity, or when two rays of light interfere, or when one animal kills another, that these are all perfectly consistent since neither matter nor energy is ever lost ; thus if a magnet attracts a piece of iron upward while gravity attracts it down, there is here no contradiction such as one finds in the ' subjective ' realm where both A is a light-house and A is not a light-house : I reply that if one will look closely enough not one of the situations described can be defined except by propositions that are contradictory. The law of attraction, for instance, whether of magnetism or of gravity, states that two masses move towards each other with a velocity that depends on their sizes and their distance apart. If the iron is held by the magnet it does *not* move toward the magnet, neither does it move toward the earth. The law of both attractions is negatived, and there is no motion. The forces still operate, but they merely ' oppose ' each other. So they do ; as to direction of motion they contradict. Had then motion not ceased the iron would have moved both up and down at the same time—which is not merely the unnatural but is equally the unthinkable. But the *propositions* or laws of motion, which are all that attraction is, have contradicted each other, and the result has been a zero motion. This contradiction is not lessened by the circumstance that no energy is lost. The case of optical interference is a similar one. Light is a form of motion in particles of ether, and the law of this motion is a proposition. When two waves meeting in ' opposite ' phase impel the same particle to move in opposite directions, that particle moves not at all. Happily the unthinkable does not happen, but the two laws of motion have nevertheless met in contradiction at that point. Nor is this fact in any way affected by the doctrine of strain, which is said to exist at the point of interference. Again, if one animal kills another, of course neither matter nor energy is lost, yet the principle of organization which would (if exactly found) describe scientifically the life activities of the victim, has been opposed and contradicted. It takes but a moment's impartial consideration to see that all cases of collision, interference, combining and separating, and, in the animal kingdom, of disease and death, are cases in which some principle of motion is contradicted by some other principle, with a resultant zero of motion at the point of contradiction and to the extent of the contradiction.

All this in no wise prejudices the doctrine either of the conservation of matter or of energy. As to the former, from the point of view of the logic of science, it should seem that if matter were to be annihilated this could be described (in the Hertzian sense) only by a proposition such as A (some term or terms) is not : for the particles of matter are the terms of the physical world. But, as Russell says, such a proposition is always either false or meaningless. So that it is hard even to conceive a meaning for the words ' annihilation of matter.'

Any two laws of motion can contradict, of course, only where they meet, and they can meet only when they simultaneously operate on the same particle or particles of matter. If the two motions are of different periodicities, the two phases will at certain points (or at certain moments) be opposed and at others not. This is illustrated by the phenomenon of Newton's rings, or of ' beats ' in sound. Both motions proceed undisturbed beyond the points (or moments) of contradiction, and presently once more combine in like phases, and these further on come again into contradiction. And there is no motion at the points (or moments) of contradiction. This persistence of the laws of motion through and *beyond* all contradictions should seem to be the logical expression of the conservation of energy. Now the annihilation of propositions is as meaningless as that of terms, and the laws of energy are propositions. It will be recalled that from our monistic point of view, the motions of matter *are* simply terms and propositions : a view which accords admirably with the scientific programmes of Kirchhoff and Hertz. If now in the physical world propositions can meet in contradiction and yet continue to operate beyond such points, one is tempted to ask why such is not equally the case in purely neutral universes of discourses in which not motion but only logical change is involved. Such ordinal points of contradiction could be studied, for instance, in the case of algebraic functions. It might be worth while in some systems, as I before remarked, instead of discarding one of two postulates that are at any (ordinal) point found to be contradictory, to retain both and note their behaviour at positions further along in the deductive ordinal series. It seems to be his bias for the static that leads the symbolic logician to eschew contradictory propositions, for in static systems, truly, the contradiction is unthinkable.

If this argument is valid, the boasted consistency of the ' objective ' realm comes down to nothing but the fact that it nowhere contains the unthinkable—that is, an explicit contradiction in a system of terms in relation. Such a contradiction is called meaningless in logic, unthinkable in psychology, and in physics impossible. But we have found the only kind of contradiction that *is* at all, that is, *contradictory propositions*, to *be* in any one of three divisions of the neutral realm of being, just as much as in any other.

Now the problem of error in knowledge is virtually solved, I believe, by this view of the meaning and the being of error itself. Not a great deal more remains to be said. The errors of 'opinion' that were so early recognized, are of course always contradictory propositions,— the opinion that ' A is B ' opposed by the opinion that ' A is not B ' ; no one ever experienced B-not-B, or the lighthouse-star, for these are mere printer's ink. The errors in knowledge are, then, the presence in the knowledge-system of propositions that contradict each other : and such a situation calls for no special explanation, because it is found in most manifolds that contain propositions.

There is, further, the matter of truth and error of correspondence. Joachim is undoubtedly right that the essence of truth does not lie in correspondence ; for it lies in mutual consistency between propositions. Yet if in a system two series, or minor systems, are defined which are not alike, and if they are also defined as corresponding, there is an inconsistency because they do not correspond. The correspondence is untrue. Similarly there is true correspondence, or a truth of correspondence. So in the knowledge of time and space we have seen that the knowledge system which, while partly identical with the objects in time and space, is a system of cross-sections of these, and from the point of view of epistemology, which is a logical manifold embracing both the knower and the known and the relations between the two, this knowledge system involves either a truth or untruth of correspondence with the system of time and space. For in the manifold of epistemology the knowing system and the known are defined as being in correspondence. As the student of epistemology surveys the process of knowledge, knows some contents of the mind of another, and just there ' surrounds and surmounts ' these in his own mind, the truth or error of correspondence reduces to ordinary consistency or inconsistency of propositions. Thus if he watches one who is trying to identify a specimen of mineral his knowledge may contain the other's opinion ' This is gold ' and also his own ' It is pyrites,' and he will deem that the knowledge-mass of the other is in error of correspondence. The inconsistency, however, is between two propositions, and is not by principle different from the case of one who has a corrective experience relating to some part of one's own knowledge. But the correspondence may be true and both knower and known, which are then identical, be internally inconsistent or false : this is the case when one plans or merely perceives an interference, collision or catastrophe. It is ordinarily but wrongly called true because the correspondence is true. There is correspondence and there is truth of correspondence, but the essence of truth is consistency between propositions.

It may be asked, if knowledge of space and time is a cross-section thereof, whence may come any parts of knowledge that do not truly correspond thereto ? They come, not indeed from space and time, but from the general realm of being, for the knowledge system as a whole is a system that intersects not merely space and time but all being. There must be, however, no spatial reference in the ' whence come,' for being is not a merely spatial manifold : to ask whence comes or whither goes in a spatial sense, the false idea or indeed the true, fancy or fact, is to ask whither and whence about motion that has ceased, the contour of the clouds, the momentary shape of waves. Being is infinite in resources and prodigal.

Of course much more could be said, and indeed much more discovered, concerning propositions and the systems which they generate : and something will be said in the next chapter. In the First Chapter, too, I classed relations with propositions ; this was very summary, and more could be said about that. But in general, propositions are in any system that contains in any wise logical change, for instance, any logical variable ; and they may be recognized because such a manifold cannot be defined without the use of propositions or some sort of functions. While too it seems fantastic to speak of the nervous system as responding to propositions (and here is indeed room for empirical research), yet the sort of active entity that the word ' proposition ' means is integrally contained in the manifold responded to by the nervous system if this manifold can be logically defined only by propositions or equations (functions). We have to consider this again in the following chapter on Volition.

CHAPTER XIV

VOLITION

We have seen that if both mind and matter are logically late and superficial categories in a universe which is composed purely of neutral stuff, if they are merely modes of combination of the neutral elements of the great manifold of being, then not only errors but also volitions probably have a place there prior to either matter or mind. In other words, volitions must be shown to be neutral entities that are not limited to the individual consciousness, but that admit of logical or even mathematical discussion.

Now even such persons as admit that perceptions may be common to two or more subjects, generally account volitions and desires to be still the intimate and inscrutable possession of each soul, the very holy of holies of the ' subjective.' Most psychologists declare automatically that we can never directly experience the volitions of another person. But if we cannot experience them directly, then not indirectly either, for we have already seen what ' representative ' knowledge amounts to. Now it just happens that we can and do directly know the volitions of other persons, and that if we did not, we could not carry on our daily traffic. If a merchant did not know pretty thoroughly the purposes and aims of his colleagues and competitors, he would be in a sorry state. One reason that psychologists so persistently deny such knowledge is perhaps that they discover no special sense-organ for apprehending volitions : but neither is there a special sense-organ for time, space, or substance. All perceptions depend on the united functioning of various nervous mechanisms.

Probably the main consideration, although it is a technical one, that makes volitions seem peculiarly subjective, is one derived from the representative theory with its parallelism of mental with cerebral states. Any particular act of volition is traditionally asserted, in physiological psychology, to take place within the cerebral cortex, so that the psychologist thinks he may say with impunity that no other person can perceive his personal volitions. If merely this were the case a surgeon's hammer and chisel ought to suffice to lay bare the ineffable secret. The fact is that whatever the cerebral processes are that go on when a person is actively willing, the volition that is content of the individual's experience is such a thing as has no position in space. To inquire where a volition is, is to inquire for the habitat, for instance, of the laws of thermo-dynamics. The physiological psychologist often seems unable to comprehend that many, and indeed particular, entities have no spatial location. But we have seen that colours, sounds and the other ' secondary qualities ' are not inside the nervous system. And even less so are volitions : these are no *where :* the expanse of ocean is not within the search-light, nor is the abstract *order* of the objects illumined, in any one *place* at all.

A person who examines candidly his own wishes and desires can manage, when these are vivid enough to allow of introspection, coherently to state them. This alone proves that volitions are logico-mathematical or neutral entities and as amenable to general inspection and discussion as curvilinear motions and barometric readings. We often have, of course, vague desires which we cannot state, which elude introspection, but the same is true, as we have seen, of other conscious contents ; and the fact does not in the least prejudice the status, as neutral entities, of volitions.

I neither find in my own consciousness, nor believe that others find in theirs, the essentially subjective and by principle unimpartable volitions that are the topic of so much discussion. They are as occult as the Dinge-an-sich, or that conception of matter that Berkeley so vehemently refuted.

Now it will hardly be denied that all volitions, desires, wishes and yearnings (in so far as the latter are not emotions mistaken for desires) are *purposes ;* they are purposes to get, have, or do something. The actions of a man who has a purpose are governed by that purpose : and this is, in so far as he is able to carry out his purpose, the *law* of his actions. And in so far it may be observed by others that his actions are the logical consequence of his law or purpose. We have now to inquire what sort of entity a purpose is, and whether purposes similar to human purposes can be found in the neutral realm, and logically prior to the categories of subject and object.

In his treatment of the many and the one, Royce[1] has shown that the unity of a finite or infinite series of logical entities lies in the one formula that generates them. The positive, whole-number series, for instance,

[1] Josiah Royce : "The World and the Individual," New York, 1900–1. See especially the Supplementary Essay to volume i.

is generated by a formula of adding one entity at a time and repeating the process indefinitely many times. There are many other such formulæ, and specially all the equations of curves and surfaces in analytic geometry are of such a kind. A simple case is the equation of a circle $x^2 + y^2 = r^2$: where, given the plane surface with the axes of X and Y, the formula is the law that generates the circle. Any equation that expresses a variable quantity as the function of one or more given independent variables is such a genetic formula. These formulæ are really laws and they are ordinarily so termed when the manifold under discussion involves the concept of motion. The laws of physics are obviously this sort of thing. A body falls by gravitation with an acceleration of 32·2 feet per second per second, so that from the formula $s = 16·1 \; t^2$ the distance that the body has fallen can at any moment be logically deduced. The formula is the law by which the body falls ; it generates the fall. Similarly from the formula $v = 32·2 \; t$ the velocity at any moment can be computed.

It may be objected that laws and formulæ are ineffective to generate anything, that nothing falls because 32·2 feet per second per second are spoken of :—a ' real impact,' an *Anstoss*, *vis viva* is needed to push it, and so forth. But it is to be remembered that the notion of an effective *Anstoss* is no longer accepted in mechanics. The pioneers in doing away with this conception were Kirchhoff and Hertz, who particularly declared that the hidden, inner impetus was no part of the world of experience, and that it was not to be looked for or thought of in physics. Wherefore explanation became for these two men the same as exact description. Natural necessity became logical necessity, and all

notion of an inner repulsion was rejected. This latter
is, in fact, another survival of animism.[1]

The reason why no clouds or mountains fall when the
law of fall is stated is, as we have seen in the chapter on
universals and particulars, that the abstract law is a
universal, while clouds and mountains are particulars,
are concrete embodiments in space and time of much
more than the law of gravitation. The objection that if
natural necessity is logical necessity and laws or genetic
formulæ are the sole efficient causes, the bare verbal
statement of a law should operate like dynamite, is a
reversal of Johnson's intended refutation of Berkeley :
that if Bishop Berkeley would trouble to thwack his cane
smartly on a rock, he should find that it would encounter
an obstacle. Johnson contended that a real physical
impact was no mere idea ; and this is the reverse of the
contention that a neutral formula is no real cause in
nature. A universal law defining the motion of an X will
not tip tables or move mountains, because a table or
mountain is not merely an X but a great deal more
besides. And it is to be borne in mind that wherever
one of these neutral laws becomes a particular, as when
embodied in an algebra or other logical universe of
discourse, it does operate with unqualified efficiency ;
and this, its effective operation, constitutes precisely
that which the symbolic logician studies.

---

[1] This was a profound advance in theoretical physics, and Wundt,
for instance, has wrongly stated in his " Logik " (Stuttgart, 1893,
2te Aufl., Bd. I, S. 615) that " Kirchhoff treats mechanics as a
' descriptive ' science only by broadening the concept of description
so as to include what was formerly called explanation." By discarding the word ' explanation ' and using ' description ' in its stead,
Kirchhoff and Hertz expressly intended to do away with all notion
of inner impetus or *Anstoss*. And their contention has been accepted
by the most competent physicists.

Genetic formulæ and natural laws are of course expressed in a great variety of symbolic terms, while the typical form is that of an equation : and the natural laws that are exactly, or quantitatively known are always so expressed. Now the equation gives the values of the quantity that is considered dependently variable, if the independent variable assumes definite, successive values. If the latter are such and such values, in turn, the former is bound to be successively such and such values. The equation is a law that generates the dependent series. And the unity of any series or function lies in the formula that generates it.

Now if we examine candidly any human purpose, we shall see that it is nothing other than just such a generative law. Merely it is seldom quantitatively exact, and therefore can seldom be expressed in equational form. It is, for instance, my desire to walk along the edge of a cliff, keeping near enough to the edge so as to see the surf below and far enough from it so as to run no danger of falling over. And I will so to walk. This purpose is at once then the law of my movements ; it generates them and is itself their sole unity. If I succeed in keeping everywhere just two feet from the cliff's edge, then my volition can be expressed in an equation as a constant function of the contour of the cliff's edge. And it is to be insisted that not only is this what another person might say about my course in walking, but it is absolutely all that I can discover about it in my own most " subjective " recesses of consciousness. Simply, I wish to walk along the edge of the cliff, to have a view over, and to be safe. If I keep two feet from the edge, I am like the body that falls with an acceleration of 32·2 feet per second per second. It is quite the same, too, if my purpose is to run a race, to gain wealth, or to become a scholar. The purpose becomes the unifying and generating law of my actions. A purpose or volition is then nothing at all mysteriously subjective, and it is a law of the same type as is found in the neutral realm logically antecedent to either matter or mind.

Several objections may be raised here : first, that a purpose in consciousness is not such a simple affair as has been described ; second, that there is a difference between having a purpose and acting on it, for one may have it, yet either not wish or not be able to act on it ; third, one's actions may discover a purpose quite different from any that is in the actor's consciousness.

As to the scrutability of the purpose in consciousness and its entire likeness to a generating law ; this must be stoutly reaffirmed.   The total state of consciousness at any moment, of course, contains much else than any one purpose : it is a cross-section that includes colours, sounds, odours, emotions, time, space and very many other conceptual entities, including other purposes. These are, however, not this purpose itself, which is always distinct from the items that simultaneously crowd in.   Any person who is blessed with an ordinary degree of mental coherence, and specially anyone versed in introspection, is able to distinguish his purposes from sensations and emotions.   Inability to do so is a mark of mental deficiency.   The other accompanying items in consciousness may be, and some of them are, germane to the purpose in the sense that they con-stitute the Given, like the independent variables in an equation, of which the purposive act is to be a function. I cannot purpose to walk along a cliff if no cliff is in my consciousness.   Yet these are not themselves the purpose, which is a formula that generates a new dependent function of the independent items that are given.

Again, one may have a purpose and yet either not care or not be able to act on it. If one does not care to act on it, it is because one has some other conflicting purpose : one wishes to do this, but just here and now one wishes more to do something else ; or one desires this and would try to attain it if one did not more desire that which is inconsistent with this : and so forth. The case in which one has a purpose but *cannot* act on it, is like the previous case, except that the conflicting purpose is itself outside one's consciousness, a contradictory proposition perhaps in the form of a law of nature. Some purpose in the world of time and space, but not at the time included in one's conscious cross-section, interferes. Such a possibility in no wise invalidates the doctrine of purposes as genetic formulæ : it merely illustrates their possibility of contradiction. For purposes and laws are propositions, and propositions often meet in contradiction.

Lastly, one's actions may evince purposes of which one is not introspectively conscious at all, as when a sleep-walker successfully makes his way along the roof of a house, or as when the general trend of a person's life obeys some law (say of shiftlessness or enterprise) on which he has never consciously reflected. This is volition at the same unreflective, so-called ' unconscious ' stage that I have previously pointed out in the case of sensations. And the view that I there set forth concerning the inability of reflection to survey the content of consciousness is reinforced by the acknowledged inadequacy of reflection to take complete cognizance of

U

one's volitions. A person does something without 'thinking of what he is doing'; or a child "is just naturally good without ever even knowing it." And this goodness is not a property of the mere nervous system : it is a law governing the activities of a know-ledge-system, and none but the most brutish materialist would locate it elsewhere. Indeed it is significant that after our most trivial and habitual, voluntary acts, it is often our very most dominant life purposes that most successfully evade the scrutiny of reflection. It is in old age that one becomes reflectively conscious, often-times, of the purposes that have, unknown to reflection, governed one's life. " Why was I so determined," says the old man, " to follow every wayward course that offered : why did I not think what I was making of my life ? " And he admits that although ' unconscious,' these are his own deeds and that he rightly bears the penalties. It is indeed not too much to say that, except in the most reflective temperaments, the profoundly ethical motives (whether bad or good) that govern a person's deeds, are more adequately represented, so far as reflective consciousness goes, in the minds of other persons than in his own. So little is it true that volitions are ' subjective,' private to the inner self. But this relation to reflection does not affect the fact that volitions are laws governing life, partly selecting, partly shaping, and partly supplementing that which is Given in knowledge : and that these laws are of the same texture as the laws of nature and the generating pro-positions of the neutral realm of being. The one deciding question is, concerning either one's own or another's volitional life,—What laws describe the sequence of terms in this conscious cross-section ? for those laws

are the volitions of that mental system. It is the same
question that one asks concerning a physical manifold,—
What laws describe the sequence of terms in this system ?
In both cases alike there may be little coherence or
much, few laws or many, laws operating harmoniously
or plentifully crossed in contradiction. In both cases
the problem is strictly that of the exact description of a
neutral manifold.

A further confirmation of this thesis that volitions
are impersonal, neutral formulæ, and are in no wise
inscrutable or sacred to the ' subjective ' realm, is
afforded by social psychology. In this science the will
of a sect, nation, race or other group of individuals is
spoken of in the most objective manner : such volitions
are described as freely as the movements of plants,
animals, or any other objects of experience. And this
could not be if a volition were something peculiarly
subjective, found only in consciousness, and *toto cœlo*
different from the objects of the ' outer ' world. Nor
can the social psychologist pretend that he uses the
term volition merely by analogy, for analogy, like
representation, means partial identity, and complete
identity in all those respects for which the analogy
holds good. The statute laws of a state are as much the
volitions of that state, as the determination to take a
walk is the volition of a person. A volition is a law, a
genetic formula, and is statable, discutable, and open
to the gaze of all who care to take cognizance of it.
If one person has a purpose that another does not know,
it is equally true and important that the first person
has a spinal column, a parlour and a bank account
that the second may not have seen. But the latter can
take action to make good this deficiency, and there is no

principle that makes the former's purpose more inscrutable than his parlour or his bank account.

It is a classic tradition that the feelings have a peculiarly intimate connection with volition, and indeed of a sort that is virtually causal. Thus in Hume, the ' idea of a movement ' is not a volition until the ' feeling of pleasantness ' is joined with it ; whereupon this feeling, precisely like a psychical *vis viva*, imparts life and efficiency to the idea of movement, which is then promptly executed. We need not here consider the minuter mechanism of volition, and if, like Hume, anyone should now find that he wills no act except an agreeable feeling is connected with the idea, I should admire but not presume to gainsay his findings. In the case of some persons, at least, the spring of action is a different one. But we have already seen (p. 111) that emotions and feelings are neutral entities, or groups of these, precisely as objective as the other components of being : and their occurrence anywhere in the psychic manifold presents on this score no difficulties to our present theory of consciousness. But that the feeling of pleasantness or unpleasantness is a *vis viva* that sets in motion our activities is a pure myth. We have seen that in physical systems no such entity as the ' living force ' is now looked for ; nothing but functions, equations, laws. These are all forms of propositions, and the motions of the physical world depend on the remarkable generative property of propositions which I have termed logical activity. Now the two feelings of pleasantness and unpleasantness are qualities, that is terms, and however they may be conjoined in consciousness with purposes (propositions) they are certainly no source of activity. And this view certainly accords better than the Humian,

with the rather common experience that we will many
things in which the quality of agreeableness does not in
the least come in question. It is generally admitted,
and the inadequacy of hedonistic ethics confirms it,
that the volitions of a right-minded person, at least, are
governed not by feelings but by intentions, purposes,
propositions. And while there is no *vis viva* in either
object or subject, there is activity in both ; and activity
inheres in propositions.

There is another spurious sort of volition, that is
perhaps classed more often under ' desires ' than elsewhere : it is the case in which a conceivably attainable
end is persistently prominent in consciousness. The
waiting-maid who has fed herself on tales of high-heeled
duchesses has a gnawing ' desire' for wealth and
grandeur, as the lad who gloats on penny shockers
desires to be a bandit. But it is the end effect and not
the more or less feasible avenues of approach thereto,
that is here in consciousness : the girl wishes to be a
' regular duchess ' and the boy a full-fledged outlaw
with a hundred scalps at his belt and a thundering
reputation that sets the whole gulch quaking. Such
' desires ' are common enough in maturer and more
serious minds. But even here they should not be
classed under volitions, for they are merely *fixed ideas*.
To be sure the purpose, ' I will become rich,' is a proposition and a true volition ; but this, the true volition,
leads to anything rather than floating dreams of luxury
or fixed ideas of how to spend. The spurious desire of
which I speak, if accompanied by any volition, is
accompanied by the will to dissipate rather than to
accumulate capital. And these ' desires,' if so they
ought to be called, are more or less fixed ideas of un-

attained conditions accompanied by the emotions of
dissatisfaction and desultory yearning : and if accompanied at all by volitions, then by such as are ill-calcu-
lated to attain the end desired. The criterion of true
volition is not complicated : one has but to survey
as much of the consciousness in question as is accessible
to one, and then to see whether the proposition (re-
taining our illustration) ' X accumulates wealth ' is
necessary in order to *describe* (just as in any physical
manifold) what X does. X may never become wealthy,
for adversity or contrary volitions may remove as fast
as opportunity permits the accumulation of, money :
yet it may still be found that certain conscious sequences
there can be described by nothing but ' X accumulates
wealth.' Contradictory volitions, too, as contradictory
propositions in the physical realm, may be plentiful in
the person in question, such as the will to be extrava-
gant, and as volitions they may all cohabit : but in
the explicit life sequence the latter purpose will beget
extravagance that will deplete the accumulations
generated by the former volition ' X accumulates
wealth ' ; so that in the explicit life sequence wealth
will not result from the implicit purpose to accumulate.
This latter has been contradicted.

It should seem that a confusion of these fixed ideas of
ends with true purposes is the source of the supposed
distinction between ' final ' and ' efficient ' causes. The
time-worn debate as to whether nature is ' purposive '
and the ' argument from design ' certainly mistook the
idea of an end for a purpose ; as indeed the word ' tele-
ology ' shows. Certainly in consciousness the idea of an
end may accompany a true purpose ; but it is not the
same as this, and as often as otherwise it accompanies

a purpose which contradicts the attainment of that end. But since true volitions are precisely what the laws of nature are—formulæ that generate explicit sequences which ' fulfil ' them—it follows of course that nature is purposive and thoroughly so. The notion (which can be found in Aristotle) that conscious purposes are ' final ' purposes or fixed ideas of the end is as erroneous a notion as well can be. Where volitions were fixed ideas the impact of an ' Ego ' was indeed necessary to get anything actually to move : and this Ego " to which all objects are presented and to which everything mental is referred " is to the conscious manifold precisely what that ' God,' which was argued from teleological design, is to the physical manifold. The former has retarded physiological psychology as much as this divine clock-maker, that sat beside his mechanism to regulate it and reset it from time to time, has retarded physical science. Neither science has any room for such outside agencies. God is in and through the physical manifold, and indeed the mental ; as the ego is in and through the conscious manifold.

And this error led to another, the supposed antithesis between free will and determinism. The ' Ego ' was of course not free if she was a stagnant term watching the play of mechanical forces ; and physics found indeed that ' God ' was not free to interfere in this same spectacle. But there is really no antithesis whatsoever. That man is free whose acts fulfil his purposes :—this is ' practical freedom,' and such a man has ' the innate sense of being practically free.' The question whence come his purposes is as irrelevant and meaningless as some others that we have seen ;—whither go the shapes of bursting bubbles ? If a purpose is his purpose

and if his acts fulfil it, he is free.   Now we have seen that
the purposes of the knowledge manifold are propositions
that actively generate series, precisely as do the laws of
nature :   volition is therefore as effective, and in the
same way effective, as the laws of nature.   Now all that
is *is*, and is therefore ' determined,' but if the human will
is confronted by a determined nature, so too is that
nature confronted by a determined will.   Each can
contradict the other even as one physical motion contradicts another, or both can co-operate, or *both for a
space be identical*.   One who holds an apple in the air
contradicts for a space the law of gravity, by his voluntary purpose, quite as the supporting bough contradicted
it before the apple was plucked.   The supposed difference
in the two cases rests on two errors :   first, the notion
that nature contains no contradictions ;   and second,
the myth of the Ego that is *not in* its volitions but applies
the mythical *vis viva* from *outside* the system.   Now
nature is everywhere purposive, but it is also largely
contra-purposive ;   and it is in one system, the neutral
realm of being, with minds.   Therefore a purpose in the
mental manifold is as potent as any other, nor is the
' Ego ' something outside and *toto cœlo* distinct from the
one inclusive system.   Such an outside Ego would be
indeed as powerless as ' God ' himself to interfere with
predetermined nature :   but no more could such an Ego
interfere with predetermined mind.   Volition is then as
free and as determined as is physical nature.

But we have seen that while contradictory propositions are free to *be*, they are not free either in mind or
matter to generate contradictory systems of terms.
When this is imminent propositions nullify each other,
and the meaningless *is* not.   But in this opposition,

volition comes off no worse than nature. We believe
that Mars is inhabited by thinking beings because it is
not in the purposes of inanimate nature to produce lines
so straight as those of the canals. And inanimate
nature has conceded much to human will in every piece of
engineering construction. So has human will conceded
much to nature. No purpose then is free when it *meets*
a contradictory purpose : a man's will is not free when
on a desert island or in prison he wills to go somewhere
else : nor is nature free when men fell the virgin forest
and quarry the eternal hills wherewith to build a city.
The human will is free just as nature is free ; and each
is free to contradict itself or the other. On the whole the
gravest restriction laid on free will is its own entertain-
ment of mutually conflicting purposes. It is here that
the erroneous becomes the evil.

One more point alone remains in connection with
volition : it is the question of the *unity* of personality ;
and by the word ' continuity ' unity is often meant.
Of true continuity of course there is very little, and
indeed the unity itself has been much exaggerated.
The common idea seems to be that the complete unity
of personality is guaranteed by the ' Ego ' which is
empowered to take reflective cognizance of a person's
total conscious life from birth to death. It is said to be
like a mirror that by reflecting the whole within one
frame unifies that whole. Perhaps some child can tell
what the frame of the ' Ego ' is ; and of course it would
be better to have a second Ego to reflect the first, and
then a third, and so on to infinity. The nth Ego would
ensure a truly transcendental unity. And agreeably
to this we are offered plans of the nervous system
whereby one single ' cell-body ' sits aloft (formerly in

the pineal gland but now in the superior frontal lobe and as far mesially as anatomy permits) in splendid isolation on the pinnacle of the pyramidally planned nervous system. As McDougall says,[1] " The diagram explains itself. It clearly implies that the higher in the nervous system the impulses reach, the fewer the number of cells they pass through in each level, so that in the higher levels the same cells or centres are affected by impulses from very different lower centres. It is suggested that we have here a key to the understanding of the unity of consciousness. . . . Do not such attempts imply a careless materialism ? " But how else, pray, could the Ego ' mirror ' the totality of consciousness, and so ' unify ' it ?

We will dismiss the figure of the mirror, since all but minds at the two extremes of learning well know that the mirrored reflection of a picture has neither less nor more unity than the picture, even though it be vastly smaller. Of course this Ego cannot survey the total experience of a life at one gasp ; it takes its leisure. And of course it does not recall all the insignificant details ; it doesn't wish to. But it may still tell an interesting story, and a fairly useful withal,—though embroidered here and there with untruth in order to lend point, interest and the satisfactory air of importance to one's past self. The Ego surely is a grand unifier, and besides, what other unifier is there ?

Quite another. But so far as it goes, I will not deny the unifying power of introspective or reflective thought : which, however, is due to something besides the faculty for combining conscious details into one ' frame.' There is but one source of unity and that is law. If a

[1] William McDougall : " Mind," 1898, N.S. 7, p. 175.

system of terms, as seemingly discrete as one will, fulfils or satisfies one law or proposition, the system has unity: and under no other conditions has it unity. I should not venture such a commonplace, indeed, were not the mirror and the ' Ego ' still so popular. With this principle in mind let us inquire how far introspection lends unity to consciousness. And let us suppose that one who is near the close of his life, for only then can introspection operate on the whole to unify it, resolves, " I will recall my past life." Then follows a series of ideas that is a cross-section of the past, partially identical therewith, and having somewhat the same relation to the original past experiences, as these had to ' real ' time and space. Identicals are here repeated. Now this series is grouped together in the man's present ex-perience as ' my past ' ; and as ' framed ' by his present consciousness it has indeed a so-called unity, the unity of a collection. Now the unity of a collection is not an intrinsic unity, for a collection is a unit only as it is a group in some including system that frames it. " Intro-spection is retrospective attention to an experience which I now surround and surmount." This is the slight truth there is in the unifying power of the ' Ego ' that ' *frames* ' what it reflects. But this confers not a particle of internal unity on the past itself, *if* the past is *impartially* reproduced. It is precisely like one man's looking over the life of another, but that other life is no more unified for figuring in some other system as ' X's life.' Furthermore, as I have already shown, this recall of the past can make no pretensions to being complete, nor could it be more than a mere skeleton even if it limited itself to a short stretch of the immediate past : and in addition to this it falsifies the past by adding items, and often very many, that were never in the past. I need scarcely adduce the experiments that prove this empirical fact. Reflection, then, is inadequate and untruthful, and if it were complete and true it would confer no unity on a life.

But now reflection does not reproduce past experience impartially. It selects what is ' *significant,*' and this is invariably that which coheres by virtue of being the embodiment of some law or purpose. And the important point is that reflection is useful not in proportion to its completeness, but in proportion to its very incompleteness, its selective partiality. It is very unsatisfactory when reflection mirrors the past as old women tell stories—with all irrelevancies included. James[1] calls this ' impartial redintegration.' If mirroring within one frame were the source of unity, the degree of unity would vary directly with the number of details included and not inversely. The reflective recall of the past, then, in spite of its untruth and its inadequacy, is more coherent than the past, more orderly : and in *this* sense reflection does indeed supply some unity to consciousness. And introspection in general is less significantly a recall of the conscious past, than it is a perception of principles as opposed to discrete details ; for in life the latent period of the perception of coherencies and principles is considerable. Now reflection cannot unify by selecting coherencies of past experience if there are few or none to select : though of course it conjures up some, but this in its capacity of falsifier. Therefore the unifying power of reflection really depends on something prior : and this is the coherence or purposiveness

---

[1] W. James : " The Principles of Psychology," New York, 1893, vol. i., p. 569.

of the life itself. That conscious life has unity that fulfils a purpose, and if it fulfils a purpose it needs no introspection or retrospection to give it unity, for it *is* a unit. The only purpose that a consciousness system can fulfil is of course a volition ; and herein is a moral. The unity of personality depends directly on the presence in consciousness of purposes that do not contradict but harmonize, and the dominance of all by one supreme purpose. This purpose is the ' I ' which wills all sub-sidiary purposes. It need not reflect on itself nor know itself, and indeed it is my belief that such a process is meaningless and impossible. But *this I* is in and through the whole life ; it *is* the proposition that alone describes (as Hertz used the word) the entire activities of the conscious life in question. Of course, the traditional doctrine of the ' Ego ' is like the doctrine of the atone-ment, in that all who believe thereon shall have unity everlasting ; and those who do not believe have to look well to their ways if they hope for salvation. And it seems to me, both theoretically and practically, that aside from this spurious security borrowed from the ' Ego ' most personalities do actually have a very limited degree of unity. Their ' I ' is distinctly a logical variable. Not one, but many purposes, and these sadly contradictory, describe most human lives. And in view of this, the inscrutable subjective ' Ego ' is a relatively easy means of securing personality : and many will continue to carry one in the pocket, offered freely as they are to all students of psychology. Yet perhaps some few will lay no such flattering unction to their souls, but rather take the hardier course. The will is free : and if not free to be at one with nature, which is cross-purposed with itself, the will is free to be at one with its own self, to be but one, clean-cut, firm, and perhaps eternally enduring.

The unifying property of purposes suggests a matter of terminology which, although unrelated to will, it may not be amiss to place at the end of this chapter. It is a task for logic to discover the relation between the formula that generates a series and the series generated, the law and the motions governed by the law, the purpose and the system of terms that embody it. The two are at least not simply identical, as the two sides of an equation are not merely identical. In surveying any unfamiliar and complicated manifold, such as the oscillations of a compound pendulum, the rotations of a printing press, or the gesticulations in a foreign market-place, we get at first only an impression of chaos. We see very well the successive motions that take place, yet the " meaning," the unifying purpose does not at once appear. So we may trace successive points along a curve and yet not know that the curve is an ellipse. By persistent observation, however, we learn more and more until at length, and often suddenly, the meaning, or the law emerges. It jumps into our consciousness. And while I fully assent to the arguments of Kirchhoff and Hertz that physics discovers no active principle that ' explains why ' change takes place, so that science is only ' exact description,' I believe that we ought still to keep the word explanation to signify that completer description which not merely enumerates, for instance, the points on the ellipse but rather gives this curve's genetic formula. Descriptive knowledge would then be all knowledge that enumerates features, describes motions and so forth, but that falls short of containing the underlying and unifying rules or laws of such features and motions : while explanatory knowledge would give just these laws and would be relieved of enumerating the explicit features or motions generated thereby, that is, really, deduced therefrom. Such a use of the terms " description " and " explanation " would recognize and preserve precisely that quality of superior satisfactoriness which in popular usage now attaches to the latter term. An explanation as thus defined would be less cumbersome and more enlightening than description ; it would show the significance, " the reason why." For the law or purpose *is* the reason why : and Kirchhoff and Hertz were quite right in asserting that no further reason why is to be sought for or even imagined. Furthermore, in the acquirement of knowledge, whether by the individual or by science as a whole, the step from merely enumerating details to discovering laws is significant enough for language to recognize the distinction. To study a manifold by enumerating and classifying its several members is so utterly different from studying it deductively by means of its underlying laws when these are once discovered, and the latter knowledge is so superior to the former, that it seems scarcely just to say, as is often said, that the work of science comes down to nothing but classification. Explanation as above defined, but not in the sense in which Kirchhoff and Hertz objected to the term, is surely the true end of science.

The upshot of this chapter is that the laws of nature and the purposes of mind are alike propositions, which are the active elements of the neutral realm of being. Purposes are no more essentially private to individual minds than any other neutral entity : and it is merely an apparent distinction between these and physical laws, that many of the latter (although not all) are quantitatively known so as to be stated in equations, while most human purposes are statable less exactly. Civil and social laws are not thought to be ' subjective,' although they too are not expressed in the form of equations. The will is as much and as little free as is nature. That will is freest and that personality most unified in which the purposes are not contrary, but are duly subordinated to some single purpose.

CHAPTER XV

THE EMANCIPATION OF PHYSIOLOGY
FROM PHILOSOPHY

THE foregoing chapter completes such defence and interpretation as seem to me just now necessary to offer, of the definition of consciousness which is the theme of this volume. I have several times called this definition a ' theory,' meaning, however, by this not that it is a working hypothesis merely for which subsequent experience is to provide the foundation, but a ' theory ' in the physicist's sense, that is, a proposition or set of propositions which are already established by well-known facts and from which deductions may now be drawn. Certainly these deductions may be verified or refuted, and therewith the theory, yet I sincerely believe that an unbiased study of the knowing process so far as we are now able to study it, yields just this description of mind and no other, and this definition of consciousness.

It is generally conceded that dualistic accounts of knowledge meet insuperable difficulties when they are called on to describe inter-relations of the dual substances, that is, to define their mutual relations. Monistic theories, on the other hand, have been either materialistic or idealistic, and each has been found to deny the *being* of either mind or matter, in spite of the vast amount of dialectic offered in order to refute such a charge. But what is worse, each has virtually denied the *being* of the very entities that it asserted to be the fundamental substance by exalting this substance to a universal predicate. For if everything is, for instance, idea, then there are no entities that are more distinctly ideas than any others. And this is untrue. Clearly nothing can be predicated of the one universal substance, and if one looks for a class of entities of whose substance nothing can be said one finds precisely such a class in the logical and mathematical concepts. Their substance is strictly neutral and nothing further can be said of it. But logical and mathematical entities are composed of this neutral stuff, and *not* this stuff of those entities. The underlying neutrality of substance is best seen in these ' concepts ' merely because these are the simplest elements of the realm of being, which we know about. The substance of *being*, then, is strictly neutral, and out of this substance are composed or compounded logical and mathematical entities, physical objects, and minds : and the order here given is the order of their increasing complexity. How this is I have tried to set forth in the preceding pages. Our theory is a strictly monistic one. Such a thing one sees mentioned, now and then, as a desideratum ; but aside from the one-sided monisms of idealism and materialism, the accounts offered confine themselves to figurative hints that mind and matter are two aspects of reality, like the two sides of a shield. Recently it has been urged that consciousness is a species of ' energy ' ;[1] and this is the

---

[1] Wilhelm Ostwald : " Vorlesungen über Naturphilosophie," Leipzig, 1902, Vorl. 19; and W. McDougall : " A Contribution Towards an Improvement in Psychological Method," Mind, 1898, N.S. VII. (See specially p. 386 ff.)

solution of several physiological psychologists. Of this it is sufficient to say that if consciousness is an energy in the true sense, that is a form of motion in time and space, the view is mere materialism : whereas if consciousness is an ' energy ' in some other sense, the word is a mere figure of speech and no more able to bridge the dualistic gap than the ' two aspects of a shield.' In neither case does the view that consciousness is an energy resolve the difficulties of epistemology.

The first indication of a way of escape from Cartesian dualism, so far as I am able to ascertain, is to be found in Avenarius. And if I have referred to this author very little in the preceding pages, it is for two reasons : first, he so neglected to explain the epistemological and ontological status of his ' Aussagewerte ' that many serious readers believe him to have been a materialist ; and second, it is difficult if not impossible to translate his account of the ' System C ' and its workings into the accepted language of physiology. The great contribution of Avenarius, as I view it, is his ' exclusion of the introjection.' I have therefore aimed to provide an epistemological setting for this ' exclusion,' and in speaking of physiological processes to use physiological terms. The only other theoretical discussions which I know of that will fit unmodified, into the theory here offered, are the curiously misnamed ' antimetaphysical preliminaries ' to Mach's " Analyse der Empfindungen," and several recent articles by James.[1]

[1] W. James : " la Notion de conscience," Archives de Psychologie, 1905, t. V. " Does Consciousness Exist ? " Journal of Philosophy, Psychology, and Scientific Methods, 1904, vol. i. " How Two Minds Can Know One Thing." " Is Radical Empiricism Solipsistic ? " " The Place of Affectional Facts in a World of Pure Experience." *Ibid.*, 1905, vol. ii.

The theory of consciousness here offered is strictly monistic. I have tried to show how the manifolds called conscious must and do arise at a certain stage of complexity in the realm of being. The mental is deducible from a system that is absolutely non-mental, and mind is no new substance nor an isolated and independent system in the realm of being. Now in attempting this deductive account of consciousness, I have had one prime purpose in view, and that is to free once and for all the study of the physiology of brain and nervous system from its present mysterious and retarding association with metaphysics. For, as I have already pointed out, metaphysics has successfully imposed its *caveat* on every physiologist who straightforwardly tries to study and describe the workings of the brain. He is warned that here the trivial notions of physiology will by no means do ; the plain empirical findings derived from the study of other parts of the organism will not apply to the cerebrum. For here sits the soul ; here alone are the secondary qualities or rather the unqualified representers of these qualities ; here is performed the daily miracle of interaction ; here, in short, mystery and ambiguity must prevail. Everybody is familiar with many solemn discussions by sound and able scientists whether in the cerebrum energy is not subtracted from the physical world to be returned when and as ' consciousness ' ordains, with assurances on the one hand that this would not affect the principle of conservation of energy, and on the other that it would ; one is familiar with the guarded and almost apologetic thesis of Huxley[1] that man is an automaton, and its

---

[1] T. H. Huxley : " On the Hypothesis that Animals are Automata, and its History."

intended refutation by Lloyd Morgan[1] that "the primary aim, object and purpose of consciousness is control. Consciousness in a mere automaton is a useless and unnecessary epiphenomenon." The literature of psycho-physical parallelism is one of the most precious farces that modern science presents.

And this bedevilment of straightaway physiology continues. Here is a telling quotation from one who is probably to-day the leading English physiologist.[2] " We shall now venture a glance at certain reactions of the cerebral hemisphere itself : our survey must be circumspect for several reasons. By use of such methods as we are employing, artificial excitation and so on . . . little light is given in regard to much that goes on in an organ whose chief function is mentality itself." Thus a most competent physiologist is rendered ' circumspect,' tentative, and as it were despairing, because he cannot hope that his mere physiological methods will avail aught in the cerebrum—the dark throne of ' mentality itself.' I could multiply instances indefinitely, but this one is typical, even at the present time, of physiologists and experimental psychologists alike. I know of but one exception, Münsterberg, whose view of the relation between mind and brain will presently be discussed.

Now my main purpose has been to show that this mystery concerning the action of the brain is pure buncombe, bequeathed to us by the absurd and in every way impossible representative theory of knowledge

[1] C. Lloyd Morgan : " Introduction to Comparative Psychology," London, 1894, p. 182.

[2] C. S. Sherrington : " The Integrative Action of the Nervous System," New York, 1906, p. 269.

with its preposterous introjection. The manifold of objects to which the nervous system responds is the conscious field of that organism, and in the organ of response (the brain and other nerve tissues) nothing, *absolutely nothing*, is to be looked for except just an organ of response. Certainly nothing else will be found. And if the manifold so responded to cannot be described in terms of the little material tennis-ball of Democritus, no more can the most ordinary ' objective ' process be described by the physicist or chemist in such terms. Every manifold when analysed reveals its neutral texture, but I have already gone into this sufficiently. The response of the nervous system, which of course cannot be described except in reference to that which is responded *to*, is the subject-matter of the nerve physiologist and the experimental psychologist alike. And this book will have fulfilled its purpose if it enforces the conviction that the organ of response is in every part a nervous mechanism and nothing more, and if it so emancipates the experimenter from his paralysing dread of epiphenomenon. There is no ghost whatsoever there. But epistemology has widely advertised the ghost, and therefore I have undertaken to show on epistemological grounds that there is no ghost, that the house of the brain is not haunted. Experimentation should feel itself free to go in, and study the simultaneous and successive complications of nervous response.

It remains to consider somewhat more in detail the programme thus laid out for experimental psychology. It will be recalled that a now antiquated psychology divided the nervous system into afferent and efferent portions : the afferent nervous impulses terminated in the epiphenomena of sensations and perceptions ; while the efferent impulses were initiated in the epiphenomenal realm by the soul's volitions. Between the afferent and efferent resided the soul. The remarkable experiments on the Rolandic area, of Goltz, Munk, Goldscheider, Hitzig, Exner, Ferrier and many others were and still are, taken to corroborate this view, since they were universally regarded as experiments on soul-localization (although ' brain-localization ' was the name given) and seemed to show that the motor region was anatomically distinct from the several sensory regions. A vexing question, however, remained in regard to sensations of the body's own willed movements. " Do we feel the impulse which we impart to the motor nerves at that moment when it leaves the central organ," said Lotze,[1] " or do we feel, not the impulse itself, but rather the more or less direct effect of its action on our muscles by means of a centripetal excitation returning thence to the brain ; or, thirdly, do we feel both of these processes ? As various as the opinions are in this regard, we must assert nevertheless that the second alternative alone truly states the fact." (S. 302) " The *voluntary use* of the movements which are possible to the body will therefore depend on two things ;—we must be able not merely to reproduce within ourselves those presentations or feelings which form the basis of each separate movement, but also be able so to combine them, simultaneously or successively, that the individual movements form together one foreseen, purposeful, harmonious operation. And since we can do this not otherwise than by reproducing at least vaguely the

[1] R. H. Lotze: " Medizinische Psychologie," Leipzig, 1852, S. 305.

sensational state which accompanied the movement as previously performed, and which was evoked by it, therefore the connection between conscious state and movement must be such that not only the first may be produced by the second, but also the second by the first." The idea expressed in this last clause, together with the controversy over ' innervation ' feelings that came subsequently, gave a distinct jog to the idea that the soul arbitrarily intermediates between all afferent and efferent impulses.

Then the French savants Charcot, Richer, Charles Richet, Binet, Féré and others, discovered and experimentally established the facts of ' dynamogenesis.' The outcome was, in the words of Richet,[1] that " one must not imagine that the organism remains inactive while experiencing sensations. Between sensations and movements there is a continuous chain." The motor and sensory areas of the brain were thus seen not to be so distinct as had been supposed ; the former seemed now more like an area containing *nuclei for simple movements*, whereas stimulation of the other cortical regions, though going over into movement, produced too complicated and in part mutually antagonistic movements, to yield definite or constant results. This vindication of the functional unity and continuity of the brain left the soul rather cramped for space. Clearly the soul must be dismembered, her volitional parts assigned to the precentral convolution, sensations to the occipital and temporal lobes, and ideation sprinkled here and there ;—

[1] Charles Richet : " l'Homme et l'intelligence," Paris, 1884, p. 522.

a barbarous procedure that had been already somewhat advocated by the associationists.

Such, very briefly, was the rise of the motor idea, which restored to physiology the functional unity of the nervous system, and to psychology showed that afferent processes are as essential to volition as are efferent, and that efferent are as necessary to sensation as are afferent. Still the soul, though pulverized and all but dead, lingered to clog, in some mysterious way which no man might explain, the otherwise purely physiological activities of the cerebrum, and, as we have seen, to debar the experimentalist from his legitimate studies. At about this juncture were presented two motor theories of the dependence of consciousness on nerve activity,—the Action-Theory of Münsterberg[1] and the Drainage-Theory of McDougall.[2] It is said[3] that a third has been devised by Dewey,[4] which I regret my inability to discuss because after careful perusal of the words I have been unable to gather a connected meaning. The theories of McDougall and Münsterberg both recognize the dependence of consciousness on efferent nervous processes ; both embody the lesson of dynamo-genesis, that the afferent and efferent nervous systems are continuous ; both agree to the minute partition of the soul and the dependence of the several portions on

[1] H. Münsterberg : "Grundzüge der Psychologie," Bd. I, Leipzig, 1900, Kap. 15.

[2] Wm. McDougall : " A Contribution towards an Improvement in Psychological Method," Mind, 1898, N.S. VII, and " Physiological Psychology," London, 1905.

[3] Charles H. Judd : "Movement and Consciousness," Yale Psych. Studies, 1905, N.S. i., p. 201 ff.

John Dewey : "The Reflex Arc Concept in Psychology," Psych. Review, 1896, vol. iii., p. 357.

processes in various parts of the cerebrum ; both decline to look for the ' unity of consciousness ' in the ultimate regulation of all nerve action by any hypothetical single master-cell or small group of cells ; and finally both profess to explain the inhibition of ideas by means of that reciprocal innervation of antagonistic muscles which was first pointed out by Charles Bell, in 1823, and which Sherrington has so notably studied. In so far both theories agree, and I believe that both are correct ; but beyond this they strikingly diverge. And inasmuch as both of these are actively under discussion, and as one is almost precisely such a one as the view of consciousness which I have presented naturally looks towards, while the other is repeatedly incompatible therewith, I wish to outline a comparison of the two.

In the first place, the theory of McDougall is radically dualistic (or if not that, then materialistic), while that of Münsterberg is not. Thus, in comparing the cerebral neurons with wires, McDougall writes :[1] " Are the wires the only existents presupposed by, and necessary to, the production of these effects ? Is all else fleeting process ? No, we are compelled to postulate, as a necessary condition of the developement of the magnetic field, a medium or substance which we call the ether. Just so we are compelled to postulate an existent, an immaterial being, in which the separate neural processes produce the elementary affections which we have called psychical elements, and this we call the soul. The soul then is the ground of unity of psychical processes, of individual consciousness. Is it anything more ? " This is the plainest dualism. Moreover, if " the soul then is the

---

[1] " Physiological Psychology," p. 168.

ground of unity," I cannot see what McDougall means when elsewhere, in discussing the ' Ego ' notion, he says :[1] " The hypothesis of the conscious psychological subject, to which everything mental must be referred, fails then to satisfy any one of the three primary necessities of a good working hypothesis. For it does not enable us to describe consistently what has been already [p. 19] ascertained ; it is not well adapted for the discovery of new truth, and it fails to take account of all the facts that must be dealt with." Certainly it is generally understood that the immaterial soul substance, which is ' the ground of unity of psychical processes,' is precisely this ' Ego ' which McDougall rejects. Since his " Psychology " was published seven years later than the article in " Mind," one must conclude that McDougall is now converted to the ' Ego.' In the dualistic opinion just quoted from the " Psychology," he asks concerning the immaterial soul which is the ground of unity, " Is it anything more ? ." And if we refer back to the article in "Mind" we may read :[2] " Now there is every reason to believe that consciousness occurs not only in myself, but in other men and in all the higher animals, and the principle of continuity makes it seem highly probable that it is present in some degree in the lower animals, and even in the very lowest [p. 28]. *It is then very difficult to believe that consciousness has no useful function.* Further, it would seem that it is consciousness on which natural selection has chiefly worked, and by which it has attained its greatest triumphs " (italics mine) : and again (on page 385), in regard to ' new functional connections between neurons,' we read : " If we reject

[1] " Mind," 1898, N.S. VII, p.18.
[2] *Ibid.*, p. 27.

the doctrine of the simple concomitance of consciousness . . . [p. 386] we must believe that consciousness is one of the conditions of the establishment of the new connections. . . . And unless we assume that the mind either destroys or creates energy, we must believe that consciousness is subject to the law of the transformation of energy, and that it has its heat equivalent that may some day be determined with more or less accuracy."

I do not know whether McDougall accounts this view materialistic : to be sure energy is not matter, but all materialists admit the physical ' reality ' of energy. In any case it seems indubitable that McDougall's view of consciousness is to all intents and purposes dualistic, and would eventually embrace the representative theory of knowledge ; it countenances the unifying ' Ego ' ; and intimates a heat equivalent therefor. (The last point has bearing later on.) I have argued in the preceding pages against all of these positions.

It is also clear that this view is as well calculated to stay the hand of the physiological investigator as any other : in the cerebrum he is directed to look for a mysterious energy of which there is no trace in other nerve tissue, into which nerve impulses may be transformed, and out of which, *per contra*, they may be initiated ; in other words, he is directed to look for the transformation of demonstrable nervous energy into a ' conscious energy ' that *cannot be scientifically detected*, and then for the reverse process. What hope, then, has the experimentalist of tracing the complicated course of nerve-currents when at certain points along their course (the synapses) they are likely to have commerce with undetectable magnitudes ? It is no encouragement to be told that this hypothetical conscious energy, of which *no trace has ever been physio-logically demonstrated*, may some day be detectable and may have its heat equivalent. Of course, if such a riddle were presented by empirical facts, it would have to be faced. But I trust that I have sufficiently demonstrated that this riddle is nothing but the ghostly remains of a false metaphysic. This conscious ' energy ' is hypothecated purely in order to bolster up an anti-quated and ridiculous theory of knowledge. I have gone to some length to show that the drainage-theory still harbours this metaphysical ghost, because Mc-Dougall in his capacity of scrupulous and sound experi-mentalist offers a view of the inhibition of ideas through reciprocal innervation that is *genuinely mechanical;* and since this is one of the perplexing questions of to-day, many of his readers have given their attention to this point, and quite overlooked the fact that the drainage-theory distinctly postulates an ' immaterial ' conscious-ness ' energy ' resident in the cerebrum and distinct from any form of energy with which the physicist or the physiologist is acquainted. By this hypothesis the drainage-theory, to my mind, forfeits its title as a strictly physiological theory of nervous response. That is not a truly physiological theory in which " conscious-ness is one of the conditions of the establishment of the new connections " between neurons, even though con-sciousness be *called* an ' energy.'

In this respect the action-theory leaves nothing to be desired. Although Münsterberg arrives at his theory from considerations as different as is well conceivable from the arguments which I have advanced in the fore-going chapters, this theory is a perfectly consistent and strictly physiological explanation of the dependence of consciousness on nerve-action. " *The action-theory* in its most comprehensive form would run as follows, that every sensation and therewith *every element of consciousness is dependent on the transition of stimulation over into discharge in the cortex, and in such wise that the quality of the sensation depends on the position of the path of stimulation, the intensity of the sensation on the strength of the stimulation, the feeling-tone of the sensation on the position of the path of discharge, and the vividness on the force of the discharge.* Thus the nerve-current will be given by the peripheral stimulation and the habitual paths of association, while the discharge will be governed by the state of the sub-cortical motor centres with their reciprocal relations of innervation."[1] " Here it is of course immaterial whether the sensory excitation comes directly from the periphery or by way of co-ordinated association centres."[2]   In the exposition of the action-theory explicit exception is taken to the apperception-theory, because it is untrue to a consistent principle of causal explanation in that it ascribes mental activity to ' the psychic.'[3]   For this the action-theory leaves no place : quite on the contrary, it assures the physiologist that there is nothing in or about the cerebrum save that which he can find and examine by his legitimate physiological methods.   No other psycho-physical theory does this save that of Avenarius, which, besides being inadequately grounded philosophically, is couched in too fantastic and ambiguous terms to be of practical service.

[1] H. Münsterberg : " Grundzüge der Psychologie," Leipzig, 1900, S. 548–9 (italics in the original).

[2] *Ibid.*, S. 531.

[3] *Ibid.*, S. 527 : S. 559.

In this respect the action-theory is one which precisely satisfies the psycho-physical requirements of the definition of consciousness here previously laid down : the responses of the nervous system alone come in question. But it may be asked how any psycho-physical theory that does not look for consciousness *in* the nervous system, can account for the acknowledged facts of soul-localization. Easily enough, I believe. It must be borne in mind that the *facts* of localization are : first, that the stimulation of certain cortical regions elicits certain responses (if the pre-central convolution is stimulated), or causes certain qualities to emerge in the conscious manifold (if the sensory areas), along with eliciting some inco-ordinated responses ; second, that the extirpation of these regions precludes such consciousness and such response (yet this is true often only when the lesion is relatively recent). If now the entrance into consciousness of a certain quality is dependent, as I have defined it, on a certain specific response of the nervous system, it follows of course that that quality is or is not in consciousness according as that specific response does or does not take place. But if responses are specific to different qualities and objects, they must specifically differ and must involve different nervous paths. Wherefore in one response and for one component of consciousness a certain part of the neural network is involved, for another a certain other. The general fact of localization is deducible from the definition which I have given. But I would ask in return how it is, if the conscious qualities are *in* the brain, depending (according to the usual view) on ' specific energies ' of the various cortical cells, that cortical cells adjacent to a lesion are ever able to function vicariously for the

cells that are destroyed ? The reacquirement of specific
responses is physiologically demonstrable and explicable, but the transfer of ' energies ' specific to cells
that are dead over to neighbouring cells that supposably
already have their own ' specific energies ' is a total
mystery.

So too even when the response is most complicated,
our definition of consciousness calls for a ' localization '
even more minute than has yet been demonstrated, and
precisely such a one as the action-theory postulates,—
a distinct quality, feature or atom in the conscious manifold for each complicating element in the response, that
is, for each neurone, fibrilla or synapse. A response
to one simple entity would be simple, but to a manifold
of such, as to any physical object or to a complex
situation, must be as complicated and involve as many
part-responses as the number of entities to which response is made : and these specific components of complicated responses must involve specific components of
the neural network. Thus in the words of Sherrington,[1]
" the juxtaposition of groups of specially refined
receptors in one set of segments, the leading or head
segments, conduces toward their simultaneous stimulation by several agencies emanating from one and the
same environmental object. . . . This alliance of reaction, we have seen, finds expression as mutual rein-
forcement in action upon a final common path. Thus a
reaction is synthesized which deals with the environmental object not merely as a stimulus possessing one
property, but as a ' thing ' built up of properties [p. 351].
And it is in the exercise of the distance-receptors with
their extensive range overlapping that of other receptors

[1] *Op. cit.*, p. 347.

that the reflexes which relate to ' objects ' in the sense
that they are reflexes synthesized from receptors of
separate species become chiefly established." Such a
synthesized reflex is what I have termed a ' specific
response ' : and it is to be remembered that the final
common path is in such case not a single efferent neurone
nor even a single group of these.[1] Similarly, too, in the
case of memory and ideation, when the present stimulation is a less massive factor in the response, " there is
based upon the ' distance-receptors ' a relatively
enormous neural superstructure possessing million-
sided connections with multitudinous other nervous
arcs and representing untold potentialities for redistribu-
tion of so-to-say stored stimuli by *associative recall.*"[2]
And quite consonantly in Münsterberg's exposition
of the action-theory we read :[3] " When attention goes
over into apperception in the narrower sense, we shall
assume that through previous exercise there exists a
molecular disposition in the motor centres by virtue of
which a stimulus can initiate a more complex reaction
than its isolated application in and for itself would have
elicited ; the reaction is response [*Antwort*] to a total
situation of which the present stimulus is merely a cue,
and this more intricate reaction in its psycho-physical
ramifications among sensory processes, is the basis of
distinction between apperception and perception. To
comprehend an object means to execute a specific
[*bestimmten*] type of action." In such wise the programme is laid out for a psychological atomism such as
I have already mentioned in Chapter XI, and for a
correspondingly minute tracing out, eventually, of the

[1] *Ibid.*, pp. 142–3.   [2] *Ibid.*, p. 352.
[3] *Op. cit.*, S. 551.

Y

function which each least participating neural element has in the simultaneous and successive complications of response. Perhaps the term ' localization ' will be a convenient one to keep, but it means not localization of the soul, but identification with each neural element of the function it has in the building up of specific responses to outer objects and to each of their least, neutral components. And the soul's activity, its free volition is to be looked for elsewhere, but not here in the domain of pure physiology. " Physiologically," Münsterberg has said, " every act, including the acts of free volition, is nothing but a reflex."[1] In this respect the action-theory is tenable and the drainage-theory is not.

In the matter of the inhibition of conscious elements, both theories rely on Sherrington's reciprocal process of innervation of antagonistic muscles ;—save in so far, indeed, as the drainage-theory finds an alternative resource in the mystery of conscious energy. But I believe that McDougall has only by implication intimated this. Each theory offers an hypothesis for the mechanism by which antagonistic inhibition is brought about, and the way in which this affects consciousness. One suggests the ' drainage ' of all nervous discharges into *one* of each pair of antagonistic muscles,[2] and the other a reverse flow of assimilatory process from the muscle that is inhibited.[3] Both suggestions are highly hypothetical, yet the difference between them is so close to a diametrical opposition that experiment will conceivably yield a presumption in favour of one and

---

[1] " Die Willenshandlung," Freiburg, B., 1888, S. 18.
[2] McDougall : " Brain," 1903, vol. 26, p. 153.
[3] Münsterberg : *op. cit.* S. 543–5.

against the other. Sherrington mentions that Mc-
Dougall's " scheme fits a number of facts of reciprocal
inhibition,"[1] and enumerates these : he also mentions
(p. 203) two difficulties presented by that scheme.
Sherrington himself proposes a different view (p. 142),
and elsewhere says (p. 192) that " we do not yet understand the intimate nature of inhibition." Since this is
the case it seems to me that theory may well wait for a
while on experiment.

The drainage-theory has an advantage over the
action-theory in that the former emphasizes the importance of the *synapses* between neurones, as the latter
does not. Now Sherrington enumerates [2] in a truly
remarkable passage and for psychologists the most
important in the volume, eleven features of difference
between ' conduction in nerve-trunks and in reflex-arcs
respectively ' ; and here he assigns to reflex-arcs
properties such as fatiguability, after-discharge (' after-
image '), inhibition, *et caetera*, on which many of the
phenomena of consciousness unmistakably depend.
And he says that, " These differences between conduction
in reflex-arcs and nerve-trunks respectively appear
referable to that part of the arc which lies in grey
matter " ; that is, of course, to synapses. In this way
synapses are of a psychological importance far exceeding
that of ' cell-bodies,' if indeed these are of any except
trophic value. While this has been most justly emphasized by McDougall, it is also true that there is
nothing in the action-theory which necessitates an
emphasis on ' cell-bodies,' and the point of tension
between incoming and outgoing nervous impulses

---

[1] Sherrington : *op. cit.*, pp. 201–3.
[2] *Op. cit.*, p. 14.

may just as readily be found in synapses as in the cell-bodies. As conversely, indeed, should subsequent discoveries demand, the drainage-theory could transfer its emphasis to cell-bodies instead of the synapses.

Aside from the thorough physiological consistency of the action-theory, and the inconsistency of the dualistic drainage-theory in this same respect (a defect which I account fatal), the really crucial issue between the two theories lies in their explanation of the ' unconscious ' performance of habitual activities. It is an odd circumstance that the two adduce precisely opposite conditions as being those which determine whether a nervous process shall be ' conscious ' or not. (I quote the word ' conscious ' because both our authors here mean that which I have called reflectively conscious). McDougall says :[1] " Consciousness then varies with neither the complexity, nor the intensity, nor the purposefulness, nor the anatomical seat of the neural processes in conjunction with which it occurs." (Unless I am gravely mistaken it varies according to his own theory with all four of these factors. I can only suppose that by ' consciousness ' he here means that mode of consciousness which Münsterberg calls ' vividness.'[2]) " But as is indicated in every text-book, there is one factor with which it does vary, perhaps not exactly and solely, but still constantly, and that is the novelty of the combination of neural processes concerned." And again (p. 366) he speaks of " the proposition whose truth

---

[1] " Mind," 1898, N.S. VII, p. 160.

[2] In his " Physiological Psychology," p. 60, McDougall says : " While the organization of a system of elements is imperfect, its excitement is accompanied by psychical processes which become progressively less vivid as the organization proceeds."

I am endeavouring to establish, namely, that consciousness accompanies only the process of establishment of
new connections among neurones." And yet again
(p. 375) we learn " that, under two conditions, consciousness would become impossible, either if an animal
should become perfectly adapted to its environment,
or if an individual should have lived so long that all the
parts of its nervous system had become mapped out
into well-organized paths of automatic reaction. For
in the case of an animal perfectly adapted to a limited
environment, all its movements would be automatic, all
apprehension would be implicit, all its mental processes [!] would go on without consciousness." Happily,
however, " there is little reason to hope or fear that we
shall attain ' Nirvana ' by this route. Our environment
seems to be infinitely complex and varied," *et caetera*.
And elsewhere,[1] by way of a rough simile, the consciousness generated at the synapses by the passage of nervous
current is likened to the light emitted from the filament
of an incandescent lamp, " the heat of each filament
being likened to an unknown form of energy that plays
a part in the transmission of the impulse across each
synapse." The view is, then, that consciousness is
generated like heat in the incandescent filament, by the
resistance offered to the nervous impulse by unfrequented
synapses. In this way the fact that some habitual
activities go on ' unconsciously,' is explained with all
the facility of a theory *ad hoc*. Very similar also, I am
given to understand, is the theory of Dewey.

Now the action-theory :[2] " The transition from
centripetal to centrifugal excitation becomes automatic

[1] McDougall : " Physiological Psychology," p. 60.
[2] Münsteı berg : " Grundzüge der Psychologie," Bd. I, S. 541.

through the establishment of sub-cortical connections, whereby the disturbance coming from the periphery is conducted to paths of outlet before it reaches the psycho-physical apparatus of the cortex. The unconsciousness of automatic processes and the inhibition of sensory processes in the cortex are thus wholly incomparable." And a few lines above we are told : " Likewise it is only a specious argument against the action-theory, that impressions lose their vividness in proportion to the readiness with which they go over into movement [*facility* of discharge being the condition requisite to vividness according to this theory], and that they are apparently quite inhibited when no resistance is offered to the movement. If we were really forced to the anatomical conception that automatic reflexes led through the sensory centres of the cortex, the action-theory would be indeed untenable. . . . But this anatomical interpretation is obviously untenable."

Clearly the drainage-theory points to ' unconscious ' *cortical* reflexes, while the action-theory finds the seat of consciousness throughout the cerebrum, so that ' unconscious ' processes must invariably pass through *lower* centres. This issue is believed by many to be the most crucial, and by many to be decisive in favour of the drainage-theory. I think, indeed, that it is decisive and, with one notion eliminated, overwhelmingly in favour of the action-theory. The one point, in my opinion, to be eliminated from this theory is the assumption that the cerebral cortex alone is the seat of consciousness. In Chapter X I have explained at some length the reasons for this :—' consciousness ' as ordinarily used in this connection means *reflective* consciousness, which involves both *memory* and the analytical function. *These* functions may well be located in the highest nervous levels, and there is much reason for supposing that they are. But common prejudice to the contrary notwithstanding, I know of no facts which show that all ' living conscious quality,' including of course the important and surely conscious ' fringe,' depends on processes in the cerebrum alone. The bearing of this, however, is merely that reflection, analysis, estimation, and judgement, rather than consciousness, are involved in the slow and arduous acquiral of motor co-ordinations as they are not in the execution of such acts after they have become ' automatic.' Now if an unusual constellation of sensory impulses meets at first with *resistance* in sub-cortical centres (for all receptors have sub-cortical connections), and such resistance is undoubtedly due to their inauguration of mutually antagonistic reflexes ('inhibitory block'), this resistance must deflect a portion of the afferent energy into other paths that are open, and these are paths to both lower and higher reflex levels.[1] And if the afferent currents are intense enough they will irradiate in part even to the highest level, the cortex. And here it may indeed be that the processes of reflection, analysis and judgement go on which so characterize the ' conscious ' acquirement of co-ordinations. And now without speculating as to how the appropriate reflex-pattern is finally established which mediates a response co-ordinated to the peculiar constellation of stimuli, after their frequent repetition, we *know* that such a pattern is established and that it involves *a less widespread irradiation* of the efferent impulses than at first took place : we know this last because before co-ordination was established inappro-

[1] Cf. Sherrington : *op. cit.*, pp. 155–6, 158.

priate movements were made *along with* appropriate
ones, whereas after co-ordination the response is
invariably *simpler* and more *economically* adapted to the
situation. There is less irradiation of currents. Now
it is Sherrington's experience (p. 163) that in " the
majority of instances, irradiation has spread more easily
down than up the cord." It should follow that howsoever automatic paths are established (perhaps by
alteration of synaptic thresholds ?), they will seek as
low reflex levels as possible, so that any economy of
irradiation will diminish the amount of energy passing
through *higher* levels, including the cerebrum which is
probably the organ of reflection, analysis, and judgement. In any case the higher the level, the less it will be
disturbed by irradiation of afferent currents, and the
less too in proportion as a stable reflex pattern for co-
ordinated response becomes established.

The point which it seems to me that McDougall over-
looks is that the automatic co-ordination is demonstrably not the same as the earlier inco-ordinated
responses to the same stimuli,—the inco-ordinated are
ever diffuse, mutually opposed, and redundant. They
involve a considerable waste of nervous and muscular
energy. They employ, then, more neural paths than
does the established co-ordination, and among the more
are paths traversing the higher centres of reflection,
analysis, *et caetera*. This accounts for the greater conscious mass of activities while co-ordination is being
established : for *reflective* consciousness is here busy,
and as food for reflection there are not merely the intended movements, but also the large mass of unin-
tended inco-ordinated movements as well. Habitual
activities, then, are alleged to be performed uncon-

sciously simply because they are performed unre-
flectingly ; they are just as much *conscious* movements,
but no nervous energy is wasted, now, by irradiation
to the centres of reflection and introspection. And that
the pattern of paths involved is not the same before and
after the establishment of a co-ordination, that *pari
passu* with such habituation the irradiation of nervous
disturbance is restricted, and that in this reduction it is
limited to ever lower and lower nervous levels—all this
is not hypothesis but fact, and readily demonstrated
by examination of the (reflex) movements that are performed in the successive stages of learning. Thus the
action-theory is not forced to the anatomical conception
that automatic reflexes pass through the higher,
reflective centres,—through the cortex. But now
according to the drainage-theory the neural paths are
essentially the same before and after co-ordination,
and the decrease of conscious vividness is due to de-
creased resistance along the *same paths as were at first
employed* to the passage of nervous impulses :—resistance producing consciousness as it produces heat.
But this assumption that the same paths are used before
and after habituation and co-ordination is demonstrably
false :—the reactions are very different indeed, being
at first many, inco-ordinated, and inappropriate and
becoming later few, precise, and appropriate ; and
differing responses involve *different* reflex paths. And
for this reason the drainage-theory, not the action-
theory is untenable. The disputed issue has arisen, I
think, from the mistaking of that which is not reflectively
and introspectively conscious, for that which is unconscious.

If it were replied that what I have said applies

indeed to the very first stages in the acquirement of co-ordinations, while gross maladjustments are being overcome, but not to the later stage when co-ordinated conscious movements are growing into ' unconscious ' automatisms, I should reply two things : firstly, that the overcoming of maladjustments never quite ceases. A process of greater and greater refinement goes on, and the reflex pattern becomes ever simpler (and gradually too, in all probability, continues to settle very slowly into ever lower and lower reflex levels). And secondly, I should inquire how, if the explanation of habit which I have given were not the true one, and how according to the drainage-theory, it can happen that *certain* lifelong habits of the nervous system do *not* become ' unconscious ' ? The assurance that we shall not reach ' Nirvana ' in this life because the environment is infinitely varied, is nothing to the point ; because this environment consists of elements that are familiar and of which we are invariably conscious. The total environmental situations are indeed diverse, but the component elements are numerically related thereto about as the letters of the alphabet to the world's store of books. Now McDougall believes in the ' specific energy of nerves,'[1] and if that then I suppose that he believes in the localization of cerebral functions, and this pretty minutely down even to the individual synapses. And how is it, then, that after even ten years of life the synapses that are correlated to the common colours are not so worn and unresisting that nervous impulses can traverse them without giving off any conscious ' energy ' ? According to the drainage-theory we ought to be dead long since to the colours of bricks

---

[1] " Physiological Psychology," p. 58.

and trees. To our total environment we are indeed learning ever new modes of response, but there are innumerable part responses which are attained very early and which continue to yield conscious ' energy ' to the very end. And this applies, in my opinion, to the synaptic processes that are correlated to each of the *qualities*. How is it that the tea-taster and the perfumer does not become anæsthetic to tastes and odours, or the dyer to colours ? Instead of which their consciousness becomes more acute and discriminating. " Ah, but they are constantly acquiring new co-ordinations." Yes, but if *pari passu* the old co-ordinations by becoming habitual are lost to consciousness the man is no better off for his labour : in order to discriminate more nicely he must *retain* the old, as well as acquire sense for the new, qualities. Otherwise his range of discrimination is not enlarged. Münsterberg is undeniably right in asserting that " the unconsciousness of automatic processes is absolutely incomparable to the inhibition of sensory processes in the cortex." I know not what doctrine of synaptic shift, regeneration, or procreation can save the drainage-theory at this point. Like many another theory it is designed to explain a particular group of phenomena,—the alleged ' unconsciousness ' of habituated co-ordinations. It has no room for habitual responses that persist in remaining vividly conscious ; and these are indubitably the larger part.

Now in regard to ' unconscious ' co-ordinations, I quite deny that they are unconscious, and for reasons already set forth (Chapter X, p. 191 ff.). They are, however, so economically effected by the nervous system, after practice, that the centres of *reflection* are not brought into play. And I have shown that reflective consciousness is too often and quite erroneously mistaken for consciousness. I do not admit that the cerebrum is the sole ' seat ' of consciousness, nor do I suppose that any *sharp* distinction marks it off from lower centres as the seat of reflective processes : indeed, I have no opinion in the matter. What I have contended is that *reflective* consciousness depends in general on the higher reflex levels, and that it is in general these levels that receive less and less irradiated nervous energy as responses become co-ordinated. And so much is plain physiological fact. The assertion of the action-theory remains, then, *practically* true, that " the transition from centripetal to centrifugal excitation becomes automatic through the establishment of sub-cortical connections, whereby the disturbance coming from the periphery is conducted to paths of outlet before it reaches the psycho-physical [reflective, *et caetera*, as I believe] apparatus of the cortex." And I have tried to show that this not such a notion as is sometimes imputed to the action-theory, of a co-ordination being established at one reflex level, and then transferred to a lower without needing there to be relearned (cf. *supra* p. 200). It is merely that in inco-ordination there is a wider diffusion of nervous energy than takes place after co-ordination is more perfected, that is, after a relatively stable reflex pattern is established. The action-theory refrains from conjecturing on the usefulness or purposelessness of this irradiation to higher (and lower) levels.

There is one further point with regard to these habituated co-ordinations. After they are well established they are not removed from the possibility of being again reflectively conscious. According to the drainage-theory this ought to be impossible, particularly with the most thoroughly established co-ordinations. It is true that 'thinking about' what one is doing seriously interferes with co-ordinations that are so imperfectly established as still to be difficult, such as for some people the case of walking on a tight-rope or playing the piano. But with perfectly established reflexes this is precisely not the case. Here, where according to the drainage-theory it should be least possible, a slight effort of volition suffices to make every movement conscious without discernibly modifying the reflex itself. I find, for myself, that I cannot dive successfully if I 'think about what I am doing,' but I can swim, row, or walk and attend to the reflexes without detectably altering them : clearly the same reflex paths are still involved. But for the drainage-theory, so far as I can see, the very same reflexes, in order again to emerge in 'consciousness,' must be learned in the twinkling of an eye by a new set of synaptic paths.

So, in fine, I do fully believe that the matter of habitual activities is a deciding issue between the two theories here under discussion, and that it decides unequivocally in favour of the action-theory. The drainage-theory, besides proposing to prolong the stultifying alliance between philosophy and physiology by hypothecating a conscious 'energy' (which is no less a piece of dualistic hocus-pocus for being designated an energy), also misleads and falls into confusion with regard to habituated nervous processes. But there is a third objection to this theory which is even more fundamental and more serious than the others : indeed if there were no action-theory and no other 'working-hypothesis' of any sort in sight, this objection would be sufficient utterly to invalidate the drainage-theory. It is that this theory makes consciousness depend not on the response of the nervous system, but on the *absence of response*, and this position denies the one certain fact that has been the significance of physiological psychology ever since the days of Democritus and Aristotle. For the drainage-theory consciousness is not that to which the nervous system responds, but everything in heaven and earth and the whole realm of being *except* that to which the nervous system responds.

For the drainage-theory asserts, as is shown by the quotations I have given, that consciousness varies as the *resistance* offered by synapses to the passage of nervous impulses. It is the resistance which generates conscious ' energy,' as the resistance of an incandescent filament generates heat and light. So far this seems harmless, but let us note what it leads to. Different synapses offer different degrees of resistance, and one and the same synapse offers different resistances at different times ;[1] now when the resistance of a synapse or a synaptic path increases, and a constant pressure of nervous current is maintained, consciousness becomes by the definition more and more ' vivid,' or the conscious ' energy ' increases. But until what point ? The definition sets no limit, and the conscious ' energy ' continues to increase until, quite clearly, the resistance is so great that *no current* passes, until the synapse or synaptic path does *not* function,—and here consciousness is at or near its maximum. In other words, whenever the resistance of a reflex path is so high that it does not function at all the process (?) is most conscious : that is, in the ordinary situation, one is most vividly conscious of those objects of the environment to

[1] Sherrington : *op. cit.*, pp. 155 and 166.

which one's nervous system is *not* responding. And since the nervous system is even more completely irresponsive to what is not in the present environment, one is even more vividly conscious of all the rest of the universe. Now the attention is demonstrably connected with a setting of receptors and effectors *for* response, and so one is the more vividly conscious of those things which escape the attention. Did ever a theory more perfectly invert the facts ?

Nor can it be said in defence that a resistance so high as to inhibit response is a limiting case not contemplated by the theory ; for firstly, it is the business of theories to provide for limiting cases ; and secondly, the situation is no better before the limit is reached. Other factors remaining constant, as the synaptic resistance rises the response grows either feebler or comprehends fewer effector organs, but consciousness still increases ; and this precisely contradicts all experimental data of association, or more specifically of threshold both of sensation and of sensation difference, of latent period, duration, after-image, summation, reaction-time, dynamogenesis, *et caetera ;*—in short, the entire range of experimental knowledge. The likening of synapses to incandescent filaments is misleading ; they are much better likened to the spark-gap between electric poles. They present a resistance to the passage of energy, and to overcome this a certain tension is required, but until this tension is exceeded neither heat nor light is produced. All experimental data in psychology go to show that consciousness is directly dependent on the amount of energy that *does* cross, and is dependent temporally on the promptness with which it crosses ; and with other factors constant these directly depend on the *decrease* and *not on the increase* of resistance. But I will not prolong argument, when the entire body of experimental knowledge so emphatically speaks for itself. The very nucleus of the drainage-theory, without which it is nothing, is an idea which is the precise inversion of the most significant fact of psychology—that consciousness depends on the responsive activity of the nervous system, and not on the suppression of that activity. As I before mentioned, in this matter of vividness the action-theory is flatly opposed to the drainage-theory : for the former, vividness varies *directly* with the freedom of discharge, with the lack of resistance to the passage of nervous currents. This is so obviously called for by the facts that one can only marvel that another view is for an instant entertained.

But my motive in bringing up these two theories was not primarily to judge their respective merits, but to demonstrate in general the possibility of a ' motor-theory ' of consciousness ; and it seemed best to base the discussion on the two ' motor-theories ' that have been so far advanced. For the definition of consciousness which has occupied us in the preceding chapters is one which it would have been hard to make seem psycho-physically plausible prior to the rise of what I have called the motor-idea. And this definition comports only, in its psycho-physical application, with a strictly consequential motor-theory, and one above all which definitely emancipates physiology from any entanglement whatsoever with metaphysic. I have attempted now to establish this definition of consciousness, on both epistemological and experimental grounds, to show that it is epistemologically inevitable and that it is experimentally feasible. Indeed, experimentally nothing else would ever have been thought of had not Descartes o'er-hastily surveyed the human cortex with metaphysical line and compass and charted it with his all-but indelible dualistic ink. The definition of consciousness here offered lays no conditions on experimental physiology, but removes them, in giving the assurance that the nervous system is no more than what it seems to be—a mechanism of response, and that the house of the brain is not haunted as has been supposed. The physiologist is to look for anything he can find, and is not to be deterred by strange rumours of a something, he knows not what, which he has not found.

If in considering motor-theories and the immediate correlation of consciousness and response, we have seen that much of that which the physiologist has found out is brought together and enunciated in a psycho-physical theory, the action-theory, this is, so far as our definition goes, a happy accident. A host of facts propound that consciousness is, as it were, the cross-section of *being* that is illuminated by a search-light, and these would still be facts even if it were not on the instant clear how the search-light is manipulated. Nor is it entirely clear yet. Physiology has not mastered the secret of inhibition, and here the action-theory pretends merely to offer tentative and alternative suggestions. So too in other ways it distinctly disavows the claim either to finality or completeness. It is a matter of course that theory, in the true sense of the physicists, primarily embodies facts already learned and synthesizes them, and only secondarily anticipates further empirical discovery. But the discussion has sufficiently shown, I hope, that the strictly deductive definition of conscious-

z

ness, from a monistic, neutral realm of *being*, fits not ill with the empirical facts that are so far at hand concerning the relation of consciousness to the nervous system—of mind to body. We have seen why the body has a mind—it is because in the neutral realm of *being* the body selectively describes one ; as the compass describes a circle.

And it is for this reason that I have constantly laid emphasis on physiological psychology. The nervous response it is which selects and defines the content of consciousness, and therefore psychology is primarily the science of response, and hence is bound to be in large part at least physiological. Yet no response can be studied except with reference to that which is responded to, and so the physiology of nervous response includes, and impossibly precludes, the study of the conscious manifold itself. Conversely, however, this latter *can* be studied apart from the nervous responses that define it ; and such a study is so-called descriptive or analytic psychology. But the history of this branch of the subject seems to show that when unrestrained by the sobering guidance of physiology, psychology tends to become as speculative as any branch of philosophy and to forfeit all claim to be an empirical science. An introspective riot ensues when the Self tries to represent itself to itself for a number of times. And thus on all accounts, it seems to me, physiological psychology, which is a branch in the broadest sense of physiology, may justly claim to be the true and authoritative science of the soul.

Lastly, here at the close of this volume, it may be noted that I have said very little about ' truth ' and nothing about ' reality.' Now this is in accord with our general logical scheme. For it is clear that in any region where some consistencies and some inconsistencies are found, there are *both* truth and untruth, perhaps too, reality and unreality. Now we have found both consistencies and inconsistencies in logical and mathematical manifolds, in physical, chemical, inorganic, organic, and conscious manifolds. Clearly, then, further specifications than are involved in these systems are necessary for the definition of truth and reality. These lie higher up in that progressive, simple-to-complex, Comtean hierarchy of *being* that we glanced at in an earlier chapter. Truth as a whole and reality as a whole involve more determinants, further specifications than even consciousness or mind. And since I have aimed at nothing higher than a deductive definition of mind, I needed not to undertake a definition of truth or reality, or of any other *values*. Truth is doubtless consistency so far as any few propositions are concerned, but that leaves open a broad question as to what is the one largest system of consistent propositions, which would constitute, perhaps, *the* truth. As to the definition of consciousness which has been offered in the foregoing pages, I trust it may be found consistent with a considerable body of mutually consistent propositions in our own familiar realm of *being*. Possibly this will be the case, and especially if there be any virtue in that sadly neglected truism of the naïve realist, that—Everything is precisely what it is, and is not to be explained away as something else.

FINIS

INDEX

341

PRINTED BY
WILLIAM BRENDON AND SON, LTD.
PLYMOUTH

CLASSICS IN PSYCHOLOGY

AN ARNO PRESS COLLECTION

Angell, James Rowland. **Psychology**: On Introductory Study of the Structure and Function of Human Consciousness. 4th edition. 1908

Bain, Alexander. **Mental Science.** 1868

Baldwin, James Mark. **Social and Ethical Interpretations in Mental Development.** 2nd edition. 1899

Bechterev, Vladimir Michailovitch. **General Principles of Human Reflexology.** [1932]

Binet, Alfred and Th[éodore] Simon. **The Development of Intelligence in Children.** 1916

Bogardus, Emory S. **Fundamentals of Social Psychology.** 1924

Buytendijk, F. J. J. **The Mind of the Dog.** 1936

Ebbinghaus, Hermann. **Psychology: An Elementary Text-Book.** 1908

Goddard, Henry Herbert. **The Kallikak Family.** 1931

Hobhouse, L[eonard] T. **Mind in Evolution.** 1915

Holt, Edwin B. **The Concept of Consciousness.** 1914

Külpe, Oswald. **Outlines of Psychology.** 1895

Ladd-Franklin, Christine. **Colour and Colour Theories.** 1929

Lectures Delivered at the 20th Anniversary Celebration of Clark University. (Reprinted from *The American Journal of Psychology*, Vol. 21, Nos. 2 and 3). 1910

Lipps, Theodor. **Psychological Studies.** 2nd edition. 1926

Loeb, Jacques. **Comparative Physiology of the Brain and Comparative Psychology.** 1900

Lotze, Hermann. **Outlines of Psychology.** [1885]

McDougall, William. **The Group Mind.** 2nd edition. 1920

Meier, Norman C., editor. **Studies in the Psychology of Art: Volume III.** 1939

Morgan, C. Lloyd. **Habit and Instinct.** 1896

Münsterberg, Hugo. **Psychology and Industrial Efficiency.** 1913

Murchison, Carl, editor. **Psychologies of 1930.** 1930

Piéron, Henri. **Thought and the Brain.** 1927

Pillsbury, W[alter] B[owers]. **Attention.** 1908

[Poffenberger, A. T., editor]. **James McKeen Cattell: Man of Science.** 1947

Preyer, W[illiam] **The Mind of the Child: Parts I and II.** 1890/1889

The Psychology of Skill: Three Studies. 1973

Reymert, Martin L., editor. **Feelings and Emotions:** The Wittenberg Symposium. 1928

Ribot, Th[éodule Armand]. **Essay on the Creative Imagination.** 1906

Roback, A[braham] A[aron]. **The Psychology of Character.** 1927

I. M. Sechenov: Biographical Sketch and Essays. (Reprinted from *Selected Works* by I. Sechenov). 1935

Sherrington, Charles. **The Integrative Action of the Nervous System.** 2nd edition. 1947

Spearman, C[harles]. **The Nature of 'Intelligence' and the Principles of Cognition.** 1923

Thorndike, Edward L. **Education: A First Book.** 1912

Thorndike, Edward L., E. O. Bregman, M. V. Cobb, et al. **The Measurement of Intelligence.** [1927]

Titchener, Edward Bradford. **Lectures on the Elementary Psychology of Feeling and Attention.** 1908

Titchener, Edward Bradford. **Lectures on the Experimental Psychology of the Thought-Processes.** 1909

Washburn, Margaret Floy. **Movement and Mental Imagery.** 1916

Whipple, Guy Montrose. **Manual of Mental and Physical Tests:** Parts I and II. 2nd edition. 1914/1915

Woodworth, Robert Sessions. **Dynamic Psychology.** 1918

Wundt, Wilhelm. **An Introduction to Psychology.** 1912

Yerkes, Robert M. **The Dancing Mouse** and **The Mind of a Gorilla.** 1907/1926